THE GREAT JEWISH BOOKS

and their influence on history

The Hebrew Bible

The Talmud

The Siddur

Rashi's Commentaries

The Kusari

Guide for the Perplexed

The Zohar

The Shulchan Aruch

Introduction by
Ludwig Lewisohn

Graetz's History

Herzl's Judenstaat

Ahad Ha-am's Essays

Bialik's Poems

Horizon Press
New York

THE

*Edited by Samuel Caplan
and Harold U. Ribalow*

GREAT

JEWISH

BOOKS *and their influence on history*

The editors acknowledge with thanks the kind permission of the following publishers to reprint selections from the copyright works listed below: Jewish Publication Society of America for: Selected Essays by Ahad Ha-am; Rashi by Maurice Liber; A History of the Jews by Heinrich Graetz. Bloch Publishing Company for: The Authorized Daily Prayer Book with commentary, introductions and notes by the late Chief Rabbi Joseph H. Hertz. Histadruth Ivrith of America for: Collected Poems of Hayyim Nahman Bialik, edited by Israel Efros. Schocken Books, Inc. for: Zohar, The Book of Splendor by Gershom G. Scholem. University of Chicago Press for: The Bible—An American Translation by Smith and Goodspeed. Behrman House for: The Talmudic Anthology by Louis I. Newman and Samuel Spitz.

Fifth printing

Contents

6

Editors' Preface

The aim of this volume is to present, in popular form, the essence of those masterworks of Jewish literature which have most decisively molded the life of the Jewish people from their earliest beginnings down to the present era. The project was begun by polling a representative group of scholars, rabbis, writers and literary critics for their choices of those Jewish books which throughout the ages have played the most creative role in the survival of the Jewish people, and most deeply influenced their life and thought.

From the vast treasurehouse of Jewish learning and literature, this group suggested some fifty different books. Each of them could well have qualified for inclusion. But the list, having been limited to the dozen major books, was finally made up of those titles which received by far the largest number of votes. An acknowledged authority on each of the books was then invited to write a study, describing its authorship, its central theme or idea, its content, its original impact and subsequent influence on Jewish life and thought.

Upon their original publication as the "Great Jewish

Books" series in *Congress Weekly*, the journal published by the American Jewish Congress, there was an immediate and widespread demand for them by educational leaders of various organizations as well as by rabbis and laymen throughout the country who established study courses in their communities on "The Great Jewish Books."

The idea for this series had clearly tapped a profound need. The consistent demand continued and, to meet it, it was decided to make the work permanently available as a definitive book. This project has now been carried out with the kind cooperation of the contributors who have generously consented to the publication of their essays, many of them now expanded for permanent reference.

The editors felt that the reference value of the book would be greatly enhanced for students and lay readers by the inclusion of comprehensive selections from each of the Great Books; and again the authors of the essays themselves graciously agreed to perform the careful and intensive work of selection.

The reader is thus provided not only with authoritative discussions of each of the most important Jewish books but also with such characteristic excerpts from them as will, in the opinions of specialists, afford the best insights into the original sources.

And though there is within the essays the necessary background information on the authors, there has been included, for ready reference, an added convenience in the form of separate biographical sketches of the men who wrote the great works. These brief biographies appear in each case directly before the discussion of the book itself. A bibliography of selected readings in English is also included for those who wish to extend their knowledge of the masterpieces.

A word about spelling: There are of course no exact
equivalents in English for certain titles, phrases and sounds.
Rendered in various English forms by writers who believe
each in the desirability of their own usage, they are recog-
nizable to readers in a variety of spellings. This variety has
been frequently followed here to maintain individual pref-
erences.

Upon completing this work, the editors felt that an overall
account of the importance of the Book for the Jewish people—frequently called "The People of the Book"—would
contribute greatly to its general usefulness. And it is a privi-
lege to be able to present this introductory survey by Ludwig
Lewisohn, the renowned novelist and critic, distinguished
representative of American-Jewish letters.

It is fitting to record here our acknowledgment to Dr.
David W. Petegorsky, executive director of the American
Jewish Congress, for suggesting the idea from which the
Great Books series was developed.

We also wish to thank, for their guidance and advice in
the selection of the books, Rabbi Jacob B. Agus, Prof. Louis
Finkelstein, Dr. Nelson Glueck, Dr. Solomon Goldman, Dr.
Jacob S. Golub, Dr. Robert Gordis, Rabbi Simon Greenberg,
Dr. Abraham J. Heschel, Prof. Alexander Marx, Sh. Niger,
Menachem Ribalow, Dr. Trude Weiss-Rosmarin, Maurice
Samuel, the late Rabbi Milton Steinberg and the late Dr.
Chaim Tchernowitz.

This long-nurtured project has been prepared for the
press with considerable pleasure and absorption on the part
of the editors and the publisher, for its early reception was
a gratifying token of the intense, latent need for it. This
volume is offered as an illuminating insight into the vast
richness of Jewish creative thought. We offer it not as a

shortcut to Jewish learning but in the hope that it will stimu-
late readers to turn to the original sources of Jewish knowledge and inspiration.

SAMUEL CAPLAN
HAROLD U. RIBALOW

THE JEW AND THE BOOK

Ludwig Lewisohn

It was probably Muhammad who in his confused diatribes (*Sura III*) first addressed Jews as the "People of the Book." Until a late age of self-consciousness Jews themselves needed not to do so. A man is not conscious of his heart nor does he talk about it unless the heart is sick. Today, in this perilous age, we talk about ourselves as the *Am ha-Sefer*, the People of the Book, and we found and need Jewish Book Councils and we mark and set apart a month as Jewish Book Month, just as a sick man watches his sick heart and runs to specialists and hopes for healing and tells himself for comfort that once upon a time his heart was sound and prays that it may be again.

Sound and spiritually whole Jews needed neither the phrase nor the admonition nor the devices. They knew concerning that historic event which made Jews into Jews and which they reaffirmed each day by those acts of obedience and sanctification which marked their character and their destiny. They knew that they were here, that they existed, that they lived and rejoiced and suffered by virtue of an experience which, whatever its precise shape in space and

11

time, had made them this people with this character and
this recurring fate. They knew that the whole course of
history, *not* only their own, would have been different, had
their forefathers not had that experience which welded a
group of clans into a unique people, a people that, by the
exclusive virtue of that experience, was to tread a fiery,
tragic and illustrious path across three thousand years.

That experience was, of course, the giving and the re-
ceiving of the Law. "And Moses came and told the people
all the words of the Eternal and all the judgments: and all
the people answered with one voice and said: All the
words which the Eternal has spoken we will do. And
Moses *wrote* all the words of the Eternal . . . And he
took the Book of the Covenant and cried it into the ears
of the people." (*Exodus 24: 3, 4, 7.*) The words of the
Hebrew text are of an incomparable simplicity, severity and
grandeur. They are like granite. Yet a sublime rhythm gives
them both fluidity and expressive accent. There is no writing quite like this among all the writings of men. Nor is
there any meaning like the meaning of that passage to
mark the birth and origin of any other people. The word
in its recorded and commemorating character—the *written*
word, the Book, the *Sefer ha-B'rith,* which Moses spoke
or, more literally, cried or called into the ears of the people
—such was for Jews the beginning of the history of their
people. No wonder that our sages liked to fancy that the
Torah was created before the world, the physical universe
itself, came into being. With and through a book we were
born and appeared upon the scene of human history. Must
not that book have been in truth a book of origin?

A point of supreme importance must at once be made.
In spite of the character of the Book, the Torah, and the

character of its relation to us, we never worshiped it; we never fell into idolatry. It is treated with reverence, but so are other books on its account. Books too worn for further use are buried; the scrolls of the Torah are adorned. But what is binding is message and command; what matters is teaching and directive; what matters is the Law by which the people and the individual Jew are to live. To live— and not to die, the sages add. The book of our origin and character is a Book of Life. It is a book, moreover, that in itself brims with life. It is not only scripture; it is literature. It is not only Law and prophetism; it is epic and idyll; it treats of love and hate and death, of righteous men and sinners and of men who sin and yet are justified by the righteousness in them. It has imagination and characteriza- tion. It rivals every classic of other peoples on that classic's own ground. A thousand human hearts beat in it. All human aspiration and all despair and all hope are concen- trated in these pages. And above them and their contents broods, as it did over the primordial waters, the *ruach*, the breathing, the spirit of the Eternal whom, again and again, Israel meets and confronts upon its way.

And one more thing must be said of the Torah, the Book of Origin and of Israel's Origin, a thing in the shape of a quality, which is sustained and even heightened in certain aspects in the proclamations of the proclaimers, the *neviim*, the prophets, as well as in the *ketuvim*, the writings (note the word), of the writers. It has been spoken of already. It is style. It is art. We have no documents which point to any development of this style. We have no earlier, simpler, more tentative examples. Full-grown, mature, this sublime and soaring, this stern and lapidary style of saying and chanting—a style, moreover, meant to be recorded, to be

written down, though also brimming with the music of
speech—sprung from the midst of Israel. Whoever wrote,
to take a single phrase: *"Panim b'panim diber Adonai
imachem ba-har mi-toch ha-esh"*—whoever wrote those
level, restrained, almost factual words: *Panim b'panim
diber Adonai imachem:* "Face to face spoke the Eternal
with them"—whoever spoke and wrote those level, tran-
quil words, and then rose and soared and thundered and
blazed in those final monosyllables: *ba-hár mi-tóch ha-ésh,*
"on the mount, from the midst of the fire," whoever spoke
and wrote thus was a great artist in words, a great and not
wholly unconscious artist, an artist who foreshadowed and
foretold all the greatest prose ever written from Plato and
Thucydides to Paul Valéry and Thomas Mann.

The Jewish people became a people by virtue of a book
both divine and human. And from at least the time of
Ezra on this book, with other books soon to be added to it,
became the instinctive and necessary preoccupation of
every Jew. With every generation it became more a matter
of both conscience and insight that no Jew could aspire to
any Jewish ideal, to any fulfillment or self-fulfillment without a direct contact with the words of the book, with the
scrolls, with the letters, with the literature which was and
is quite realistically "the length of his days," the condition
of his being and survival and permanence. And so arose,
quite practically, the millennial necessity of learning, of the
education of the children, upon whose pure breath rests the
divine world: there arose the insight that the illiterate man,
the yokel, the *am ha-aretz,* could not be a sound Jew; there
arose undiminished until, alas, a generation or two ago, the
unquestioned conviction that learning, learning with the
right *kavanah,* the right intention, the right *attention* fixed

upon the immortal and transcendent, is the highest function
of such a creature as man in such a world as the present.

The tradition became flesh. It became instinctive practice. "If three eating at one table have spoken words of the
Torah, it is as though they had been eating at the table of
God, blessed be He." But the text reads: "at the table *shel
maqom*," of that "place" of God, which is the universe,
though the universe is not His place. Those three are, in
other words, in the divine and intelligible world, not in the
world of mere contingency. And this normative maxim of
Rabbi Simon bar Yohai became through the ages a matter
of practice. No one who has sat at many tables in many
lands with many Jews can fail to have observed that three
Jews, even remote and alienated Jews, do not sit long at a
single table before in some sense they begin to discuss
Torah, to "speak" Torah, to immerse themselves in some
aspect of the character and destiny of Israel by adducing
Torah, remembering Torah, commenting Torah. This circumstance marks, as perhaps no other does with equal
emphasis, the relation of the Jewish people to the Book
and to books.

We have here a phenomenon unique and incomparable,
which measurably but theoretically only, Christians and
Muslims borrowed from us. For among us the Book never
became rigid or doctrinal or dispensable or capable of sub-
stitution by credal or other formulae. On the contrary, the
Torah in the original sense became by expansion and pene-
tration, by comment and enlargement, Torah in the broader
sense. It broadened into Mishnah and Gemara and Midrash;
it soared strangely in the *Zohar*; it was defended in Yehudah
Halevi's *Kitab al Khazari*. Age after age it was reexamined
under the aspect of the world's philosophies. Maimonides

reestablished it under the aspect of Aristotle; long before
that Philo of Alexandria had sought a reinterpretation under the aspect of the Platonists; in our own day Hermann
Cohen sought confirmation in the philosophy of Kant. From
it sprang the liturgy—*Siddur and Machsor*; based upon it
were the mighty compendia of Joseph Karo, the *Shulchan
Aruch*, and the unrivalled intellectual powers of Rashi were
used in commentaries upon it. Yet—and this is of ultimate
import—the original text never lost life and freshness. It
was never submerged in the seas of interpretation and commentary. Its original words remained words of life to all
men and a light to all peoples, so that in our own generation a supremely great artist from among the Gentiles,
Thomas Mann, wrote a great creative super-Midrash upon
a few chapters of the Torah in the tetralogy of novels, *Joseph and His Brothers.*

Nor was even this all. A period of moral and spiritual
nihilism arose in the Nineteenth Century in which all sanc-
tities were trodden under foot and all faith failed. Jews
were necessarily not untouched by this phenomenon. But it
happened that in precisely this period prophetic souls saw
that the old Emancipation had failed, that the apparent
splendors of Western Jewry were hollow and meretricious,
the while the more wholesome gloom of East-European
Jewry deepened and that, for all these reasons, a new insight and a new willing and a new shaping of destiny were
needed. And Ahad Ha-am wrote those essays which were
later gathered under the title *Al Parashat Derahim*, At the
Parting of the Ways, and Chaim Nachman Bialik wrote
those poems which stirred the authentic Jewish people as
that people had hardly been stirred since the days of the
prophets, and last of all Theodor Herzl wrote the *Juden-*

staat and prophesied that within fifty years a Jewish State would come into being and the Jewish State, the *Medinath Yisrael* was proclaimed at the appointed time. And so it is clear that Ahad Ha-am, the nineteenth century rationalist, and Bialik as well and Herzl, the Viennese man of letters in whose diaries the word Torah does not occur, all wrote, all proclaimed, as it were, from within the spirit and destiny of Israel and so added to and expanded Torah and deepened and broadened that immortal stream.

In that last sentence the relation of the authentic Jewish writer to the book, to literature has been defined. He writes from within the spirit and destiny of Israel. In some sense and in whatever language he adds, however humbly, to Torah. Whenever there are health and life and the creative onward spirit in Jews or in any group of Jews, they seek out these Jewish books, the old ones and the new ones, as no other men in all the world seek out books, for these books are in some sense to them books of life, books of living, books of destiny.

In our own day in America the Jewish spirit has burned low and its fire has been all but quenched and the authentic Jewish book has often been left bleak and alone. But there are signs here and there that the embers are glowing and that a flame may yet again spring forth. To that end the learned and eloquent essays in this book on the central Jewish classics will powerfully contribute. No group of Jewish scholars could have set their hands to a better or a nobler or a more needed task. Those who hope and strive for a rebirth of authentic Judaism in America, will welcome this volume with gratitude and joy.

THE HEBREW BIBLE

Solomon Goldman

The Bible is the outgrowth of the divine wrestlings, endless frustrations, and deep optimism of the Jewish people. Strictly speaking, from the opening word of Genesis to the closing word of Chronicles, the Hebrew Bible pursues but a single theme, unfalteringly and without digression. Changes of names, shifts of locale, the overlapping of centuries, are immaterial. It is of little import who it was that killed Abel, pleaded for Sodom, battled with Amalek, slew Goliath, loved the Shulamite maiden, or at what point in the narrative and in what epoch these incidents are placed. Whether the protagonists were Cain, Abraham, Moses, David, Solomon in the long ago, or whether they were our contemporaries but yesterday, is irrelevant. The idea, the purport, and the passion alone matter and remain the same. *Mutato nomine, de te fabula narratur.* Change only the appellation, and the story is about you. Times and names are but existents or variants of the same theme; and the people of Israel itself are but incidental to it.

Yet the Hebrew Bible is witness to the havoc that early

19

centuries have wrought among Hebrew books; for not all
the Hebrew books that were ever written have been preserved. It mentions and quotes an appreciable number of
writings no longer in existence, although some of them, as,
for example, the Book of Yashar and the Book of the Wars
of the Lord, seem to have enjoyed considerable popularity
in their days. However, the books that have been preserved,
except for the few that were declared apocryphal, have
been transmitted as a unit.

Several of the late stages in this process are discernible
in the Hebrew Canon to this day. The fact that it consists
of larger and smaller groupings makes obvious that it was
not in its beginnings a collection of individual books but of
units. These units were presumably formed independently
of one another and at various times. That was one stage in
the growth of the Canon. Another stage resulted when
these units were combined into larger groups, and canonized. The final stage was the formation of the Hebrew
Canon as a whole with its threefold division: Law, Prophets, Writings.

It is generally agreed that the Torah was the first division
to be canonized. Its only units are actually the five members of which it is composed: Genesis, Exodus, Leviticus,
Numbers, Deuteronomy.

The second division of the Canon, or Prophets, falls into
two parts, which are arranged in the following order:

Earlier Prophets—Joshua, Judges, First Samuel, Second
Samuel, First Kings, Second Kings.

Later Prophets—Isaiah, Jeremiah, Ezekiel.

The Twelve—Hosea, Nahum, Joel, Habakkuk, Amos,
Zephaniah, Obadiah, Haggai, Jonah, Zechariah, Micah,
Malachi.

The order of the books in *Ketuvim,* or Writings, is as follows: Psalms, Proverbs, Job, Five Scrolls, The Song of Songs, Ruth, Lamentations, Ecclesiastes, Esther, Daniel, Ezra, Nehemiah, First Chronicles, Second Chronicles.

The Bible had its beginnings in the tales of a bold skeptic of whom it was recounted that, having rejected the beliefs universally adhered to in his day, he set out to transform the face of the earth. How he came by his skepticism or new faith is a question easier asked than answered. The past buries its secrets deep down beyond the reach of the archaeologist's spade or historian's acumen. Of this much we are certain: once, in the ancient world, there lived a Jew, or one whom the Jews came to regard and claim as their own, who, repelled by idolatrous creeds and pagan practices, groped his way to a glimpse of the One God, perfect in all perfections.

His descendants, or at any rate some of them, brooded on this God with such constancy and concentration that it became the passion of their being to mold humanity in His likeness. Never again would they recognize progress or see any purpose in the dazzling civilization upreared by the empire builders and hoarders of wealth on the misery and poverty, sweat and blood of the slave, the soldier and the drudge. For they had discovered in the holiness of their father's God man's sanctity, his common origin and destiny; in His eternity the principle of the consistency of history; and in His goodness the coherence of humanity or the brotherhood of men. They desired nothing more out of life than to make of their people the agent that would bring the whole world to live by these insights.

The people responded readily and agreed to do and

obey. They resolved never again to be like unto the nations
—but could not abandon their ways. They accepted the
Eternal as God—but upon every hill and under every green
tree they erected altars to wood and stone. They urged that
man was God's image—but they would not abolish slavery.
They apprehended the vanity of life—but were tempted by
the gold of Ophir. They longed for justice—righteousness
had made Jerusalem its lodging-place—but, fond of bribes,
they neither judged the orphan nor did they plead the
cause of the widow. They looked forward to peace but
periodically became enmeshed in the web of imperialistic
ambitions of Egypt, Assyria, or Babylonia as the case might
be. In a word, they dreamed and prophesied of the ideal
society and even legislated for it, but never got down to
build it.

Yet, this disparity between faith and conduct, these habit-
ual backslidings and innumerable frustrations, much as
they tormented the people, never hardened into cynicism
or pessimism. Israel wrestled with its conscience and no
less with an inscrutable Providence that paid it double for
all its sins. If it laid bare in its national literature its own
evil-doing with an openness and candor that no people was
ever to emulate, it also demanded of the Judge of all the
earth an accounting for chastising the innocent and making the guilty to prosper. It would neither desert its God,
nor cease to vex Him; nor would it despair either of its own
ultimate regeneration or of the salvation of mankind. And
it was out of these apostasies and wrestlings and aspirations
that the Bible came into being.

The Bible's inspired authors unfolded their theme of
themes in language as fluent and popular, as vivid and near

to the comprehension of the senses as they did with all other ideas. They wrote history instead of theology or philosophy, and dramatized the destiny of all mankind in the career of a people, in a manner which across the centuries engages the uncultivated imagination of the common man as much as the subtle wit of the philosopher. They developed the vast, eternally evolving theme in a drama built around the earliest stories current among the people, in which the climax appeared ever imminent and ever remote. These stories, in which the great Biblical values seem to have been germinally present at the beginning, were told with such simplicity, conviction, and eloquence that their imprint never faded from the national mind. Generation after generation retold them with variations in detail but unaltered in essence, often employing the imagery of the originals.

The first of these stories is that of Creation. It remains, to this day, unequaled in majesty and sublimity. Who, indeed, can speak of it without ecstasy? No poetry in the world, said Herder, exhibited the beginnings of all things in greater purity. "If all the oceans were ink," said the Rabbis, "all reeds pens, the heavens parchment, and all men writers, it would not suffice to describe the infiniteness of the universe." The Biblical author nevertheless did it with a few strokes of his pen, and revealed the purpose and design of God in creation, in language that wins as easily the heart of the child as of the sage.

The Sabbath peace that settled upon creation and the bliss of the Garden of Eden are short-lived. Man is perfectible but not perfect. Compounded of impulses and desires, he is easily tempted and easily misled. For a moment it is made to appear that the creation of man was a divine

error, to be rectified by a cataclysmic recall. One righteous
man suffices to justify the existence of the human race. Un-
contaminated by the evil of his generation, Noah is chosen
to continue the thread of creation.

The descendants of Noah failed to learn the lesson of the
doomed generation. As they multiplied and prospered, they
sank to the level of the antediluvians. Again the purpose of
creation must be renewed, but in another fashion. Abraham,
turning his back on the arrogance and frivolity of Ur, its
vices and violence, its impotent gods and depraved men,
treks across the desert to enter into an eternal covenant
with God. Later generations never ceased to dwell on the
story of his life and of the lives of Isaac and Jacob, of Joseph and Joseph's brethren. The idyllic sketches of their simplicity, humility and dignity, their concern for their fellow
men, their mutual affection, are the more poignant for the
honest references to their weaknesses and family rifts; but
above all weaknesses rises their unswerving faith in God;
an eternal pattern graven in an eternal style.

The Exodus has become perhaps the most universal store-
house of liberative ideas and literary allusion. It has entered
almost bodily into the folklore of humanity, a symbol of
freedom, a source of vital metaphors.

Then comes an unforgettable climax. We see Sinai in travail, its metallic veins ablaze; the heavens are rent like a veil,
and amidst the rolling of the thunder and the succession of
lightning flashes a voice speaks unto man. It is the voice of
God, revealing Himself in the purity of the absolute, not
under an image, but as a form of power, calling man to redemption and offering him a law, a discipline, a way of
righteousness, and the path of love, peace, and freedom.
The sublime imagery of the revelation from the mountain-

top haunted forever the minds of the prophets and psalmists. When the world was in commotion, apprehensive of disaster or tremulous with expectation of glad tidings, they saw the glory of God descend again on Sinai's summit.

In its incomparable account of Creation, *le dernier effort du genie,* Chateaubriand called it, the Bible avoided precipitating intricate metaphysics by maintaining, in reality, silence concerning the creative process and never going beyond sensuous connotations. It achieved clearness by having limited itself to a description of observable phenomena, of things as they are, of things as they are perceived by the senses and are within the ken of children—heaven and earth, water and land, tree and grass, sun, moon and stars, fish and fowl, beast, reptile, and insect—having studiously refrained from expatiating on how they had come into being. By the aid of grace or as a result of a stroke of genius, as you will, it conceived of the "hid beginnings" as darkness, a darkness in whose "unbottom'd infinite abyss" the boundless and formless realms of space had lain buried for countless aeons of time, and of Creation as light that made all things visible. It said hardly anything else. If anything, it was even more concise respecting the essence of the Deity. Though it cast its God in anthropomorphic mold and ascribed to Him human functions, He remained immaterial and invisible; though it represented Him as Personality, His impact was no less one of infinite process. He speaks, as it were, out of the fire. You hear the sound of words, but you see no form, there being only a voice. What it did reiterate untiringly, deliberately, it would seem, or with clerical preciseness and monotonousness, as some would have it, was that God was the Creator, that He alone called forth Creation. He spoke "the word and they were made."

By being reticent and laconic, eschewing, on the one hand, the hypotheses of metaphysics and, on the other, the fantasies of polytheism—in all of whose accounts of beginnings creation is invariably pictured as a copulative act, where someone is forever ravishing somebody else, if not Enlil Ninlil then it is Zeus Themis—the Bible, by avoiding all this and metaphysical abstractions as well, actually formed a combination of the two that has proved to be as fruitful as it was remarkable. Investing the former with imagery and vitality and ridding the latter of grossness and superstition, it made itself acceptable *mutatis mutandis,* to the many and the few. The people found in it a conception of a Creator and Creation that was not far removed from their perception of the phenomena of nature, and consequently was not altogether beyond their comprehension or outside their experience. The world of sense impressions, of material objects was there. This much they knew, and they had learned from experience that anything that was had had to be made, and making suggested a maker, one inevitably fashioned in the image of man. What the Bible actually did was to make explicit that which was already implicit within their mind. It organized their experience in the light of a few simple ideas, co-ordinated their subconscious perception, and transfigured and fused their unreflective awareness into intelligible and sublime expression. If they believed in it it was only because it spoke their mind. Their faith was neither blind nor superimposed, but pragmatic. They were believing not what they read or were told, but what they saw and felt. Of course, many centuries were to elapse before they would become habituated to the idea of an incorporeal and unseen Maker, and many more before they would bring themselves to think of Him as

being only one, without a family, and without peers or
rivals. However, this brand of skepticism did not clash with
the Biblical account of Creation. For the masses of antiquity, as for those of the Middle Ages and more recent
times, the mystery of the origin of things had been successfully unraveled.

Likewise its representation of the Deity was of a character not to make any circles about the imagination. Emanating from a conviction that man cannot by searching find
out God—find Him to perfection—it spoke of Him in a manner corresponding to no experienced object, and consequently admitted of almost any sense. He could be thought
of, to be sure, as "a masculine being," but He could also be
apprehended as the sustaining principle of the universe
and, indeed, as a "floating symbol."

But the truth or riddle of the divine essence and the actuality or miracle of Creation apart, the majesty, omnipo-
tence, omniscience, and solitariness of the Biblical God
reached deep into the heart and captivated the mind. Man,
child and poet that he is, incurable lover of the fantastic
and fabulous, always bent to awe by the gigantic and un-
excelled, quite expectedly thrilled to the infinite might, the
exalted sovereignty, the transcendent wisdom, the veiled
remoteness of Him who was beyond and above all grandeur
and whom the heaven of heavens could not contain. For,
whether fact or fiction, no imagination had ever conceived
a being, no Hellenic muse had ever formed a shape to stand
beside Him. "The Jupiter of Homer," Chateaubriand wrote,
"shaking the heavens with a nod of his brow is without
doubt most majestic; but when Jehovah goes down into
chaos and says *Fiat Lux*, the extraordinary son of Saturn
collapses and turns to nothing." No! No one else had ever

encompassed the air with a sphere of fire or covered himself with light as with a garment or stretched out the heavens like a tent or walked upon the wings of the wind or
measured the waters in the hollow of his hand or weighed
the mountains with a balance and the hills in scales or
lifted lands like a grain or marshaled the elements like ro-
bots. No one else had ever created a world of such breath-
taking variety and magnificence. And in the doing of all
this the God of Genesis or Isaiah or Psalms or Job was
alone, alone in the ordered and peopled universe as He had
been when before the beginning of things He was brooding over chaos. And yet despite His being intangible and
invisible beyond perception, transcendent and infinite beyond conception, He was at the same time near to the humblest of His creatures anywhere in the wide world. He
would stop to converse with a handmaid in distress, embrace the wayward in His mercy, and pity the lowly and
weak as a father pities his children. To whom, then, was
He to be likened? Or what likeness could be placed over
against Him? To whom else would men be drawn as irresistibly as to Him?

What particularly made Him unique was that to comprehend Him in His omnipotent Oneness was to recognize
in Him the sole arbiter of the destiny of all things in the
heavens above and the earth below, the one being a corollary of the other. It was dreadfully enchanting to contemplate a God who was the only Ruler as He was the sole
Creator, who could, if He would, trifle with nations and
toy with their armed hosts, shatter the bow of the hero and
unnerve the arm of the lionhearted. He alone could judge
all creatures, bring them to birth and send them to death,
impoverish and make rich, raise from the dust and lower to

the refuse heap. There was no power anywhere in the world to challenge His will or stay His hand. Unlike the pagan gods, He set *Anagke*, or Necessity, at nought and held in derision the triformed Moirai who could entangle even the mighty Zeus in a web from which the hurler of thunderbolts would struggle in vain, despite all his *téchne*, or craft, to extricate himself. The very thought that anyone could design anything He had not wished was preposterous, the bare supposition that there was anything fated which He had not ordered was blasphemous, to say nothing of the suggestion that He could be ensnared in a contrivance either of His own making or that others had devised for Him.

This conviction that God was steersman of all things, that nothing lay outside His knowledge or beyond His power, in a word, the belief that He held the world in the hollow of His hand, went far to enlighten man's understanding of nature. For to conceive of God as One was to embrace the world in its unity, to view it also as basically one. In other words, monotheism, from the start, harbored the intuition, though seen only through a glass darkly, that all the elements nature comprised together with the shifting phenomena observed in it were without exception subject to the law and order God had established in the universe, there being not the remotest probability that any of them might at any time disregard the place or function assigned to it in the universal system He had contrived and go its own way.

But even more than the congeniality of its metaphysics to ever-changing views about God and the coming of the universe into existence, it was the portrayal of man in the Bible, the place it assigned him in the general scheme of things, the endless number of marvelous, multicolored, giant figures it portrayed, the pattern it designed for associative living, the proportionate rights and duties it granted to and imposed upon society and the individual, the coherence it perceived in humanity, the element of consistency it introduced into history—these were the things that have drawn men to it as iron is drawn to the lodestone. Both Egypt and Mesopotamia expatiated at great length on the coming of the physical universe into existence. But as to man—the former had no specific account of his creation and the latter brought him into the world only to be the slave of the gods. The Genesis account of creation, on the other hand, is brief, giving every evidence of having been intended only as a prologue to the more important human drama. Elsewhere the Bible practically draws the curtain on cosmological speculations, and, as to God, though He is ever the burden of its message, in whom all the threads of its enormous story converge, He is more Father, King, or Providence than Creator. Once it had arranged the stage and supplied it with all the necessary properties, it paused to express its delight in the work of God, reflected for a moment on the Sabbath peace that pervaded it all, and proceeded to fix its attention on the protagonist and what he was about. Man became its preoccupation, the enthralling purpose of His creation as contrasted with the mortal clay that was to bring about its fulfillment, dominating its every page.

They must have brooded long and tenaciously on man, those farmers and shepherds of ancient Judea, on the subtleties and depths of his being, to have become aware, subconsciously to be sure, of what was many centuries later to be described as his subconscious self, and thus to have come by his enigma; that is, to have apprehended in the

division of his nature the sorrowful grandeur of his destiny.
They must have seen far into the hungers of his flesh to
have concluded that the whole bent of his thinking was
never anything but evil, and have touched the chord of his
aspirations to have come to believe that he was stamped
with the image of the Creator of heaven and earth. The dis-
cord between the one and the other never eluded them and
never gave them rest. Nor were they any less sensitive, despite their absolute faith in the benevolence and lovingkindness of God, to the wretchedness and insufficiency of
man, to the intolerable sick anguish in his heart, the speech-
less, incommunicable sorrow brought on by those inexpli-
cable and terrifying blows of Providence which periodically
laid low the innocent and guilty alike. Who had ever seen
as clearly as Job that man was even more fragile than sin-
ful, as much the target for the arrows of the Almighty as he
was the victim of the snares of Satan? Who had ever written with greater candor and realism of the vanity of human
life, the emptiness of its pleasures, the extent of its travail
and trouble, its ills and its brevity than had Ecclesiastes?
Who has ever articulated with more wonderful pathos the
ebb and flow of human misery, the timorousness and loneliness, the rootless desolation and sense of insecurity, the woe
of the sorrow-laden and grief-stricken than have the
Psalmists?

They were masters of the word, these Judeans, adepts at
inventing the forms of sensations or thoughts and creating
visions, images, or phrases that touched the chords of the
heart to exactest nicety. Endowed with a native gift of observation and taking their illustrations from what was near
at hand, from things natural and congruous, perceptible
and tangible, they expressed the impact of experience con-

cretely and fully. But, though their work bears the super-
scription and imprint of their surroundings, it is stamped with
the likeness of no particular place or time. For, whereas
most pagan writers of antiquity were satisfied to present
the object itself, the Biblical writers were more eager to
represent what it implied. Even the Greek masters, Homer
not excluded, seem to have aimed at reproducing the object
complete, inclusive, finished, abounding in everything that
might conceivably be said of it, congealed into its unalter-
able identity, and imprisoned in a continuous present, fearful lest the reproduction be lacking in a single shade of
color or nuance of sound or thread of texture. The Judeans,
on the other hand, fashioned illustrative fragments, carved
out symbolic torsos, and left them *res infectae*, that is, un-
finished, mutable, a kind of restless, prying question marks.
This undoubtedly accounts for the dynamic, pervasive and
suggestive quality of their language, its sensory and emotional associations, and the ease with which it has evoked
out of the minds of men infinite words of beauty and
thought.

selections from THE BIBLE

The Sacrifice of Isaac

After these things had occurred, God put Abraham to the test.

"Abraham!" He said to him.

"Here am I," he said.

Then He said,

"Take now your son, your only son whom you love, Isaac, and go to the land of Moriah, and offer him there as a burnt-offering on one of the hills, which I will name to you."

Abraham rose early in the morning, saddled his ass, took two of his servants with him and his son Isaac, cut the wood for the burnt-offering, and set out for the place of which God had told him.

On the third day Abraham, raising his eyes, saw the place afar off. Then Abraham said to his servants,

"Stay here with the ass, while I and the boy go a short distance to worship, after which we shall return to you."

Abraham took the wood for the burnt-offering and laid it on his son Isaac; the fire and the knife he carried in his own hand. So they went both of them together.

Isaac spoke to his father Abraham and said,

"Father!"

And he said,

"Here am I, my son."

"I see," he said, "the fire and the wood, but where is the lamb for a burnt-offering?"

"God will provide Himself," Abraham said, "with the lamb for a burnt-offering, my son."

So the two of them went on together.

They came to the place of which God had told him. There Abraham built the altar, arranged the wood, bound his son Isaac, and laid him on the altar on top of the wood. Then Abraham put out his hand, and lifted the knife to slay his son.

But the angel of the Lord called to him from heaven, and said,

"Abraham, Abraham!"

He said,

"Here am I."

And he said,

"Do not lay hands on the boy, do him no harm! For I know now that you are a God-fearing man, since you have not withheld your son, your only son, from Me."

Abraham raised his eyes and saw, there was a ram caught in the brushwood by its horns. So Abraham went and took the ram, and offered it as a burnt-offering in place of his son; and Abraham called the name of the place Adonai-jireh—hence the saying to this day, "In the mount of the Lord He is seen."

Then the angel of the Lord called to Abraham a second time from heaven, and said,

"I swear by Myself," the Lord reveals it—"since you have done this thing, you have not withheld your son, your only son, I will indeed bless you, I will indeed make your descendants as numerous as the stars of heaven and the sand on the seashore. Your descendants shall take possession of the cities of their enemies; through your descendants shall all the nations of the earth be blessed; because you have obeyed My word."

Abraham then returned to his servants, and they set out together for Beer-sheba, as Abraham lived in Beer-sheba.

Genesis, Ch. 22, v. 1-19

(Translated by Solomon Goldman)

The Burning Bush

While Moses was tending the flock of his father-in-law, Jethro, the priest of Midian, he led the flock to the western side of the desert, and came to the mountain of God, Horeb. Then the angel of the Lord appeared to him in a flame of fire, rising out of a bush. He looked, and there was the bush burning with fire without being consumed! So Moses said,

"I will turn aside and see this great sight, why the bush is not burned up."

When the Lord saw that he had turned aside to look at it, God called to him out of the bush.

"Moses, Moses!" he said.

"Here I am!" said he.

"Do not come near here," he said; "take your sandals off your feet; for the place on which you are standing is holy ground." "I am the God of your father," he said, "the God of Abraham, Isaac, and Jacob."

Then Moses hid his face; for he was afraid to look at God.

"I have indeed seen the plight of my people who are in

Egypt," the Lord said, "and I have heard their cry under
their oppressors; for I know their sorrows, and I have come
down to rescue them from the Egyptians and bring them
up out of that land to a land, fine and large, to a land flowing with milk and honey, to the country of the Canaanites,
Hittites, Amorites, Perizzites, Hivvites, and Jebusites. Now
the cry of the Israelites has reached me, and I have also
seen how the Egyptians are oppressing them; so come now,
let me send you to Pharaoh, that you may bring my people,
the Israelites, out of Egypt."

But Moses said to God,

"Who am I, to go to Pharaoh and bring the Israelites out
of Egypt?"

"I will be with you," he said; "and this shall be the sign
for you that I have sent you. When you bring the people
out of Egypt, you shall serve God at this mountain."

"But," said Moses to God, "in case I go to the Israelites
and say to them, 'The God of your fathers has sent me to
you,' and they say to me, 'What is his name?' what am I to
say to them?"

"I am who I am," God said to Moses. Then he said, "Thus
you shall say to the Israelites: ' "I am" has sent me to you.' "

God said further to Moses,

"Thus you shall say to the Israelites:

'Yahweh [the Lord], the God of your fathers, the God of
Abraham, Isaac, and Jacob, has sent me to you.' This has always been my name, and this shall remain my title throughout the ages. Go and assemble the elders of Israel, and say
to them, 'The Lord, the God of your fathers, the God of
Abraham, Isaac, and Jacob, has appeared to me, saying, "I
have given careful heed to you and your treatment in
Egypt, and I have resolved to bring you up out of your

tribulation in Egypt to the land of the Canaanites, Hittites, Amorites, Perizzites, Hivvites, and Jebusites, to a land flowing with milk and honey." ' They will heed your appeal, and then you and the elders of Israel shall come to the king of Egypt and say to him, 'The Lord, the God of the Hebrews, has paid us a visit; so now, let us make a three days' journey into the desert to offer sacrifices to the Lord our God.' I know, however, that the king of Egypt will not let you go without the use of force; so I will stretch out my hand and smite Egypt with all the marvels that I shall perform in it; after that he will let you go."

Exodus, Ch. 3, v. 1-20

Song of Moses

"Hearken, O heavens, that I may speak;
And let the earth hear the words of my mouth.
May my message drop as the rain,
My speech distil as the dew,
As the mist on the fresh grass,
And as showers on the vegetation.
For I proclaim the name of the Lord:
Give glory to our God!
He is a rock; what he does is right;
For all his ways are just;
A trustworthy and never deceiving God;
True and upright is he.
Their imperfection has been the undoing
        of those undutiful to him,
A twisted and crooked generation.
Is this the way to treat the Lord,

You foolish and senseless people?
Is he not your father who created you,
Who made you and fashioned you?
Remember the days of the old,
Review the years, age after age;
Ask your father to inform you,
Your elders to tell you.
When the Most High gave heritages to the nations,
When he made divisions among mankind,
He assigned the realms of the nations
To the various deities;
While the Lord's apportionment was his own people;
Jacob was the allotment for him to hold.
He found them in a desert land,
In the howling waste of a wilderness;
He encircled them, he cared for them;
He guarded them like the pupil of his eye.
Like an eagle stirring up its nestlings,
Dashing against its brood,
Spreading its wings to catch them,
And carrying them on its pinions,
The Lord alone was their leader,
And no foreign god was with him.
He made them mount the heights of the earth,
And they ate the products of the field;
He had them suck honey from crags,
And oil from flinty rocks.
Curds from cows and milk from sheep,
With the fat of lambs and rams,
Herds of Bashan and goats,
With the very choicest wheat,
And the blood of the grapes, a foaming draught,

Jacob ate to the fill;
Jeshurun grew fat, and kicked—
Gorge yourself, and you do become fat and corpulent—
So they forsook the God who made them,
And scoffed at the Rock of their salvation;
They provoked him to jealousy with alien gods,
They vexed him with abominable practices;
They sacrificed to demons that were not at all God,
Gods of whom they had had no experience;
New ones, but lately arrived,
Whom your fathers never revered.
You neglected the very Rock who bore you,
And forgot the God who gave you birth.
When the Lord saw it, he spurned them,
Because he was vexed with their sons and daughters;
And he said, 'I will hide my face from them;
I will see what will become of them;
For a fickle race are they,
Children in whom there is no sense of honor.
They provoked me to jealousy with what is no god;
They vexed me with their vanities;
So I will provoke them to jealousy with what is no nation,
With an impious people I will vex them;
For a fire shall blaze within me,
And burn to the very depths of Sheol;
So that it shall consume the earth and its produce,
And set the bases of the mountains on fire.
I will exhaust calamities upon them;
I will use up my arrows on them.
The devastation of famine, and the ravages of fever,
And malignant pestilence,
And ferocious beasts I will send on them,

Along with poisonous reptiles.
On the street the sword shall cause bereavement,
And terror at home,
For youth and maiden alike,
For the babe as well as the man of gray hairs.
I would have said, "I will cut them in pieces;
I will extinguish the memory of them from men,"
Except that I dreaded irritation from the enemy,
Lest their foes should misinterpret it;
Lest they should say, "It is our might that has triumphed,
And not at all the Lord who did this";
For a people lacking in sense are they,
With no intelligence among them;
If they had any sense, they would perceive this;
They would see through to their own end.'
How could one person chase a thousand,
Or two put ten thousand to flight,
Unless their Rock had sold them,
And the Lord had given them up?
For their rock is not like our Rock,
Nor is our God a thing of nought;
For their vine comes from the stock of Sodom,
And from the fields of Gomorrah;
Their grapes are poisonous grapes;
Bitter clusters are theirs;
Their wine is the venom of dragons,
And the pitiless poison of cobras,
'Is it not stored up with me,
Sealed up in my treasuries,
Against the day of revenge and requital,
Against the time that their foot slips?
For their day of calamity is at hand,

And their doom is coming apace.'
For the Lord will vindicate his people,
And take compassion on his servants,
When he sees that their power is gone,
With neither bound nor free remaining,
And that it is being said, 'Where is their **God**,
The Rock in whom they sought refuge,
He who ate the fat of their sacrifices,
And drank the wine of their libations?
Let him come to your help;
Let him be a shelter over you!'
'Know now that I, I am he,
And that there is no god besides me;
It is I who slay, and bring to life;
When I have inflicted wounds, it is I who heal them,
With none to give deliverance from my power;
For I lift my hand to the heavens,
And declare, "As I live forever,
I will whet my flashing sword,
And my hand shall lay hold on justice;
I will wreak vengeance on my foes,
And punish those who hate me;
I will drench my arrows with blood,
With the blood of captives slain;
And my sword shall devour flesh
From the shaggy heads of the enemy." '
Shout among the nations, O you, his people,
That he shall avenge the blood of his servants,
And wreak vengeance on his adversaries,
And purge his people's land of guilt."

Deuteronomy, Ch. 32, v. 1-43

The Way of Kings

Then Samuel told all the words of the Lord to the people who were asking of him a king; and he said,

"This will be the procedure of the king who shall reign over you: he will take your sons and appoint them for himself for his chariots and for his horsemen; and they shall run before his chariots; and he will appoint for himself commanders of thousands and commanders of hundreds, and some to do his plowing and to reap his harvests and make his implements of war and the equipment for his chariots. He will take your daughters for perfumers, for cooks, and for bakers. He will take the best of your fields and your vineyards and your olive orchards, and give them to his servants. He will take the tenth of your grain crops and of your vineyards and give it to his eunuchs and to his servants. He will take your male and female slaves, and the best of your cattle and your asses, and make use of them for his work. He will take a tenth of your flocks; and you yourselves will become his slaves. Then you will cry out on that day because of your king whom you will have chosen for yourselves; but the Lord will not answer you on that day."

First Book of Samuel, Ch. 8, v. 10-18

Song of the Vineyard

Let me sing for my Loved One
My love song of his vineyard.

My Loved One has a vineyard
On a fertile hill;

He dug it, and cleared it of stones,
And planted it with choice vines;
He built a watchtower in the midst of it,
And hewed out a winevat;
And he expected it to yield grapes,
But it yielded wild grapes.

Now, O inhabitants of Jerusalem, and men of Judah.
Judge, I pray, between me and my vineyard!
What more could have been done for my vineyard
Than that which I have done for it?
Why, then, when I expected it to yield grapes,
Did it yield wild grapes?

So now, I pray, let me tell you
What I will do to my vineyard:
I will remove its hedge, so that it shall be ravaged;
I will break down its wall, so that it shall be trampled
        down;
I will make it a waste, unpruned and unhoed,
That shall spring up with briers and thorns;
And the clouds will I command
That they rain no rain upon it.
For the vineyard of the Lord of hosts is the house of Israel,
And the men of Judah are his cherished plantation;
He looked for justice, but lo! bloodshed,
For righteousness, but lo! a cry.

Isaiah, Ch. 5, v. 1-7

The Coming Utopia

A shoot will spring from the stem of Jesse,
And a sprout from his roots will bear fruit.
And the spirit of the Lord will rest upon him,
The spirit of wisdom and understanding,
The spirit of counsel and might,
The spirit of knowledge and the fear of the Lord—
And his delight will be in the fear of the Lord.
He will not judge by that which his eyes see,
Nor decide by that which his ears hear;
But with justice will he judge the needy,
And with fairness decide for the poor of the land;
He will smite the ruthless with the rod of his mouth,
And with the breath of his lips will he slay the wicked.
Righteousness will be the girdle round his loins,
And faithfulness the girdle round his waist.
Then the wolf will lodge with the lamb,
And the leopard will lie down with the kid;
The calf and the young lion will graze together,
And a little child will lead them.
The cow and the bear will be friends,
Their young ones will lie down together;
And the lion will eat straw like the ox.
The suckling child will play on the hole of the asp,
And the weaned child will put his hand on the viper's den.
They will do no harm or destruction
On all my holy mountain;
For the land will have become full of the knowledge of the
        Lord,
As the waters cover the sea.

Isaiah, Ch. 11, v. 1-9

Ephraim My First-Born

"At that time," is the oracle of the Lord, "I will be the
God of all the families of Israel, and they shall be my
people."

Thus says the Lord:
"The people that escapes from the sword
Shall find grace in the wilderness;
When Israel goes to seek rest,
The Lord from afar shall appear to him.
With an everlasting love have I loved you,
Therefore with kindness will I draw you to me.
Once more will I build you, and you shall be built,
O virgin of Israel!
Once more shall you take your timbrels,
And go out in the dances of those who make merry.
Once more shall you plant your vineyards
On the hills of Samaria;
The planters shall plant, and shall raise their praises;
For a day shall come when the vintagers shall call
On the hills of Ephraim:
'Arise, and let us go up to Zion,
To the Lord our God!'"

For thus says the Lord:
"Raise a peal of gladness for Jacob,
And shout on the top of the mountains;
Publish, praise, and say,
'The Lord has saved His people,
The remnant of Israel.'
Behold, I am bringing them out of the north land,

And will gather them from the uttermost parts of the earth,
Among them the blind and the lame,
The woman with child, and her that is about to give birth—
A great company shall they return hither.
With weeping they went away, but with consolation will
        I bring them back;
I will lead them to streams of water,
By a level way on which they shall not stumble;
For I have become a father to Israel,
And Ephraim is my first-born.

"Hear the word of the Lord, O you nations,
And announce it in distant coastlands;
Say, 'He who scattered Israel shall gather him,
And shall keep him as a shepherd keeps his flock.'
For the Lord has ransomed Jacob,
He has redeemed him from the hand of those that were
        stronger than he.
They shall come and be jubilant on the height of Zion,
They shall be radiant at the goodness of the Lord—
At the grain, the wine, and the oil,
At the young of the flock and the herd.
They shall be like a well-watered garden,
And they shall languish no more.
Then shall the maiden rejoice in the dance,
And the young men and the old shall make merry;
For I will turn their mourning to joy,
I will comfort them, and will give them gladness
        instead of grief.
I will satisfy the priests with fat things,
And my people shall have their fill of my goodness,"
Is the oracle of the Lord.

Thus says the Lord:
"Hark! in Ramah is heard lamentation, bitter weeping!
It is Rachel weeping for her children,
Refusing to be comforted for her children,
        because they are not."

Thus says the Lord:
 Restrain your voice from weeping,
And your eyes from tears!
For your labor shall have its reward,"
Is the oracle of the Lord;
"And they shall return from the land of the enemy.
There is hope for your future,"
Is the oracle of the Lord;
"And your children shall return to their own domain.

"Truly have I heard Ephraim bemoaning:
'Thou has chastened me, and I let myself be chastened,
Like an untrained calf;
O restore me, that I may be restored!
For thou art the Lord my God.
Since I was exiled, I have repented,
And since I was disciplined, I have smitten upon my thigh;
I am ashamed and confounded,
For I bear the disgrace of my youth.'
'Is Ephraim my precious son?
Is he my darling child?
For as often as I speak of him,
I cherish his memory still.
Therefore my heart yearns for him,
I must have pity upon him,'
Is the oracle of the Lord.

"Set up waymarks for yourself,
Make yourself guideposts;
Pay heed to the highway,
The way by which you went.
Return, O virgin of Israel,
Return to these your cities!
How long will you hesitate,
O backturning daughter?
For the Lord has created a new thing on the earth—
The woman woos the man!"

Thus says the Lord of hosts, the God of Israel:
"Once more shall they use this speech,
In the land and the cities of Judah,
When I have restored their fortunes:
'The Lord bless you, O home of righteousness,
O holy mountain!'
Yea, the people of Judah shall dwell there,
And all her cities as well—
The plowmen, and those who wander with flocks.
For I shall have satisfied the weary spirit,
And every drooping spirit I shall have filled."

Jeremiah, Ch. 31, v. 1-25

The Dry Bones

The hand of the Lord was upon me; and the Lord carried me out by the spirit, and set me down in the midst of a valley which was full of bones. He led me all round them, and lo! there were very many of them on the surface of the valley, and lo! they were very dry. Then he said to me,

"O mortal man, can these bones live?"

And I answered,

"O Lord God, thou knowest."

Then he said to me,

"Prophesy over these bones, and say to them, 'O dry bones, hear the word of the Lord! Thus says the Lord God to these bones: Behold, I am causing breath to enter you, and you shall live. I will put sinews upon you, and will clothe you with flesh, and cover you with skin; then I will put breath into you, and you shall live; and you shall know that I am the Lord.'"

So I prophesied as I had been commanded; and as I prophesied, there was a sound; and lo! there followed a rustling; and the bones came together, bone to its bone. And as I looked, lo! there were sinews upon them, and flesh came up, and skin covered them over; but there was no breath in them. Then he said to me,

"Prophesy to the breath; prophesy, O mortal man, and say to the breath, 'Thus says the Lord God: Come from the four winds, O breath, and breathe into these slain men, that they may live!'"

So I prophesied as he had commanded me; and the breath came into them, and they lived, and stood upon their feet—an exceedingly great host. Then he said to me,

"O mortal man, these bones are the whole house of Israel. Behold, they keep saying, 'Our bones are dried up, and our hope is lost; we are completely cut off.' Therefore prophesy, and say to them, 'Thus says the Lord God: Behold, I am opening your graves, and will raise you out of your graves, O my people, and will bring you into the land of Israel. And when I open your graves, and raise you out of your graves, O my people, you shall know that I am the Lord.

Then I will put my spirit into you, and you shall live; and
I will settle you on your own land; and you shall know that
I am the Lord. I have spoken it, and I will do it,' is the
oracle of the Lord."

Ezekiel, Ch. 37, v. 1-14

When a People Sows the Wind

Thus the Lord God showed me;
And lo, a basket of summer fruit!
And he said, "What do you see, Amos?"
And I said, "A basket of summer fruit."
Then the Lord said to me,
"The end has come to my people Israel;
I will never again pass them by.
The songs of the palace shall become dirges on that day,"
Is the oracle of the Lord God;
"Many shall be the carcasses; in every place they shall be
        cast out."

Hear this, you who trample upon the needy,
And would bring the poor of the land to an end,
Saying, "When will the new moon pass
That we may sell grain,
And the Sabbath that we may offer wheat for sale,"
Making the ephah small and the price great,
And falsifying the scales;
Buying the poor for silver,
And the needy in exchange for a pair of sandals,
And selling the refuse of the grain.

The Lord has sworn by the pride of Jacob,
"I will never forget all their deeds!"
Shall not the land tremble because of this,
And all who dwell therein mourn;
And all of it rise up like the Nile,
And be shaken and sink like the Nile of Egypt?

"And it shall come to pass on that day,"
Is the oracle of the Lord God,
"That I will cause the sun to set at noon,
And I will darken the earth in broad daylight;
And I will turn your festivals into mourning,
And all your songs into dirges;
And I will put sackcloth upon all loins,
And baldness on every head;
And I will make it like the mourning for an only son,
And the end of it like a bitter day."

"Behold days are coming,"
Is the oracle of the Lord God,
"When I will send famine upon the land;
Not a famine of bread,
Nor a thirst for water,
But for hearing the words of the Lord.
And they shall wander from sea to sea,
And run from north to east,
To seek the word of the Lord;
But shall not find it.

"On that day they shall faint,
The fair maidens and the young men, for thirst;
They who swear by Ashimah of Samaria,

And say, 'As thy god lives, O Dan'
And 'As thy God lives, O Beer-sheba';
They shall fall, never to rise again."

Amos, Ch. 8

God's Word and God's Torah

The heavens are telling the glory of God,
And the sky shows forth the work of his hands.
Day unto day pours forth speech,
And night unto night declares knowledge.

There is no speech, nor are there words;
Their voice is not heard;
Yet their voice goes forth through all the earth,
And their words to the ends of the world.

In them he has pitched a tent for the sun,
Who is like a bridegroom coming forth from his chamber,
And rejoices like a strong man to run the course;
From one end of the heavens is his starting-point,
And his circuit is to the other end;
And nothing is hid from the heat thereof.

The law of the Lord is perfect, renewing the life;
The decree of the Lord is trustworthy,
        making wise the simple;
The precepts of the Lord are right, rejoicing the heart;
The command of the Lord is pure, enlightening the eyes;
The fear of the Lord is clean, enduring forever.
The judgments of the Lord are true, they are also right;

They are more valuable than gold, and much fine gold;
Also sweeter than honey, and the droppings of
      the honeycomb.

Thy servant also is instructed by them,
In keeping them there is great reward.
Who can discern his errors?
Of unconscious ones, hold me guiltless!
Moreover, restrain thy servant from wilful ones,
May they not rule over me!
Then shall I be blameless, and be acquitted of much
      transgression.
May the words of my mouth and the meditation of my
      heart
Be acceptable before thee,
O Lord, my rock and my avenger!

Psalms, Ch. 19

God Speaks

    Then the Lord answered Job from the whirlwind, saying,
"Who is this that obscures counsel
By words without knowledge?
Gird up, now, your loins like a man,
That I may question you, and do you instruct me.

"Where were you when I laid the foundations of the earth?
Declare, if you have insight.
Who fixed its measurements, for you should know?
Or who stretched a line over it?
Upon what were its bases sunk,

Or who laid its cornerstone,
When the morning stars sang together,
And all the heavenly beings shouted for joy?

"Who enclosed the sea with doors,
When it burst forth, issuing from the womb,
When I made the cloud its covering,
And dense darkness its swaddlingband;
When I imposed upon it my decree,
And established its barrier and doors;
And said, 'Thus far shall you come and no farther,
And here shall your proud waves be stayed'?

"Have you ever in your life commanded the morning?
Or assigned its place to the dawn,
That it should lay hold of the corners of the earth,
And the wicked be shaken out of it?
It changes like clay under the seal,
And is dyed like a garment.
Their light is withdrawn from the wicked,
And the arm of the proud is broken.

"Have you gone to the sources of the sea,
Or walked in the hollows of the deep?
Have the gates of death been revealed to you,
Or can you see the gates of darkness?
Have you considered the breadth of the earth?
Tell, if you know all this.

"Which is the way where light dwells,
And which is the place of darkness,
That you may take it to its border,

And that you may perceive the paths to its home?
You know, for you were born then,
And the number of your days is great!

"Have you been to the storehouses of snow,
Or do you see the storehouses of hail,
Which I have reserved against the time of distress,
Against the day of war and battle?
Which is the way to where light is distributed?
Where does the east wind spread itself over the earth?
Who cleaved its channel for the torrent,
And a way for the thunderbolts,
To send rain on a land without people,
On the steppe where there is no man;
To satisfy the waste ground and desolate,
And to cause the blade of grass to spring up?

"Has the rain a father?
Or who brought forth the dew drops?
From whose womb did the ice come forth?
And who gave birth to the hoarfrost of the skies,
When the waters congeal like a stone,
And the surface of the deep is frozen solid?

"Can you bind the chains of the Pleiades,
Or loosen the girdle of Orion?
Can you send forth Mazzaroth in its season,
And lead forth the Bear with its satellites?
Do you know the laws of the heavens?
Or do you appoint the arrangements of the earth?
Can you lift your voice up to the clouds,
That a flood of waters may cover you?

"Can you send forth the lightnings that they may go
And say to you, 'Here we are!'
Who put wisdom in the inner parts,
Or who gave insight to the mind?
Who counts the clouds by wisdom?
And who tilts the waterskins of the heavens,
When the dust runs into a mass,
And the clods stick together?

"Do you hunt prey for the lioness,
Or satisfy the hunger of young lions,
When they crouch in dens,
Or lie in wait in the thicket?
Who provides its prey for the raven,
When its young ones cry unto God,
And wander without food?

Job, Ch. 38

Beauty

"Ah, you are beautiful, my love; ah, you are beautiful!
Your eyes are doves, behind your veil.
Your hair is like a flock of goats, streaming down from
        Mount Gilead.
Your teeth are like a flock of ewes ready for shearing,
        that have come up from the washing,
All of which bear twins, and none of which loses its young.
Your lips are like a thread of scarlet, and your mouth is
        comely.
Your temple is like a slice of pomegranate,
        behind your veil.
Your neck is like the tower of David, built as an armory,

With a thousand bucklers hung upon it,
    all kinds of warriors' shields.
Your two breasts are like two fawns, twins of a gazelle,
    that pasture among the hyacinths.
Until the day blows, and the shadows flee,
I will betake myself to the mountain of myrrh,
    and to the hill of frankincense.
You are altogether beautiful, my love,
    and there is no blemish in you.

                    Song of Songs, Ch. 4, v. 1-7

Vanity

    The words of Koheleth, the son of David, who was king in Jerusalem.

"Vanity of vanities," says Koheleth,
"Vanity of vanities, all is vanity!
What does a man gain from all his toil
At which he toils beneath the sun?
One generation goes, and another comes,
While the earth endures forever.
The sun rises and the sun sets,
And hastens to the place where he rose.
The wind blows toward the south,
And returns to the north.
Turning, turning, the wind blows,
And returns upon its circuit.
All rivers run to the sea,
But the sea is never full;
To the place where the rivers flow,
There they continue to flow.

All things are wearisome;
One cannot recount them;
The eye is not satisfied with seeing,
Nor is the ear filled with hearing.
Whatsoever has been is that which will be;
And whatsoever has been done is that which will be done;
And there is nothing new under the sun.
Is there a thing of which it is said, 'Lo, this is new'?
It was already in existence in the ages
Which were before us.
There is no memory of earlier people;
And likewise of later people who shall be,
There will be no memory with those who are later still."

"I, Koheleth, was king over Israel in Jerusalem; and I set my mind to search and to investigate through wisdom everything that is done beneath the heavens. It is an evil task that God has given the sons of man with which to occupy themselves. I have seen everything that has been done under the sun; and lo, everything is vanity and striving for the wind.

"The crooked cannot be made straight,
     And that which is lacking cannot be counted.

"I thought within myself thus: I am great and have increased in wisdom above all that were before me over Jerusalem; and my mind has seen abundant wisdom and knowledge. So I set my mind to knowing wisdom and to knowing madness and folly. I am convinced that this too is striving for the wind.

"For with more wisdom is more worry,
     And increase of knowledge is increase of sorrow."

Ecclesiastes, Ch 1

THE TALMUD

Simon Federbush

The Talmud is unique among the classics of world literature. No other book has exercised such an overwhelming influence upon the spirit of men as the Talmud upon the Jewish people; no other book has been the focus of such a bitter struggle between its admirers and its enemies throughout the ages; no other literary production has ever been exposed to such malicious misrepresentations. It is only in recent times that an unbiased evaluation of the Talmud has dawned among the Christian scholars, who are now trying to make good the injustices done to the Talmud either by malevolence or ignorance.

Actually, the Talmud is not a book; it is a whole literature—the result of the collective work of many successive generations. Its more than 6,000 folio pages contain the spiritual creativeness of a period of nearly 1,000 years (about 450 before and 500 after the Christian Era). More than 2,000 scholars from various countries, especially Palestine and Babylon, made contributions to it.

The Talmud is divided into the Babylonian Talmud, or Talmud Babli, and the Palestinian Talmud, called the Tal-

mud Yerushalmi. The Talmud Babli is much better known
and more widely studied than the Palestinian Talmud.
There was a time when the Talmud Yerushalmi was entirely unknown, even among Jewish scholars. Consequently,
the name "Talmud" refers frequently only to the Talmud
Babli. The Babylonian Talmud is considerably more vo-
luminous than the Palestinian (which is less than one-third
its size), because it was completed about 200 years later
and contains the contributions of the latest Amoraim.

Each Talmud consists of two parts: The Mishnah and
the Gemara. The Mishnah was edited by the Patriarch
Rabbi Jehuda about the year 200 of the Christian Era. It
contains the first codification of the Jewish law since the
Bible, and is written in the Hebrew language. The Gemara
contains a commentary and amplification of the Mishnah.
In addition, it includes many portions of Amoraic teachings which have only a very loose connection with the contents of the Mishnah. The Gemara is written mainly in
Aramaic, and only a small part of it in Hebrew. The scholars of the Mishnah are the Tannaim (teachers), and those
of the Gemara are known as Amoraim (interpreters).

The Talmud Babli was compiled and edited by Rab Ashi
and Rabina in the Academy of Sura in Babylon, about the
year 500. These scholars concluded the era of the Amoraim.
There are, however, in the Talmud Babli additions and supplements of the later scholars, the Saboraim, who followed
the Amoraim, and put the finishing touches to the Talmud
Babli. The Talmud Yerushalmi was compiled in Tiberias by
Rabbi Johanan, the greatest sage and teacher of his generation, in about the year 300, but the final edition was completed 150 years later by Jona ben Mani and Jose ben Abin.

The Talmud Babli is distinguished by its dialectic pro-

fundity and the clarity of its definitions, and analyses. The
characteristics of the Talmud Yerushalmi are its simplicity
and logic. `

Between the academies of Palestine and those of Babylon,
the most famous of which were Nehardea, Sura, and Pum-
bedita, there was maintained a constant inter-communica-
tion by roving scholars called "Nehuti." Their mission was
to secure a continuous exchange of teachings, so that the
Palestinian scholars and their concepts were well known in
the Babylonian academies, and vice versa. This collabora-
tion between the spiritual centers of Palestine and the
Diaspora—which could well serve as an example for cultural alliance between Israel and the Diaspora in our own
time—ensured the unification of Jewish spiritual life during
the Talmudic period. This unification also found expression
in both Talmuds, as the Palestinian scholars are among the
most significant contributors to the Babylonian Talmud,
and the Babylonian sages are frequently cited in the Talmud Yerushalmi, thus giving both works a unified character
despite many variances rooted in the differences between
Palestinian and Babylonian Jewry.

The Talmud represents the Jewish tradition transmitted
orally through the centuries, the unwritten teachings which
were handed down from generation to generation, just as
the written law was. The Bible frequently mentions customs and laws prevailing in Israel besides the written law.
The Talmud is the oral law put into writing. In the beginning, however, this undertaking encountered many difficulties, one reason being that, according to an ancient
stipulation, oral teachings were prohibited from being put
into writing (*Gittin 60b*).

After the canonization of the books of the Bible, no other

religious book was allowed to be added to the Holy Scriptures; all additional religious teachings had to remain unwritten. Rabbi Sharira Gaon therefore assumed that Rabbi Jehuda the Patriarch compiled and edited the Mishnah by memorizing its vast contents, a feat which appears incredible. There is evidence, however, in the Talmud itself, that the Tannaim, such as Rabbi Akiba and others, possessed written compilations of the oral law.

The compiling of the Talmud was therefore an innovation in that it committed the oral lore to writing—now the authoritative source of the oral law—both in private studies as well as in public teaching.

This departure from the traditional stipulation became necessary because Talmudic literature had so expanded that it was impossible for one to master it by sheer memorizing. In order to preserve them the traditional teachings had to be put into written form, lest they fall into oblivion as a result of the homelessness of the Jewish people and the instability of Jewish life. Rabbi Johanan, the first compiler of the Talmud in written form, decreed this significant deviation from the accepted system by saying: "It is preferable to violate one law of the Torah lest the whole Torah be forgotten" (*Temura, 14b*).

From the literary point of view, the Talmud is composed of two main parts: the Halakah and the Agada. The Halakah contains the Jewish law. The Talmudic law is, in its basic precepts, a direct continuation of the Biblical teachings, with amplifications to meet the challenge of changing circumstances. The Jewish conception of pure monotheism led both Biblical and Talmudical law to recognize the equality of men, for they are the children of one Creator. Both have in common the protection of the weak, abhorrence of all tyranny, and devotion to freedom. The Halakah teaches the highest esteem for manual work, and contains progressive regulations for the protection of labor which are unrivaled even by the most modern legislation. It is merciful in its penal code, tending toward the abolition of capital punishment, conceiving of legal penalties not as vengeance but as protection for society and treating crime more as a pathological phenomenon than anything else. It asks, therefore, for sympathy and compassion in the execution of punishment. Restricting private ownership in the interest of public welfare, it calls for a most liberal social order. It considers ethical family life as a prerequisite for a happy society.

In a word, Talmudic law is the application and fulfillment of the lofty humanitarian ideals of the Torah.

The Agada, comprising approximately one-third of the Talmud Babli and only one-sixth of the Talmud Yerushalmi, contains metaphysical meditations, theology, philosophy, ethics, poetry, historical events, traditions, and descriptions of personalities, philological and exegetical portions, and scientific passages dealing with medicine, mathematics, astronomy, psychology, botany, etc.

It is for the Jewish people the only historical source for many events which occurred during the centuries of the Talmudic era, treating as it does, the happenings, ideas, personages and conditions of those times. The Agada also contains superb literature in prose and poetry, an inexhaustible fountain of edification and joy for the masses of Jews who were unable to follow the rather intricate study of Halakic jurisprudence.

The difference between the Halakah and the Agada is illustrated in the Talmud by the following story: Rabbi

Abahu and Rabbi Hia ben Aba met at a certain place. Rabbi Hia lectured on Halakah while Rabbi Abahu preached Agada. The people deserted the gathering of Rabbi Hia and joined the audience of Rabbi Abahu. Rabbi Hia thereupon felt depressed. Said Rabbi Abahu to him: "I shall tell you a parable. Two people came to a city, one selling gems and the other vending simple necessities. To whom do most people flock? Is it not to the one who offers the plain necessities?" (*Sota 40*).

Rabbi Abahu, being an Agadist, disregarded in his modesty the fact that the Agada, too, contains in its store many precious gems.

The first edition of Talmud Babli was completed in 1520 in Venice, Italy, by Daniel Bomberg. In order to publish it, he had to receive permission from the Vatican. To the first edition there were attached the commentaries of Rashi and Tosafoth, on the right and left margins of each page, which set a pattern for all subsequent editions. In 1523, Bomberg published the first edition of the Talmud Yerushalmi. Among the many subsequent editions of the Talmud, the most significant was the Basel edition which appeared during 1578-1581, mutilated by the censor. In this edition, on which most subsequent editions were based, many passages considered reprehensible to Christianity were omitted and many phrases arbitrarily modified. In some later editions, the original text of the Talmud was restored.

The external history of the Talmud reflects the ordeals in the history of the Jewish people. The defamation of the Talmud was one of the tactics used in the crusade against them. The anti-Semites could not assail the Hebrew Bible because it was recognized by the Christian Church as a sanctified source of Christianity. So they concentrated their attacks upon the Talmud, which was regarded as the core of Jewish resistance to conversion to Christianity. At the very time that the Babylonian Talmud was completed, Emperor Justinian issued an edict prohibiting the use of the traditional exposition of the Holy Scriptures according to the teachings of the Talmudic scholars. This was the forerunner of the unceasing fight against the Talmud through the Middle Ages, which has lasted to modern times. Condemnation of the Talmud was frequently used as justification for contemplated persecutions of the Jews.

The attacks on the Talmud were usually initiated by apostate Jews, who were considered by Christians as experts in Jewish literature. The charges against the Talmud launched by a convert, Nicholas Donin, led to the first public disputation between Jews and Christians, which resulted in the first burning of the parchments of the Talmud in Paris in 1244. Popes and kings participated in the campaign to suppress study of the Talmud and to destroy its editions. One of the best known disputations on the Talmud took place in Barcelona in 1263 between Nachmanides, the famous Jewish scholar, and Pablo Christiani. In spite of Nachmanides' brilliant and convincing defense of the Talmud which was commended by the King—although with the derogatory remark: "I have never witnessed such an excellent defense of an unjust cause"—the dispute resulted in a papal Bull against the Talmud. In 1415, Pope Martin V issued a Bull forbidding Jews to read the Talmud and ordering the destruction of its copies. On the very day of the Jewish New Year, 1520, the Talmud was confiscated and burned publicly in Rome, in accordance with a decree of the Inquisition. The same occurred in Cremona, Italy, in 1559. Popes Gregory XIII and Clement VIII renewed in 1593 the interdiction against reading and owning the Talmud. In Poland, Bishop Dembowski ordered the burning of the Talmud in 1757.

In all these disputes, the accusers were also the absolute judges, and the resulting condemnation was inevitable. There was no appeal to an impartial body.

The historian Josephus Flavius tells the story of the first attempt of Apion of Alexandria to slander Jews and their religion by distortion and forgery. This design against Israel was repeated by the converted Jew, John Pfefferkorn, in the early 1600's. According to Graetz, he was a butcher by trade and illiterate, who was jailed for burglary. On his release he forsook the faith of his ancestors, placing himself under the protection of the Dominican Friars who exploited his treacherous service in promoting their anti-Jewish policy. Pfefferkorn published, under the auspices of the Dominicans, several pamphlets to show that Talmudic literature was hostile to Christianity. The Christian scholar, Johann Reuchlin, defended the Talmud valiantly in his publications, and demanded freedom of religion for the Jews. Some of these historic documents are contained in the famous *Epistolae Obscurorum Virorum.* Reuchlin's rebuke of the wicked vilifiers of the Talmud is noteworthy: "The Talmud does not exist for the purpose that each scoundrel should trample on it with dirty feet and boast: 'I know it too.' "

Curiously enough, this passionate dispute about the Talmud had far-reaching consequences for the militant Christian Church. The controversy about the Talmud between bigots and the liberal-minded humanists resulted in a deep schism which paved the way for the Reformation.

A new crusade of incitement against the Talmud began with Johann Andreas Eisenmenger, who set a pattern for all subsequent forgers of the Talmud, such as the Russian Paraneites and the Nazi falsifiers. His book *Uncovered Judaism* contains a deliberate distortion of the spirit and character of the Talmud, and it contributed a great deal to the spreading of intolerance against Jews. The Bishop and Elector of Mainz asked the Kaiser to prohibit the publication of Eisenmenger's book which, in the Bishop's words, "arose from evil motives and must lead to fatal consequences." The first edition was banned. Eisenmenger proposed to the Jewish community of Frankfurt that he would withdraw his book, if given 30,000 talers. But this blackmail was rejected. The book appeared after Eisenmenger's death in 1711, and was a source for the instigation of Jew-hatred.

The German Orientalist Gildemeister, reviewing the increasing anti-Talmudic literature, remarked: "The less they know about the Talmud, the more they write about it."

In order to remedy this situation, Reuchlin called for an objective and scientific study of the Talmud, which led to a new orientation and, finally, a new appraisal of Talmudic literature. Aware of the injustice done to the Talmud by anti-Semitic pseudo-scholars, and anxious to undo it, scholars placed Talmudic research on a new, unbiased basis. Prominent among the representatives of this school were Travers Herford, the author of *The Pharisees* and George Foot Moore, author of *Christian Writers on Judaism*, and *Judaism*. They attempted to rectify all the misinterpretations and misquotations of the text. Drawing upon authentic sources, they tried to rehabilitate the Pharisaic teaching contained in the Talmud, which was charged with hypocrisy by some Christian Church Fathers on the basis of the con-

demnation of the Pharisees found in the New Testament
(*Mat. 23*). Thus a false impression, still prevalent among
some Christian writers, was created concerning the Pharisees. The Pharisaic sages themselves chastised some of their
followers, enumerating five examples of hypocritical Pharisees (*Sota 22b*), as did the Jewish prophets in regard to
their generation. The spiritual leaders of the Pharisees,
however, preached purity of heart and absolute sincerity
and single-mindedness in thought and in action. Moreover,
the unbiased Christian scholars showed that the teaching of
Jesus in regard to love of man and mercy to the enemy is
no more than an elaboration of the religious and humanitarian concepts of the Pharisaic sages.

This new trend in the evaluation of the Talmudic literature was facilitated by the translation of the Talmud into
modern languages. The Palestinian Talmud was translated
by M. Schwab into French; the Babylonian Talmud was
translated into German by L. Goldschmidt, and into English by Radkinson. A Hebrew translation is in preparation
by the publishing house Dvir in Tel Aviv.

Because of its didactic significance as a religious and
ethical code, the study of the Talmud is considered to be
one of the greatest virtues in Judaism. The study of Torah,
both the written and oral, is conceived as an outgrowth of
a sincere love of Torah, not merely as an imposed obligation. This found expression in the prayers for "a life which
is dedicated to the love of the Torah." (*Ahavath Torah*)
The Talmudic scholar was held in the highest esteem; a
gifted Talmud student was the dream and the pride of all
parents.

Devotion to Torah constituted the unshakable rock of

Jewish survival, defying all ordeals of the Diaspora. This experience through the ages manifested itself in the words: "The Torah is our life and our preservation." The Talmud was moreover a stimulating factor in fostering the intellectual abilities of the Jews in other spheres as well.

It has ruled supreme in Jewish life because of the admiration for and faith in the sages of the Talmud prevailing among Jewish people, of whom they were the spiritual and political leaders, the judges and teachers. These services were performed without compensation in conformity with the Talmudic doctrine: Hillel instructed his disciples: "He who makes use of the toga of the Torah for personal advantage should perish."

In accordance with this conception, the Talmudic scholars earned their livelihood mostly by manual labor. The famous Hillel was a woodchopper; Rabbi Joshua ben Hananiah produced charcoal; Rabbi Johanan was a shoemaker and Rabbi Itzhak a blacksmith. They held their occupations in honor and are referred to in the Talmud as Johanan the shoemaker, Itzhak the blacksmith, etc. It was the realization of their own teaching: "Love work, and avoid public office" (*Aboth I*).

The Jewish people saw them as martyrs for the Torah and its principles; and many famous scholars willingly gave their lives for the sanctification of the Jewish religion. Among the martyrs were the greatest of the Tannaim, Rabbi Akiba, Rabbi Ismael, Rabbi Hanina ben Taradion, Rabbi Jehuda ben Baba, and many others. Rabbi Akiba defied Rome's decree prohibiting the study of the Torah and continued to study in his numerous academies. Finally he was caught and sentenced to death. When he was tortured, his face displayed blissful elation. As his disciples expressed

astonishment at this unusual composure, Rabbi Akiba replied: "During all of my life, I had a deep desire to fulfill
the commandment 'Thou shalt love God with all Thy soul,'
and now that I am about to realize it, should I not be
happy?"

It is no wonder then that the glory of men of such great
stature so deeply influenced the Jewish people. They were
indeed examples of unflinching faithfulness to professed
ideals. Israel, the "People of the Book," embraced the Talmud as the Book of the people.

Paraphrasing Ahad Ha-am's saying about the Sabbath, it
may rightly be said: "More than the Jewish people preserved the Talmud, the Talmud preserved the Jewish people."

selections from THE TALMUD

Against Cruelty to Animals

No man may buy a beast, an animal or a bird until he has provided food for it.   *Y. Yebamot, 15, 3*

Rab Huna and Rab Hisda were seated together. Gneiba passed by, and the one Rabbi said to the other: "Let us rise before him because he is a sage."

The other answered: "Shall we rise up before a quarrelsome person, who torments Mar Ukbah, the Chief Justice?"

Gneiba halted, however, and took his seat near them, and said: "Greetings to you, O Kings!"

The Rabbis asked: "Why do you greet us so?"

Gneiba replied: "Because we read in Proverbs 8:15: 'By me (wisdom) kings reign.'"

They invited him into the house and set food before him. He said: "I have not yet fed my beast, and Rab Judah has said in the name of Rab that a man is forbidden to eat unless he has fed his beasts, as it is written (Deut. 11:15): 'I will give grass in thy fields for thy cattle, and thou shalt eat and be satisfied.'"   *Gittin, 62*

The Patriarch, Rabbi Judah I, suffered from toothache for many years. Why was he thus punished? Because he

71

once saw a bound calf being taken to the slaughter. The calf bleated and appealed for his aid, but the Rabbi said: "Go, since it is for this that thou hast been created."

And how was the Patriarch cured? He once saw a litter of mice being carried to the river to be drowned. He said: "Let them go free, for it is written that 'The Lord is good to all; and His tender mercies are over all His works.'" (*Ps. 145:9*)   *Y. Kilaim, Chap. 9*

Zion and the Diaspora

Rabbi Hananiah, the son of Rabbi Joshua's sister, emigrated to Babylonia. Believing himself to be the greatest sage in his generation, he usurped the prerogatives of the Palestinian sages and fixed the calendar for the year. When this became known in Palestine, two sages were sent to him. When they arrived and declared themselves as disciples, he proclaimed them to be great men in Israel. Determined, however, to decrease his authority, the newcomers continually rendered opinions opposed to his. Rabbi Hananiah thereupon declared them to be men of no merit. They replied: "Thou hast built and canst not destroy; thou hast made fences and canst not now make a breach."

He inquired: "Why do you continually oppose me?"

They answered: "Because thou usurpest the privileges belonging to Palestine."

"But Rabbi Akiba also fixed a calendar outside of Palestine," said he.

They said: "But he left none like him in Palestine."

"Neither did I," rejoined Rabbi Hananiah.

The two sages replied: "The kids thou hast left behind have become goats with horns. They instructed us to tell thee: 'If Rabbi Hananiah gives ear, well and good; if not, we will excommunicate him.' Therefore are we to tell the people: 'if ye care naught for Zion, go ye up on the mountain. Your chief, Ahiah, will erect an altar, Hananiah will play before it with a harp, and all will say: "We have no share in the God of Israel." ' "

The populace cried out: "Of surety we have a share in the God of Israel."

"Then follow the law that comes out of Zion, not the laws of each community."   *Berakot, 63*

Authors and Translators

"Wealth and riches are in his house, and his benevolence standeth forever." This describes the man who writes excellent books and makes them easily available to others.

Ketubot, 50

Rabbi Judah ben Ilai said: "He who translates a verse with strict literalness is a falsifier, and he who makes additions to it is a blasphemer."   *Kiddushin, 49a*

The day on which the Torah was translated into Greek was a mournful day unto Israel. It was like unto the day when the Golden Calf was made. Why? Because the Torah cannot be translated exactly as it ought to be.

Soferim, Chap. 1

The Men of the Great Synagogue observed many fasts in order that the writers of the Scrolls of the Torah, of the Tefillin, and of the Mezuzot might not grow rich, lest, in becoming rich, they might be tempted to write no longer.

Pesahim, 50b

Torah

What is the most important verse in the Bible? "In all thy ways know Him." (*Prov. 3:6*)   *Berakot, 63*

"Is not My word like as fire? said the Lord; and like a hammer that breaketh the rock in pieces?" (*Jer. 23:29*). As a hammer divideth fire into many sparks, so one verse of Scripture has many meanings and many explanations.

Sanhedrin, 34a

The Rabbis said: Let not the Mashal (Parable) be lightly regarded, for by means of it a man can understand the words of Torah. It is like a king who has lost a pearl and finds it with the aid of a candle worth only a centime. Solomon clarified the Law by means of parables. R. Nahman, R. Jose, R. Shila and R. Hanina illustrated the idea thus: The wise king tied a rope at the entrance of a labyrinth, and was able to find his way out of it; he cut a path in a wild thicket of reeds; he fashioned a handle for a heavy case of fruit so that it could be lifted; he formed a handle for a cask of hot liquid so that it could be moved; he joined rope to rope, and was able to draw water from the deep well. Thus from word to word, from Mashal to Mashal, Solomon attained the uttermost secret of the Torah.

Kohelet Rabbah on 2, 11, etc.

Earned Bread

It was said of Rabbi Phinehas ben Jair that he never ate a slice of bread that did not belong to him by purchase. Even in his father's house he ate no food, since he had adopted this fixed norm of conduct.

Once Rabbi Judah I invited him to a meal. Out of honor to the Patriarchate, he was prepared to make an exception. He explained that in one instance a man invites a guest even though he must deprive himself; another invites a guest unwillingly even though he can afford the hospitality. Rabbi, however, was both willing and able to afford the courtesy; therefore, no good reason presented itself to decline it. As it happened, Rabbi Phinehas entered through a side door, and beheld in an enclosure several white mules. He said: "These animals are accustomed to injure people severely; a pious man should not possess them." And he refused to enter the house. *Hullin, 7*

R. Hanan said: The mind is not contented unless one eats of the fruit of his own labor. Even the baker's bread is unpalatable, though a man pay for it with money earned by his own labor. *Shekalim, 3*

Business Methods

"He performed no evil against his fellow man," (Psalm 15:3) namely he began no competitive enterprise or trade where there was no demand for it. *Makkot, 24*

Rabbi Judah ben Ilai declared that a shopkeeper should not give to children-customers sweetmeats to attract their patronage. The other Rabbis permitted this, since the merchant does not prevent his competitor from doing likewise. . . . The others declared: The public owes him grateful remembrance, since this will prevent high prices on foodstuffs, and will also work against the practice of holding goods back for a higher market.

Baba Metzia, 4, 12, Mishnah

Rab Gidal was bargaining for a certain piece of ground,
but Rab Abba bought it instead. Rab Gidal complained to
R. Zeira, and when Rab Abba visited him, R. Zeira inquired: "If a poor man bends down to pick up something
that belongs to no one else, and, as he does so, another
person snatches it away, what would you call the latter?"

"I would call him a wicked person," replied R. Abba.

"Then why did you snatch the property away from R.
Gidal?"

"I did not know that he was bargaining for it."

"Will you sell it to him now?"

"No," answered R. Abba. "It was my first purchase, and
I do not care to admit a mistake in my initial land enterprise. However," he continued, "R. Gidal may have it as a
gift from me."

R. Gidal refused to accept it, however, and R. Abba declined to use it; hence it was turned over to the Disciples.

Berakot, 10

Certain officers of the Exilarch were designated to seal up
weights and measures, and also to regulate prices. Samuel
said to his Disciple Karna: "Go and tell them they have no
right to regulate prices." But they answered: "What is thy
name?" And when they were told: Karna, meaning a horn,
they laughed at him and said: "Thou shouldst have a horn
on thy forehead."

They accepted the opinion of R. Isaac, who favored the
regulation of prices in order to obstruct the tactics of swin-
dlers. The latter would wait until the honest merchants had
sold at a fair price the bulk of the produce, and then they
would raise prices.   *Baba Batra, 89*

R. Zeira would curse those who pretended to seek an
article for which they knew others were looking, so that the

would-be purchasers would be forced to pay a high price. He also cursed those who conspired with the merchants to raise the price of articles which they knew a bona-fide purchaser was seeking.

R. Abba b. Abba would sell his produce early in the season, thereby establishing a low price.

His son, Samuel, wished to improve upon his father's procedure. He would, therefore, keep his produce until prices were higher, and then he would sell at the season's lowest price.

They sent word from Palestine: "We prefer the father's action to the son's. The father established a low price at the very beginning, but the son's action did not serve to lessen the price of the produce, since a higher price had already been established."

Baba Batra, 90. Y. Kiddushin, 3

Charity

He who closes his eyes against giving to charity is like an idolater.   *Ketubot, 68*

He who does charity and justice is as if he had filled the whole world with kindness.   *Sukkah, 49*

Better is he who gives little to charity from money honestly earned, than he who gives much from dishonestly gained wealth.   *Kohelet Rabbah, 4*

A man may give liberally, and yet because he gives unlovingly and wounds the heart of the poor, his gift is in vain, for it has lost the attribute of charity; a man may give little, but because his heart goes with it his deed and himself are blessed.   *Baba Batra, 9b*

If one gives only the kind word, and speaks comfortably
to the poor, he has done true charity, for doth not Holy
Writ say: "Because of this *word* will God bless thee"?

Sifre Deut., 15:10

Charity knows neither race nor creed.   *Gittin, 61a*

If a poor man comes to thee for aid in the morning, give
it to him. If he comes again in the evening, give it to him
once more.   *Bereshit Rabbah, 61, 3*

If a man sees that his income is meagre, let him practice
charity.   *Gittin, 7*

He who gives charity serves the Holy One daily, and
sanctifies His Name.   *Zohar, iii, 113b*

Ipra Hurmiz, the Queen Mother of Persia, sent a purse to
Rab Joseph on behalf of a great Mitzwah. "What is a great
Mitzwah?" mused Rab Joseph. Abbaye replied: "Rab Samuel
bar Judah has taught: no charity tax may be levied on the
property of orphans, even for the ransoming of captives.
This proves that the ransoming of captives is the greatest
of charities."

A community must maintain two kinds of charity: a free
kitchen and a Chest for the Poor. The free kitchen should
be open every day, and should be enjoyed by the poor
from out-of-town as well as by the local poor. The Chest
shall be open every Friday and is for residents only. Other
Rabbis declare: for both residents and non-residents.

Rab Judah said: Investigate before you give a garment to
a poor man, but do not investigate before giving him food.

·   ·   ·

Rabbi Assi said: Charity is equal to all Mitzwot.

Rabbi Eleazar said: Greater is he who persuades others
to give than him who gives.

Rabba said to the people of Mehuza: Do charity among yourselves so that you will enjoy peace.

Rabbi Eleazar said: . . . Give charity now, for if you do not, it will be forcibly taken from you by officials.

Said R. Eleazar: He who gives charity in secret is as great as Moses.   *Baba Batra, 8-9*

R. Eleazar ben Jose said: Kind deeds and charity achieve peace between Israel and their Father in Heaven.

R. Judah said: Great is charity for it brings Redemption nearer.

R. Judah said: Come and see how great is charity. Ten strong things exist in the world: a mountain is strong, but iron breaks it; iron is strong, but fire softens it; fire is strong, but water extinguishes it; water is strong, but clouds bear it along; clouds are strong, but the wind spreads them out; the wind is strong, but the body of man withstands it; the body is strong, but fear breaks it; fear is strong, but wine overcomes it; wine is strong, but sleep dispels it; sleep is strong, but death is stronger still. But charity rescueth even from death.

R. Dosetai ben Hannai said: When you bring a gift to a ruler, it may or may not be accepted; if accepted, you may or may not be called to see the monarch. It is different with God. If a man gives a small coin to the poor, he has a satisfaction equal to beholding the Shekinah, as we read: "As for me, I shall behold Thy face in Zedek" (righteousness). (*Psalm 17:15*)   *Baba Batra, 9-10*

R. Hiyya bar Abba said: The best way to give charity is to drop it into the Collection Box. The donor thus knows not to whom he gives, and the poor man knows not who is giver. Care should be taken, however, that the distributor is an excellent person.   *Baba Batra, 10a-b*

If a man gives with a sullen face, it is as if he gave nothing; but he who receives the needy person with a cheerful
countenance, even if he was not able to give him anything,
it is as if he gave him a good gift.   *Abot de-R. Nathan, 13*

R. Eleazar of Bertota said: Give unto Him of what is His,
seeing that thou and what thou hast are His; this is found
expressed in David who said: "For all things come from
Thee, and of Thine own have we given Thee." (I Chronicles 29:14)   *Abot, 3, 8*

More than the householder does for the beggar, the beggar does for the householder.   *Wayyikra Rabbah, 34, 8*

A Rabbi advised his wife: "When a beggar comes, hand
him bread, so that the same may be done to your children."
She exclaimed: "You are cursing them!" He replied: "There
is a wheel which revolves in the world: the poor become
rich and the rich become poor."   *Shabbat, 151b*

Greater is he who practices charity than all the sacrifices.
                                               Sukkah, 49b

If the funds in the Community Chest are low, the relief
of the women takes precedence over the relief of the men.
                                          Tos. Ketubot, 6, 8

Mar Ukba was accustomed to throw four zuzim every
day in the hole of his neighbor's door, and walk away unseen. Once the poor recipient wished to know his benefac-
tor, and ran out of his home to detect him, but he was too
late.

Rabbi Abba would lose a kerchief with coins among the
poor. He was careful, however, to chase away rogues.
                              Ketubot, 67; Hagigah, 5

Mar Ukba was accustomed to send a sum of money to a
poor neighbor before Yom Kippur. Once his son, who took
the money, reported: "The poor man was indulging in old

wine, and I did not give him the money." His father re-
torted: "He must have seen better days since he has such
dainty tastes. I will double the amount of my gift."

Ketubot, 67b

There was a pious man with whom Elijah would visit and
walk. However, when that man made a watchman's door
at the gate of his yard, and thus prevented the poor people
from entering the house, Elijah refrained from visiting him.

Baba Batra, 7b

In years of famine, King Monobaz of Adiabene distributed all his treasures to the poor. His kinsmen remon-
strated with him: "Your fathers laid up treasures, but you
squander them."

He replied: "My fathers laid up treasures for below: a
place where force prevails—treasures which bear no fruit;
treasures of money, treasures for others to enjoy; treasures
of consequence only in this world. I, however, have laid up
treasure for Above: a place where no force prevails—
treasures bearing fruit; treasures for souls, treasures which
I, myself, will enjoy; treasures of value in the World-to-
Come." *Baba Batra, 11a*

Rabbi Tarfon was very rich, but did not give enough to
charity. Rabbi Akiba asked him for a large sum to purchase
a village, but when he received the money, he distributed
it among the poor. When Rabbi Tarfon asked for the deed
to the village, Rabbi Akiba opened the Psalter to 112:9,
and read to him: "He hath scattered abroad; he hath given
to the needy; his righteousness endureth forever. This
have I purchased for thee," added Rabbi Akiba, and Rabbi
Tarfon embraced him.

Wayyikra Rabbah, 34, 16; Baraita Kallah

Greater is he that lends than he that gives, and greater

still is he that lends, and, with the loan, helps the poor man
to help himself.   *Shabbat, 63a*

Charity is rewarded according to the benevolence it contains. It is appreciated by God only in proportion to the
love within it.   *Sukkah, 49b*

R. Akiba related: When I was once at sea I witnessed a
boat sinking and mourned for a friend of mine on it. When
I came to Cappadocia, lo, my friend was safe. I inquired:
Who saved thee? He answered: Before my departure I gave
a loaf of bread to a beggar, and he blessed me, saying:
Thou savest my life; may thy life be saved. When the boat
sank, great waves carried me to land. I quoted to him the
words from Ecclesiastes.   *Kohelet Rabbah, 11*

The daughter of Rabbi Akiba stuck her knitting needle
into the wall. It went into the eye of a snake. Rabbi Akiba
said to her: "What good deed hast thou done?" She answered: "While we ate, I noticed a beggar at the door, and
I gave him my portion of the food."   *Shabbat, 156*

Benjamin, the Zaddik, was keeper of the Poor Box, and a
woman came to him at famine-time to ask for food. "By
the worship of God," he replied, "there is nothing in the
Box!" She exclaimed: "O Rabbi, if thou dost not feed me,
I and my seven children will starve." He then gave her relief from his private purse.

In the course of time he fell ill and was close to death.
Then the Angels interceded with the Lord, saying: "Lord
of the Universe, Thou hast said that he who preserveth the
life of one single soul . . . is as if he had preserved the
lives of the whole world. Shall Benjamin, the Zaddik, who
preserved a poor woman and her seven children, die so
prematurely?" Instantly the death-warrant which had gone

forth was torn up, and twenty-two years were added to his
life.   *Baba Batra, 11a*

Rabbi Johanan ben Zakkai was once riding out of Jerusalem, and saw a woman picking grain left over on the
field. She halted him and said: "Dost thou not recognize me,
Rabbi; I am the daughter of Nakdimon ben Gorion." The
Rabbi pityingly gazed at her, and queried: "Art thou not
the same at whose marriage I was present, and whose
Ketubah was that of a multi-millionaire? What became of
thy riches and of thy father's?"

She answered: "Dost thou not remember warning us that
charity preserves riches as salt preserves food? We stinted
in our gifts to the poor, not giving according to our wealth,
and our wealth was lost through many mishaps."

The Rabbi aided her to establish herself in another town.
                                                        Ketubot, 66b

Nahum Ish Gamzu, one of R. Akiba's teachers, narrated
the following experience: I was once travelling to the house
of my father-in-law, taking with me three donkey-loads of
food and drink. A starving man asked me for food. I answered that I would give him some when I unloaded, but
before I could do so, he fell dead. I greatly grieved over his
death, and prayed that the Lord send sufferings upon me in
expiation for my sin. I should not have delayed my help,
but should have cut through the load and given him food at
once.   *Taanit, 21*

Comforting the Bereaved

When Rabbi Abbahu's child died, he said: "We are
taught that (in Israel) after the execution of a person condemned by an earthly Court, where lies, deception,

favoritism, and bribery may have existed, whose judges are but mortal beings, the kinsfolk come and pleasantly greet the judges and witnesses to demonstrate that they have no grievance in their heart against them, because they have judged truthfully. How much more then, after a person has surrendered his life according to the decree of the Heavenly Tribunal, where no human defects and shortcomings exist, should we not receive with humility and submission the verdict of Heaven?"   *Y. Sanhedrin, 6*

When Rabban Johanan ben Zakkai's son died, Rabbi Eliezer ben Arak came to offer consolation. He said: "To whom may I liken you? To a man who has received for safekeeping a jewel from his king. As long as he has it beneath his roof, he is troubled with anxiety regarding it; when the king takes it back in the same good condition, the man rejoices. You, O Master, have received for safe-keeping a dear soul. He studied much and well, and died without sin. You have returned it in perfection, and you should find comfort in the knowledge of this."

Rabban Johanan thanked him heartily.

Abot de-Rabbi Nathan, 14

In times long ago funeral expenses were so high that kinsmen would leave their dead and move away. Rabban Gamliel ordained in his testament that he be buried in simple linen raiment, and thus the burden was lifted.

Moed Katon, 27

The Rabbis have taught: formerly those who came to a wealthy mourner with the first meal after the funeral would bring him the food in golden baskets; to the poor mourners, however, they brought food in wicker baskets. The poor felt humiliated, and therefore it was ordained that food should be brought to all mourners only in wicker baskets.

To wealthy mourners, they brought wine in decanters of white glass; to the poor, in vessels of colored glass. Again the poor felt humiliated, because white glass was more costly. Therefore it was ordained that wine should be brought to all mourners in colored glasses.

Formerly the deceased of the wealthy were buried in fancy caskets, of the poor in cheap coffins. This, too, was altered, and now all who die, whether rich or poor, are buried in inexpensive caskets.   *Moed Katon, 27*

Ulla's home was in the Land of Israel, but he died in Babylonia. Before he breathed his last, he wept bitterly. "Cease thy weeping," he was told. "We promise to take your body for burial to the Land of Israel." "Of what avail is this to me?" he replied. "I am losing my jewel in an unclean land. Can ye compare one who gives away his dearest [1] while on the lap of his mother,[2] to one who gives it away in the lap of a strange woman?"   *Y. Kilaim, Chap. 9*

When R. Eliezer was on his death-bed, he was visited by R. Akiba and his companions. R. Eliezer sighed and said: "Much Torah have I learned, yet I have not received from my Teachers any more than a dog who licks the salty water of the sea. Much Torah have I taught, yet my disciples have received from me only as much as a tiny brush absorbs by one dip into a vessel of paint."

When he died, R. Akiba beat his hands against his breasts, and cried out: "Father, Father, I have much money, and there is no banker to change it into small coins." [3]

                                        Sanhedrin, 68

---

[1] His soul.
[2] Palestine.
[3] Many difficult passages in Torah, and no one to explain them.

Dress

R. Hiyya bar Abba asked R. Assi: "Why do the Sages in Babylonia dress in so distinguished a manner?"

R. Assi replied: "Because they are minor scholars, they desire to be respected because of their attire."

R. Johanan overheard him and said: "Thou art wrong. They dress well because they are emigrants there; and the popular saying runs: 'In my own town I am respected for the name I have achieved; in another town I receive my respect because my clothes lend me distinction.'"

Shabbat, 145

Eretz Israel

Why did Sennacherib deserve to be recorded in the Bible (Ezra 4:10) as the great and noble Asenappar? Because he did not speak derogatively of Palestine, as it is written: "I shall bring you away to a land like your own land" (Isaiah 36:17) and not better than your land.   *Sanhedrin, 94*

More beloved is a small school in Eretz Yisrael than a large Academy outside of it.   *Y. Nedarim, 6, 5*

Living in Eretz Yisrael is equal to the weight of all Mitzwot. (Said also of the Sabbath, Charity, and the *Tzizit*.)

Sifre, Reeh

He who resides in Palestine, reads the Sh'ma and speaks Hebrew is a son of the World-to-Come.   *Sifre, Berakah, 13*

"In your Land (Eretz Yisrael) you can sit in safety," but you cannot dwell in safety in a strange land.

Sifre Behukotai

In the days to come Eretz Yisrael will be redeemed little by little.   *Tanhuma, Debarim, 1, 2*

Why is the Sea of Tiberias called Kinnereth? Because the fruit which grows around it is sweet, like the melody of a Kinnor (a harp).   *Megillah, 6*

R. Eleazar b. Shamua and R. Johanan, the Alexandrian, planned to study with R. Judah of the family Ben Beteirah, who resided in Netzibin outside of Palestine. When they reached Sidon, they reminded themselves of Palestine, and their eyes were filled with tears. They said: "To live in the Land of Israel is a duty equal to any other Mitzwah. Why should we leave Palestine and forego one Mitzwah in order to perform another?" They returned to their home.

Sifre to Deut. 12:29

When R. Zeira came to Eretz Yisrael he understood more clearly the arguments of his opponent, R. Illa, and surrendered his own viewpoint in a certain matter, saying: "This demonstrates that the very air of Eretz Yisrael makes one's brain clearer."   *Baba Batra, 158*

Abbaye said: A student in Palestine grasps the reasons of a law twice as quickly as a student in Babylonia.

Rabba added: Even a Babylonian student who goes to Palestine becomes twice as keen as he who has remained in Babylonia. Take the case of Jeremiah. When he was here, he did not understand the teachings of the Rabbis, but since he has been in Palestine, he calls us: Those foolish Babylonians.   *Ketubot, 75*

There is no Torah like the Torah of Eretz Yisrael, and no wisdom like the wisdom of Eretz Yisreal.

Bereshit Rabbah, 15

When R. Zeira went up to Palestine he came to the river-boundary. Since there was no ferry, he took hold of a rope, and crossed the river on a narrow board. When asked why he had not waited for the ferry, he answered: "How do I

know whether I shall be worthy to enter a place which
Moses and Aaron did not merit entering?" When R. Abba
reached Acco, he kissed the very stones out of love for
Zion.

R. Hanina labored to repair Palestine's roads.

R. Jose b. Hanina said: "Why is the boundary city
called Acco? The word is a contraction of 'Ad Ko,' 'until
here' (is holy)."   *Ketubot, 112; Y. Shebiit, 4*

R. Shimeon b. Abba asked R. Hanina for a letter of
recommendation, since he wished to settle in another country for his livelihood. R. Hanina answered: "Tomorrow if
I went to thy parents, they would say to me: 'We left a
desirable plant in the Land of Israel, yet thou hast permitted it to be transplanted to a strange land.'"

                                                    Y. Moed Katon, 3

Labor

Work is more beloved than the merit of the fathers.
                                                    Bereshit Rabbah, 74, 12
Great is labor, for it brings its master to honor.
                                                    Nedarim, 49b
The right of the workingman always has precedence.
                                                    Baba Metzia, 77
Great is labor! All the prophets engaged in it.
                                                    Midrash Gadol u-Gedolah, 14
Great is labor! It honors the doer.   *Nedarim, 49*
If a man works, he is blessed.   *Midrash Tehillim, 23, 3*
Greater even than the God-fearing man is he who eats
of the fruit of his toil; for Scripture declares him twice-
blessed.   *Berakot, 8a*
Beautiful it is when the study of the Torah goes with
worldly work; it is a safeguard against sin.   *Abot, ii 2*

The Rabbis said: "Do not think that the blessing will be yours even if you stand idle. Oh, no! God's blessings rest only 'on all that thou doest'—on all that thou shalt labor!"

Sifre, Reeh, 99b

Even though God assured the Patriarch Isaac: "I will bless thee and increase thy seed," Isaac set to work and planted, because he knew that blessings cannot come except through the labor of one's own hands.

Tosefta Berakot, 7, 8

To the employer of workmen the Rabbis said: "This poor man ascends the highest scaffoldings, climbs the highest trees. For what does he expose himself to such danger if not for the purpose of earning his living? Be careful, therefore, not to oppress him in his wages, for it means his very life."   *Sifre Ki Teze, sec. 279, p. 123b*

"And thou shalt choose life"—namely, a trade.   *Y. Peah, 1*

He who does not teach his son an occupation is as one who has taught his son to rob.   *Kiddushin, 29*

Rabban Gamliel III, the son of Rabbi, said: "Study, combined with a secular occupation is a fine thing, for the double labor makes sin to be forgotten. All study of the Torah with which no work goes, will in the end come to naught, and bring sin in its train."

Abot, 2, 2. See Mishnah
Kiddushin, 1, 10

Skin a carcass in the market-place, take the fee, and say not: "I am an important man."   *Baba Kamma, 106*

No labor, however humble, is dishonoring. *Nedarim, 49b*

Justice

Rabbi Simeon ben Lakish said: "A lawsuit about a small coin should be esteemed of as much account as a suit of a hundred gold coins."   *Sanhedrin, 8a*

Rab once boarded with a certain man who treated him with great respect. Several years later he came to Rab to have a lawsuit decided before him. He whispered to Rab: "Dost thou remember how well I treated thee when thou wast my boarder?"

"Yes," replied Rab, "and what is thy business?"

"I came to have a trial before thee."

"I cannot try thee, since thou remindest me of thy favors," said Rab.   *Sanhedrin, 7*

The judge must not say to himself: "This man is poor; and, inasmuch as this rich man is under obligation by the general duty of charity to support him, I will give judgment in his favor, and he will be able to make an honest living."

In the converse case, the judge must not reflect: "This man is rich, this one well connected. Can I see him shamed? How much less put him to shame myself?

"One is not to be allowed to state his case at length and the other bidden to cut it short; one must not be allowed to be seated in court and the other kept standing, and the like."   *Sifre Kedoshim, Perek, 4*

The Rabbis ask: "Why is the word justice written twice? (Deut. 16:20). To teach us that we must practice justice at all times, whether it be for our profit or for our loss, and towards all men—towards Jews and non-Jews alike!"

Sanhedrin, 32b; Tanhuma, Buber to Shofetim, 5 and 7

There are three whom God dislikes: he who speaks one

way with his mouth, and another way in his heart; he who knows of testimony on behalf of a fellowman, but does not go forth to present his testimony; he who beholds an immoral act and testifies against it in his role of a single witness.   *Pesahim, 113*

The investigating judge would say to witnesses: "If you have evidence to offer which some one else has seen and mentioned to you, or if you wish to offer as testimony that which a man whom you trust has told you, know that you must desist. This is not like taking money unjustly, for in such a case the mistake can be rectified. In this case, however, if an innocent man is executed his blood will be upon you and the blood of his descendants for all generations. But, the injunction is that by giving evidence in a court of law, and, assisting in the execution of a murderer or another criminal, you bring security into the world."

Sanhedrin, 37

THE SIDDUR (Prayer Book)

Samuel Rosenblatt

Although the Bible is the basis of the Jewish religion, there is one book which—at least during the past 2,000 years—has been even more familiar to the average Jew than the Holy Scriptures and has more fully reflected his thoughts and feelings throughout the ages. This book is the *Siddur*, or order of daily prayers. It was better known than the Bible because it was the daily companion of the Jewish people, who used it not only at each of the three daily services of the synagogue but also in the recitation of grace after meals, and on every occasion of joy or sorrow. It mirrors more completely the reactions of the Jewish mind and heart to the vicissitudes which the Jew experienced during his long career, from the time he appeared on the horizon of history until this very day, because the stretch of time covered by its contents extends far beyond the period of roughly one thousand years during which the Hebrew Scriptures were committed to writing. Certain important parts of it, such as the *Shema* (*Deuteronomy 6.4-9; 11.13-21* and *Numbers 15.37-41*) and the Psalms, are, to be sure, derived from the Bible and therefore of great antiquity. Others, however, are of much more recent date, having been composed during that long interval of nearly nineteen centuries in which the Jew lived as a homeless wanderer on the face of the earth, exiled from the land in which his fathers had dwelt and to which he longed so ardently to return, and exposed to every kind of humiliation and oppression.

The foundations of prayer, "the service of the heart" as the rabbis called it, as the chief feature of the liturgy of the synagogue, were laid during the days of the second Temple of Jerusalem. It is to the Men of the Great Assembly, said to have been organized by the scribe Ezra in the fifth century before the common era, that the Talmud ascribes the formulation of the *Berakot*, benedictions containing the expression "Blessed art Thou, Oh Lord," which earmarks every important Jewish prayer. However, it was only after the national sanctuary had been destroyed and the sacrifice of animals, which had until then been the chief mode of Jewish worship, was replaced entirely by "the offering of the lips," that the need was felt for uniformity in prayer and regularization of the liturgy of the synagogue as a means of preserving the unity of the scattered fragments of the Jewish people, no longer held together by a central government.

One of the prime advocates of such a policy was the patriarch Gamaliel, who headed the Jewish community of Palestine during the first generation after the destruction of the Temple of Jerusalem by the Romans in the year 70 C.E. Under his direction the *Amidah*, the "prayer" par excellence in the phraseology of the Mishnah, which constitutes the nucleus of every synagogue service, obtained its definitive order. It was also at this time that the hours of the daily service were fixed, although the text of those prayers that were not of Biblical origin remained fluid, allowing for variations that gave rise to the different rituals of later eras.

The first complete *Siddur* known to us was drawn up during the ninth century of the common era by Rabbi Amram, the *Gaon* or rector of the Academy of Sura, in Babylonia, the seat of the foremost Jewish religious authority at the time. The practice of making additions to the basic prayers in the form of *piyutim*, a new type of liturgical poems composed for the various festivals as well as the distinguished Sabbaths, had then already been in vogue for more than two hundred years. Some of the Babylonian *Gaonim* were violently opposed to these interpolations which they regarded as an interruption of the fundamental prayers. Moses Maimonides, whose monumental code was completed in Egypt in the year 1180 of the common era, disapproved of them, while his French contemporary, the father of the *Tosafists*, Rabbenu Jacob Tam, grandson of the king of commentators, Rashi, was in favor of them. Even at that late date the *Berakot* and psalms now recited at the beginning of the morning service were apparently not yet included in the order of public prayers.

The trend toward standardization in ritual during the Middle Ages may seem to have reached its peak in the *Sefer Minhagim* (Book of Customs) of Jacob Moelln. This fifteenth century German rabbi looked upon every Jewish practice as possessing the weight of law from which there must be no deviation. Nevertheless, although the Ashkenazic rite had then apparently received its final form, it was only a century and a half later to be enriched by the incorporation in the Friday night services of the hymn in welcome of the Sabbath, *Leka Dodi* (Come, my beloved),

composed by the Palestinian poet and mystic, Solomon
Alkabez. The Hassidic movement, begun around the middle
of the eighteenth century, also made its contributions to the
liturgy of the synagogue. The latest additions to the traditional prayerbook are the prayers for the governments of
countries in which the various Jewish communities happen
to be located.

Although according to Talmudic law it is permissible to
pray in any language comprehensible to the worshipper,
and Jewish women, who until the twentieth century rarely
received a formal Jewish education, were accustomed to re-
citing their private devotions in the vernacular of the lands
of their residence, the public prayers of the synagogue were
composed almost exclusively in Hebrew. Certain liturgical
selections, such as the *Kaddish, Yekum Purkan* and *Berik
Shemey,* either partly or entirely in Aramaic were included.
But it must be remembered that this idiom, spoken by the
Jews of Palestine and Babylonia during the ages of the
Talmud and the *Gaonim,* was to them a second holy tongue.
For parts of the Biblical books of Daniel and Ezra as well
as the two Talmuds, the Palestinian and the Babylonian,
were written in Aramaic.

The scheme of arrangement generally followed in the
printed texts of the traditional prayerbook is to list first the
prayers recited most frequently and those said less often
afterwards. Most *Siddurim,* accordingly, open with the
daily morning, afternoon and evening prayers; followed by
the weekly Sabbath prayers, namely the Friday evening, the
Sabbath morning, the *Musaf* (additional) and the afternoon services. After these come the additional prayers for
the evening service at the outgoing of the Sabbath. The
Hallel (*Psalms 113-118*) and the *Musaf* service for *Rosh*

Hodesh (new moon) are next in order. Following these come the *Kiddush* (benediction declaring over a cup of wine at the beginning of the holiday meal the sanctity of the occasion) and the *Amidahs* of the three pilgrimage festivals of Passover, Pentecost and Tabernacles; and finally, the services of the High Holidays, that is of the New Year and the Day of Atonement. Often also appended at the end of the *Siddur* are the blessings recited before the kindling of the *Hanukkah* lights on the Feast of Dedication and those pronounced prior to the reading of the Book of Esther on *Purim* (the Feast of Lots). In this section there are also the grace after meals, and bedtime and other private prayers.

The nucleus of every synagogue service (the three daily services, the four held on Sabbaths, new moons and all major festivals, and the five of the Day of Atonement) is the *Amidah*. It consists of three parts, the first devoted to the praise of God and the last to thanksgiving, etc.; the middle section contains the actual petitions. In the *Amidah* for the weekdays these petitions are divided into thirteen paragraphs or *Berakot*, making a total, with the introductory and closing benedictions which are virtually the same for all occasions, of nineteen. Originally there were eighteen *Berakot* altogether, whence the name *Shemoneh Esreh* (eighteen). In the *Amidahs* of the Sabbath and the festivals the middle section consists of but one paragraph. The sole exception is that of the *Musaf* service of the New Year in which it is divided into three parts.

The *Amidah* of the morning and evening services is preceded by the *Shema,* which contains the essence of Jewish belief, and its introductory and concluding benedictions.

That of the morning and afternoon services of weekdays that are not half-holidays is followed by penitential prayers called *Tahanun* (entreaty). Psalms and other quotations from the Bible as well as liturgical selections of predominantly rabbinic authorship round out the regular prayer ritual of the synagogue.

Despite the great disparity in the dates of composition—there is a lapse of as much as three thousand years between the earliest and the latest—a remarkable unity of thought and sentiment pervades the component elements of the traditional prayerbook. The expressions of the experiences of Jewish religious geniuses in different ages are woven together into a harmonious pattern in which no clash of ideas is felt; one supplements or adds to the other. Thus, for example, the simple belief, expressed in the Biblical *Shema*, that "God is one" is amplified in poems like *Adon Olam* (Lord of the World) and *Yigdal* (Magnified be) emanating from the rationalist schools of medieval Jewish philosophy, which call attention to the Creator's uniqueness:

"For He is one, no second shares His nature or His loneliness."

"One Being, yet unique in unity; a mystery of Oneness measureless."

This incomparable, eternal, spiritual being which, according to the philosopher poets, has "neither form nor body" and whose nature is not shared by any one of His creatures, is omnipotent. "Thou are mighty forever, Oh, Lord" are the opening words of the second paragraph of the *Amidah*, and in the first of the benedictions preceding the *Shema*,

God is described as "the creator of light and darkness" and "the author of all things."

It is particularly during the High Holiday season, when He is pictured as being seated on the throne of judgment, that God's majesty and power are felt by the Jew. "Reign over all the universe in Thy glory, and in Thy splendor be exalted over all the earth. Shine forth in the majesty of Thy triumphant power over all the inhabitants of Thy world, that every living thing may know that Thou hast formed it." These are the terms in which this view finds expression in the *Amidah* of the New Year's Day. Yet, notwithstanding His great and unending power, the Master of the universe stands by no means aloof, nor is He indifferent to the needs of His creatures. As the psalmist put it—and this psalm is recited three times every day in the synagogue—"The Lord is near unto all who call upon Him . . . He fulfilleth the desire of them that fear Him, and heareth their cry so as to save them." The *Amora* Rabbi Johanan observes—and the statement of this third century teacher of the Talmud is quoted in the ritual of the outgoing of the Sabbath—"In every passage of Scripture in which the greatness of God is spoken of, there findest thou also His humility mentioned."

It is but natural that this "Lord who is good to all and whose mercies extend over all His works" should be adored by those who on every festival assert in the *Amidah:* "Thou hast chosen us from all peoples," as their savior and redeemer; and that they should declare in the benediction following the third paragraph of the *Shema,* which ends with a reference to Israel's deliverance from Egypt: "Thou hast been the help of our fathers from of old, a shield and a savior to their children after them in every generation."

God's special solicitude for the seed elected manifested

itself, in the opinion of the compilers of the *Siddur,* not so much in the worldly fortunes enjoyed by it as in the gift of the Torah. This is evident from such declarations as the one with which the second of the benedictions preceding the *Shema* of the evening service begins, namely: "With everlasting love hast Thou loved the house of Israel, Thy people; a law and commandments, statutes and judgments hast Thou taught us." In the holiday *Amidah* it is corroborated by linking Israel's exaltation with its sanctification by God's commandments. True, Israel did not live up to its high vocation while it was still settled on its own soil. "But because of our sins," so the Jew confesses in the *Amidah* of the *Musaf* service of the festivals, "we were exiled from our land." So intense at times were the sufferings of Jewry in exile that the medieval liturgist did not exaggerate when he said, in the words of the *Tahanun* recited on Monday and Thursday mornings: "Look down from heaven and see how we have become a scorn and a derision among the nations; we are accounted as sheep brought to the slaughter, to be slain and destroyed, or to be smitten and reproached."

The attribution of Israel's national misfortunes to its iniquities is a favorite motif of the Jewish fast-day ritual. If the Jew appeals to the heavenly judge for mercy and forgiveness, it is not on account of his virtues. "Not because of our righteous deeds" he admits every morning "do we lay our supplications before Thee." It is rather out of regard for the weaknesses of man's nature that he hopes to obtain his Master's pardon. "For He knoweth our inclination; He remembereth that we are dust" (quotation in the daily *Tahanun* from *Psalms 103.14*). Also in spite of its sorrows, Israel has not altogether forgotten the name of its God.

Hence the prayer: "We beseech Thee, forget us not" (from the *Tahanun* of the Monday and Thursday morning services).

The gathering of Israel's exiles, the rebuilding of Jerusalem, the return of the Jewish people to its ancestral soil and of the Divine Presence to Zion are ever-recurrent themes in the liturgy of the synagogue. They are found in the daily *Amidah* as well as the special *Amidahs* of the holidays, in the second benediction preceding the *Shema* of the morning service, and in the grace recited after meals. Indeed, most of the prayers contained in the traditional prayerbook are couched in the plural, indicating that they were intended for public recitation and that they were concerned with the needs, aspirations and well-being of Jews as a group. This fact is borne out by an analysis of the middle section of the weekday *Amidah,* more than half of which consists of petitions for the national welfare of the Jewish people.

There are also, however, liturgical selections written in the singular. These were originally private meditations of a didactic character. Notable among these is the one attributed to a fourth century teacher of the Talmud, who was accustomed to pray after the conclusion of the *Amidah:* "Oh my God, guard my tongue from evil and my lips from speaking guile; and to such as curse me let my soul be dumb." Another such appendix to the daily prayers, purported to have been composed by Rabbi Judah the Patriarch, the editor of the Mishnah who flourished during the last half of the second century of the common era, is: "May it be Thy will, Oh Lord my God and God of my fathers, to deliver me this day and every day from arrogant men and from arrogance." The moral value of such prayers is self-evident.

On the whole, the traditional prayers of the synagogue are singularly free from narrow, self-seeking requests of a materialistic nature. Although on Sabbaths preceding the new moon it is customary to pray for material prosperity and sustenance, only one of the *Berakot* of the weekday *Amidah* is dedicated to this end. It is such spiritual gifts as knowledge, the power of repentance, forgiveness and redemption, that the Jew asks for, after having uttered the praises of his Maker, in his communion with Him, before imploring Him for physical health and the blessing of the fields, on the ordinary days of the year. On Sabbaths and festivals he is silent about his private wants altogether. Instead of pressing his personal demands, he pleads only for the opportunity to enjoy the Sabbath rest or rejoice on the holiday, as the case may be, and to dedicate himself through consecration to the service of God. "Purify our hearts to serve Thee in truth." On the High Holidays he utters, in the *Amidah,* the hopes for the advent of the day when "iniquity would close her mouth and all wickedness would be consumed like smoke" and when "all men would form a single band in order to carry out God's will." The *Alenu* prayer, which is recited at the conclusion of every synagogue service and which is taken from the *Amidah* of the *Musaf* service of the New Year as formulated by the Babylonian *Amora* of the third century Rab, speaks of "the improvements of the entire human world through the establishment of the kingdom of the Almighty and the casting out of the idols from the earth." The keynote of the last portion of another concluding prayer, namely the *Kaddish,* which has become the official Jewish requiem for the dead, is peace, which is also the theme of the final *Berakah* or paragraph of the *Amidah*. Then, again, there is the call upon man "to fear heaven in private as well as in public," and other such exhortations.

Our listing of the main ideas or trends of thought contained in the basic prayers of the synagogue is by no means exhaustive. We have left out of account the mystical description of the adoration of God by the elements of the universe given in the *Kedushah,* the amplification of the third benediction of the *Amidah* that celebrates God's holiness. We have mentioned neither the glorification of the Creator in the various nature psalms, nor the marvellous expressions of faith voiced in that collection of hymns known as *Hallel (Psalms 113-118)* and recited on the pilgrimage festivals, new moons and the Feast of Dedication. Last, but not least, we have not touched on the confessional or *Vidduy* appended to the *Amidahs* of the Day of Atonement in which are enumerated in alphabetical order the various moral sins on account of which the Jewish worshipper feels contrite and for which he craves the forgiveness of "the king who forgives and pardons the iniquities of His people Israel."

It is of course impossible within limited confines to treat so vast a subject with any degree of completeness. However, the examples cited suffice to indicate that the prayers included in the *Siddur* cover in their totality the entire range of Jewish religious thinking. They reflect the views of a religion with the broadest possible humanitarian outlook. They aim at the spiritual refinement and elevation of the individual's character, and are at the same time bound up with the hopes and aspirations of the Jewish people. Thus the *Siddur* is one of the most precious heirlooms of Jewry. It is the book which, more than any other, reveals the soul of the Jew in all its richness and spiritual grandeur, besides having served as a mighty force for Jewish unity and as a most important means of Jewish survival.

selections from THE SIDDUR

Lord of the World

Lord of the world, He reigned alone
While yet the universe was naught
When by His will all things were wrought,
Then first His sov'ran name was known.

And When the All shall cease to be,
In dread lone splendour He shall reign,
He was, He is, He shall remain
In glorious eternity.

For He is one, no second shares
His nature or His loneliness;
Unending and beginningless,
All strength is His, all sway He bears.

He is the living God to save,
My Rock while sorrow's toils endure,
My banner and my stronghold sure,
The cup of life whene'er I crave.

I place my soul within His palm
Before I sleep as when I wake,
And though my body I forsake,
Rest in the Lord in fearless calm.

Immortality of the Soul

O my God, the soul which thou gavest me is pure; thou didst create it, thou didst form it, thou didst breathe it into me. Thou preservest it within me, and thou wilt take it from me, but wilt restore unto me hereafter. So long as the soul is within me, I will give thanks unto thee, O Lord my God and God of my fathers, Sovereign of all works, Lord of all souls! Blessed art thou, O Lord, who restorest souls unto the dead.

Prayer for Divine Help in Daily Life

And may it be thy will, O Lord our God and God of our fathers, to accustom us to walk in thy Torah, and to make us cleave to thy commandments. O lead us not into sin, or transgression, iniquity, temptation, or disgrace: let not the evil inclination have sway over us: keep us far from a bad man and a bad companion: make us cleave to the good inclination and to good works: subdue our inclination so that it may submit itself to thee: and let us obtain this day, and every day, grace, favour, and mercy in thine eyes, and in the eyes of all who behold us; and bestow lovingkindnesses upon us. Blessed art thou, O Lord, who bestowest lovingkindnesses upon thy people Israel.

Frailty of Man

Sovereign of all worlds! Not because of our righteous
acts do we lay our supplications before thee, but because
of thine abundant mercies. What are we? What is our life?
What is our piety? What is our righteousness? What our
helpfulness? What our strength? What our might? What
shall we say before thee, O Lord our God and God of our
fathers? Are not all the mighty men as nought before thee,
the men of renown as though they had not been, the wise
as if without knowledge, and the men of understanding as
if without discernment? For most of their works are void,
and the days of their lives are vanity before thee, and the
pre-eminence of man over beast is nought: for all is vanity.

The Creator of All Things

Blessed art thou, O Lord our God, King of the universe,
who formest light and createst darkness, who makest peace
and createst all things:

Who in mercy givest light to the earth and to them that
dwell thereon, and in thy goodness renewest the creation
every day continually. How manifold are thy works, O
Lord! In wisdom hast thou made them all: the earth is full
of thy creatures. O King, who alone wast exalted from afore-
time, praised, glorified and extolled from days of old; O
everlasting God, in thine abundant mercies, have mercy
upon us, Lord of our strength, Rock of our stronghold,
Shield of our salvation, thou Stronghold of ours!

Hear, O Israel

HEAR, O ISRAEL: THE LORD IS OUR GOD, THE LORD IS ONE.

BLESSED BE HIS NAME, WHOSE GLORIOUS KING-DOM IS FOR EVER AND EVER.

And thou shalt love the Lord thy God with all thine heart, and with all thy soul, and with all thy might. And these words, which I command thee this day, shall be upon thine heart: and thou shalt teach them diligently unto thy children, and shalt talk of them when thou sittest in thine house, and when thou walkest by the way, and when thou liest down, and when thou risest up. And thou shalt bind them for a sign upon thine hand, and they shall be for frontlets between thine eyes. And thou shalt write them upon the door-posts of thy house, and upon thy gates.

For the Righteous and Proselytes

Towards the righteous and the pious, towards the elders of thy people the house of Israel, towards the remnant of their scribes, towards true proselytes, and towards us also may thy tender mercies be stirred, O Lord our God; grant a good reward unto all who faithfully trust in thy Name; set our portion with them for ever, so that we may not be put to shame; for we have trusted in thee. Blessed art thou, O Lord, the stay and trust of the righteous.

Recognition of the One God

We therefore hope in thee, O Lord our God, that we may speedily behold the glory of thy might, when thou wilt remove the abominations from the earth, and heathendom will be utterly destroyed, when the world will be perfected under the kingdom of the Almighty, and all the children of flesh will call upon thy Name, when thou wilt turn unto thyself all the evil-doers upon earth. Let all the inhabitants of the world perceive and know that unto thee every knee must bow, every tongue must swear allegiance. Before thee, O Lord our God, let them bow and worship; and unto thy glorious Name let them give honour; let them all accept the yoke of thy kingdom, and do thou reign over them speedily, and for ever and ever.

Hymn of Glory

Sweet hymns shall be my chant and woven songs,
For Thou art all for which my spirit longs—

To be within the shadow of Thy hand
And all Thy mystery to understand.

The while Thy glory is upon my tongue,
My inmost heart with love of Thee is wrung.

So though Thy mighty marvels I proclaim,
'Tis songs of love wherewith I greet Thy Name.

God the Teacher of Israel

With everlasting love thou hast loved the house of Israel, thy people; a Torah and commandments, statutes and judgments hast thou taught us. Therefore, O Lord our God, when we lie down and when we rise up we will meditate on thy statutes; yea, we will rejoice in the words of thy Torah and in thy commandments for ever; for they are our life and the length of our days, and we will meditate on them day and night. And mayest thou never take away thy love from us. Blessed art thou, O Lord, who lovest thy people Israel.

God the Guardian

Cause us, O Lord our God, to lie down in peace, and raise us up, O our King, unto life. Spread over us the protection of thy peace; direct us aright through thine own good counsel; save us for thy Name's sake; be thou a shield about us; remove from us every enemy, pestilence, sword, famine and sorrow; remove also the adversary from before us and from behind us. O shelter us beneath the shadow of thy wings; for thou, O God, art our Guardian and our Deliverer; yea, thou, O God, art a gracious and merciful King; and guard our going and our coming unto life and unto peace from this time forth and for evermore. Blessed art thou, O Lord, who guardest thy people Israel for ever.

Sabbath Prayer

Our God and God of our fathers, accept our rest; hallow us by thy commandments, and grant our portion in thy Torah; satisfy us with thy goodness, and gladden us with thy salvation; purify our hearts to serve thee in truth; and in thy love and favour, O Lord our God, let us inherit thy holy Sabbath; and may Israel, who sanctify thy Name, rest thereon. Blessed art thou, O Lord, who hallowest the Sabbath.

"Renew Our Days As of Old"

But on account of our sins we were exiled from our land, and removed far from our country, and we are unable to go up in order to appear and prostrate ourselves before thee, and to fulfil our obligations in thy chosen house, that great and holy temple which was called by thy Name, because of the hand of violence that hath been laid upon thy sanctuary. May it be thy will, O Lord our God and God of our fathers, merciful King, that thou mayest again in thine abundant compassion have mercy upon us and upon thy sanctuary, and mayest speedily rebuild it and magnify its glory. Our Father, our King, do thou speedily make the glory of thy kingdom manifest upon us; shine forth and exalt thyself upon us in the sight of all living; bring our scattered ones among the nations near unto thee, and gather our dispersed from the ends of the earth. Lead us with exultation unto Zion thy city, and unto Jerusalem the place of thy sanctuary with everlasting joy.

Repentance

Thou dost put forth thy hand to transgression, and thy right hand is stretched out to receive the penitent; thou hast taught us, O Lord our God, to make confession unto thee of all our sins, in order that we may cease from our unrighteous acts, and thou wilt receive us when we come unto thee in whole-hearted repentance, even as upon fire offerings and sweet savours, for thy words' sake which thou hast spoken. Endless would be the fire offerings required for our guilt, and numberless the sweet savours for our trespasses; but thou knowest that our latter end is the worm, and hast therefore shown us manifold ways of forgiveness.

Closing Confession

O my God, before I was formed I was nought; and now that I have been formed, I am but as though I had not been formed. Dust am I in my life: how much more so in my death. Behold I am before thee like a vessel filled with shame and confusion. O may it be thy will, O Lord my God and God of my fathers, that I may sin no more, and as to the sins I have committed, purge them away in thine abounding compassion, though not by means of affliction and sore diseases.

Rashi

Rabbi Solomon ben Isaac, better known as Rashi (an abbreviation of his formal name), was born in Troyes, France, in 1040. He died in his native city in 1105. Throughout his life, quiet and uneventful but intellectually exciting, Rashi wrote historic commentaries on nearly all the books of the Bible, and on most of the Talmud. The popularity of his work led to his commentary on the Torah; it was the first Hebrew book to be printed (in 1475). His commentaries have been translated into Latin, German, English and many other languages. And on his own work, more than a hundred commentaries have been written.

Rashi studied in Worms and at 25 he was a rabbi in Troyes where he founded a yeshiva. An owner of vineyards, he probably earned his livelihood by the making of wine. Rashi had three daughters, all of whom married noted rabbis. In 1940, the 900th anniversary of Rashi's birth was celebrated by Jews all over the world.

RASHI'S COMMENTARIES

Samuel M. Blumenfield

Rabbi Shlomo Itzhaki, better known by his initials Rashi, holds a unique place in the history of Jewish culture. Neither a lawgiver nor a prophet, neither ruler nor philosopher, he nevertheless exercised a powerful influence upon the thinking and feeling, the expression and mode of living of millions of Jews for some nine hundred years.

Rashi contributed to many fields of Jewish learning and literature. However, his fame rests upon his commentaries on the Bible and the Talmud, the classical sources of Judaism. These works represent an interesting phenomenon of an interpreter becoming completely identified with the material he interpreted, for Rashi's commentaries have for centuries appeared side by side with the original texts and his utterances have become grafted to these sources as skin to flesh.

Elementary Jewish education has for ages revolved around the study of "*Humash mit Rashi*"—the Pentateuch with the commentary by Rashi. The printed texts of the Pentateuch and the Talmud were accompanied as a matter of course by Rashi's commentary, which enriched the imagination and warmed the hearts of generations of school children and older students alike. In fact, some of the writings of Rashi were among the first to see print and appeared in 1475—seven years before the printing of the Bible itself in 1482. Because of the type of script used by the first printer (which was the handwriting current among the Jews in Spain) and reproduced by the printers in succeeding generations, this script became associated with the name of Rashi. To this day it is known as Rashi script—a tribute of a people to its favored teacher.

Jews of all walks of life, from laborer to man of means, from young student to accomplished Rabbi, have been profoundly influenced by the Jewish and secular lore contained in Rashi's interpretations. Indeed, Rashi stands as a rare example of the power of a teacher to impress himself upon a whole people.

The factual data about the life of Rashi, as about other great Jewish personalities of his time, can be summed up in several sentences, for Rashi did not deem it worthwhile to record the details of his life. Like other pious medieval Jewish writers, he preferred to present even his own views in terms of Rabbinic tradition and scriptural quotations.

Rashi was born in Troyes, Northern France, in 1040, of a typical Franco-German Jewish family. He received the traditional Jewish schooling in Bible and Talmud in his home town. In order to become an accomplished student, he journeyed to the then centers of Rabbinic learning, Worms and Mayence. He married young and was poor. To use his own words: "Lacking bread and decent clothes, with a millstone on my neck, I served before them [the masters]." Following his studies he returned to his native Troyes, where he opened a Talmudic school of his own.

Like many other Jews of that part of France, he was a wine grower. His three daughters were married to scholars who became heirs to his views and interpretations of Jewish law and letters. One of his grandsons, Rabbenu Tam, became the founder of the school of Talmudic interpretation known as the Tosafaists.

During Rashi's lifetime, the relations between the Jews and their neighbors appear to have been comparatively peaceful and even friendly. Rashi's worldly knowledge and use of French indicate contact with French life and culture. Toward the end of his days, however he sensed the gathering storms of hatred and persecution which reached their climax in the Crusades of the 12th century.

While our knowledge of the details of Rashi's personal life is limited, we have abundant information on his literary and Rabbinic labors and the influence he exercised over his contemporaries and generations of students of the Bible (Jewish and non-Jewish) and the Talmud, up to our own days.

Rashi's greatest contribution consists in his commentaries which helped transmit the accumulated experiences and cultural heritage of his people to succeeding generations. The Rabbis of the Talmud had to cope with the problem of adjusting the civilization of the Hebrews to the Roman regime in Palestine and later to an oriental diaspora. Rashi and his disciples had the even more difficult task of transmitting the twofold heritage of the Bible and the Talmud to a Jewry which had to adapt itself to the new and different environment of Europe. This accomplishment was made possible by the unique method of interpretation Rashi used in teaching the Jewish heritage to his people.

At a very early period in the history of Judaism one finds

the question of how to hand down Jewish ideals and practices to be a bone of contention. While still in Palestine and
enjoying a comparatively free and independent existence,
Israel was shaken by a violent controversy between the
Sadducees and Pharisees, one of the major points of dis-
sension being whether the Scripture should be understood
and transmitted literally or interpreted and evaluated according to its spirit. This same controversy later led to the
differences between the Karaites and Rabbinites and
brought about a serious schism in Jewry.

One can readily see that Rashi's problem was a difficult
one. To interpret Jewish lore literally or to explain it only
rationally would render the Torah a dogmatic, spiritless
code. This danger was sensed by some of the Gaonim and
by Rashi himself. In commenting on the Talmudic injunction of "keep children away from *higayon*" (meditation),
Rashi says, "Do not accustom them to Scripture more than
is necessary, for it may lead to heresy," as indeed it did
when followed to its extreme by the Karaites.

On the other hand, the method of free interpretation had
its dangers, for once one departs from the literal sense and
the rational approach, one incurs the risk of lapsing into
far-fetched allegory and mysticism. That Rashi was conscious of these dangers appears from such a comment as,
"Let the interpreter keep on interpreting, but we are interested in the simple natural meaning of the text;" or from
his denunciation of those "who pervert the sense of the
Torah by wrong and misleading exegesis."

The contribution of Rashi consists in his blending of both
peshat and *derash*, literal exegesis combined with free interpretation and homiletic comment. In his *peshat* Rashi
strives to explain the text and convey its meaning in terms

of logic, grammar, common sense, and personal experience. This rational treatment helped clarify many obscure ideas and practices embodied in the Bible and the Talmud, and to this day Rashi remains by far the most widely used commentator by students of Bible and Talmud.

Not being too far removed from the Talmudic age, Rashi was able to project himself into the world of the Talmud and share in it as though he were a contemporary. At home in the Rabbinic environment, Rashi found no difficulty in bridging over to the world of the Bible, which he correctly sensed to be closely related to that of the Talmud. Having shared vicariously in the life of Biblical and post-Biblical Jewry, Rashi was able to interpret the civilization of Israel to his contemporaries in a lucid, vivid style which is to this day a model of precise Hebrew writing.

When Rashi was in doubt as to whether his contemporaries would understand a Hebrew term, he did not hesitate to translate it into French. When he was not certain that words alone would suffice to convey the meaning of a passage, Rashi used drawings or cited graphic illustrations from daily life and the experiences of artisans and men of affairs. When Rashi himself was not certain of the meaning of the text, he would quote an authority, adding that he was not convinced; or confess, "I do not know." At times he pointed out his own errors. Even in his old age, when men's minds ordinarily tend to rigidity, Rashi confided to his grandson that if he had the time, he would rewrite his Biblical commentary in the light of more recent findings. Considering the authoritarian spirit of the age, such freedom from dogmatism is all the more significant.

While Rashi employed the rational approach, he was fully cognizant of the place of emotion and imagination in the scheme of education. He could not have been influenced by Plato's theory of character building through the arts, but as a true teacher he must have sensed the power of myth and poetry in elevating the spirit and enriching the imagination. This explains how a man with as clear and realistic a mind as his could so often be at one with the world of imagery and poetic fantasy—the Midrash. Practically all the references used by Rashi are taken from this rich treasure of Rabbinic lore. However, Rashi chooses his selections with discriminating taste and a sense of harmony.

"There are many *midrashim*" (dealing with a particular quotation), he remarks a number of times, "but I have chosen the Agada which interprets Scripture according to its proper meaning in its appropriate place." In many instances, Rashi, in order to convey a thought or image more graphically, departs from the original text and freely uses his own intimate style. That his versions have proved to be more appealing than the original can be judged from the fact that the one hundred Rabbinic dicta which are most current in Yiddish are those quoted from Rashi and in his style.

The celebrated remark of Pascal, that "the heart has reasons which reason does not know at all," may well apply to the realm of legend which has a rationale that rationalism does not have. Some scholars of the Rationalist School have deprecated Rashi's flights into what they called the "irrational" and "unscientific," but the present generation, cognizant of the educative value of legends and mytho-poetry, is better able to understand why Rashi used them so freely.

An example of Rashi's effectiveness in selecting Midrashic material rich in emotional content and human appeal, is his often quoted commentary on *Gen. 48:8.* "And as for me, when I came from Padden, Rachel died unto me in the land of Canaan in the way, when there was still some way to come unto Ephrath; and I buried her there in the way to Ephrath, the same is Bethlehem." Rashi's commentary reads as follows:

> *And although I trouble you to take me into the land of Canaan for burial, and I did not do this for your mother, though I might easily have done so since she died quite close to Bethlehem . . . , do not imagine that it was the rains which prevented me from bringing her to Hebron for burial. It was the dry season, when the ground is riddled and full of holes like a sieve, and yet I buried her there, and did not carry her even the short distance to Bethlehem, to bring her to a city. I know that in your heart you feel some resentment against me. Know, however, that I buried her there by the command of God, that she might help her children when Nebuzaradan will take them into captivity. When they pass along the road, Rachel will come forth from her grave and stand by her tomb weeping and seeking mercy for them as it is said, "A voice is heard in Ramah . . . the sound of weeping . . . Rachel weeping for her children." And the Holy-One-Blessed-Be-He replies to her, "For thy children will return to their own border."*

The tender voice and the moving appeal of Mother Rachel pleading for her perpetually wandering children as expressed by Rashi in these lines have found their echo in the hearts of millions of Jews who studied the Pentateuch with Rashi's commentary and had much to do with the preservation of the hope of Zion rebuilt through the ages.

In Jewish history, it is the Rabbi and teacher, rather than the ruler or priest, whose leadership has guided the development of the people. Moses, the lawgiver and the father of the prophets, is known to Jewish tradition as Moshe Rabbenu, "our teacher." The reconstruction of Jewish religious life after the Babylonian exile is associated with Ezra, the leading teacher of his day. Following the destruction of the Second Temple the continuity of Jewish development was ensured by the activity of a third great teacher, Rabbi Johanan ben Zakkai. The significance of Rashi therefore lies not only in his contributions to Judaism but also in the fact that as Rabbi and teacher he personifies the ideal type of Jewish tradition.

In Rashi's writings, as well as in his practices, one finds sublime expressions of the value of study and teaching. There is hardly an utterance on this subject, recorded by generations of scholars and pietists who preceded him, which is not quoted directly or indirectly by him. Education, or its Hebrew equivalent, Torah, was to Rashi as to his predecessors, more than a means of imparting knowledge, the training in skills, or even the building of character. Education to the Jew has been an integral part of religion itself, constituting one of the three foundations upon which Judaism rests: God, Israel and Torah. It is this conception of Torah, as an essential element of Jewish religious faith and observance that accounted, more than anything else, for the widespread interest in and practice of education among Jews, even in an age of universal illiteracy.

Many a great Jewish personality sensed the role of education in the centuries-old struggle for survival and devoted his creative abilities to teaching. Rashi shows a particular appreciation of the historic mission of the teacher in the destiny of his people. Teaching to him was not a chore to be relegated to someone else as was the case among the Greeks and the Romans, where the slave performed the function of the teacher. To Rashi, as in Jewish tradition which he helped fashion, teaching was a divine function and the teacher a spiritual father. By bringing out the potentialities of the learner, the teacher helps recreate human personality and thus partakes of the function of God. Indeed, God himself is often referred to in Jewish tradition as scholar and teacher.

As a born pedagogue Rashi had a wholesome appreciation of the importance of developing the interest of the learner. "There is no comparison," says Rashi, "between one who does things out of love and one who does them out of fear. He who does things for his teacher out of fear, leaves him the moment they become burdensome." Rashi has, therefore, a high regard for one "who teaches his students with gentleness" and advises that, "If the teacher approaches the learner in a pleasant way, the pupil will succeed in his studies; if not, he will not." Rashi also warns against harsh punishment and admonishes, "You are not to punish him more than is necessary, nor to remove him from your presence."

This attitude to the pupil is no small achievement considering the practices of his time, based upon the teachings of St. Augustine, that "a birch, a strap, a cane" are indispensable "to overcome ignorance."

Rashi sought to develop the reasoning faculties of the student. He advised him to ask many questions and, if need be, subject himself to the abuse of those who may consider

him foolish. It is not enough, according to Rashi, for a
teacher to say "This is the tradition that I received"; his
duty is to give reasons which will satisfy the learner. Indeed, Rashi himself, despite his reverence for his teachers,
did not hesitate to express himself vigorously against them
when their views were not acceptable to him.

One who gathers mere information without understanding, Rashi describes as "a basket full of books," carrying a
load without appreciating its contents. Rashi used, therefore, all possible devices to simplify his subject matter and
make it understandable to every type of student. That is
why his commentaries on the same subject may differ in
form, depending upon the kind of student for whom the
explanations were intended.

Rashi's method is noteworthy for its sense of fitness and
balance. He neither leaves passages unexplained, nor does
he explain more than is necessary, veering carefully between "not enough" and "too much," and aiming "to help
the student to help himself," to use the apt expression of
William Kilpatrick in his description of the ideal teacher.
Drawing upon the distinction made by the Rabbis between
the *Hacham* who relies upon authority, and the *Nabon*,
who from his knowledge of one situation understands another, Rashi advises one who received instruction from his
teacher, "Do your own investigation in order to be able to
infer one case from another." Rashi, in his interpretations,
instead of doing the work of the student, stimulates him,
thus achieving one of the highest ideals of good education.

What emerges in all of Rashi's writings is the warm personality of a kindly, loving teacher, whose honesty of purpose and sincerity of motive are sensed by anyone who
comes in contact with him. In many ways, he reminds us of

the humble and patient Talmudic teacher, Hillel. Like him, Rashi would rather explain than command, forgive than reproach. "It is better to listen to one who is lenient and permits, rather than to one who forbids," says Rashi regarding disagreements between Rabbinic authorities. "Anyone can be strict and forbid," hence, "Since I began to understand the words of the Talmud, my heart leans toward those who permit."

His influence on the Rabbinate in later centuries can be judged from the fact that more than two hundred super-commentaries have been written upon Rashi's commentary on the Bible and the Talmud. There is increasing evidence that knowledge of Rashi was not limited to the Jews alone and that his influence on Christian Bible commentators was more far-reaching than hitherto recognized by scholars. It is well known that Rashi's commentaries were used copiously by Nicholas de Lyra (d.1349), the commentator who exercised a great influence on Luther. Recent studies show the great influence of Rashi and his disciples on Christian scholars as early as the 12th century. One author places Rashi on the same level with Philo and Maimonides as "three stages distinct though overlapping" in the history of Jewish influence on Christian students of the Bible.

Of greater significance is the fact that Rashi brought the Rabbinic world into the very life of his people. Jewry for many centuries, therefore, did not know of the distinction that existed in Christendom between the clergy and the laity. Because of his lucid, warm style, his intimate manner of interpretation, Rashi helped bring an ancient heritage to life, not to the scholar alone, but to the Jewish people as a whole. While education was until modern times restricted to the few, and in the days of Rashi, to the clergy, Jewish learning because of Rashi was so widespread that the average Jew could quote Scripture and adorn his quotations with Rashi's commentaries. He was indeed an architect of Jewish destiny, for he succeeded in opening the vast treasures of Jewish lore to the masses of Jewry, thereby setting a unique example of democracy in education.

Rashi's colossal systematic labor on the Bible and the Talmud is to this day the only comprehensive treatment of the most creative period of Judaism written by one man, and is justly mentioned in Jewish tradition in the same breath with the Bible and frequently with the Talmud. Jewish tradition has valued its teacher-commentator greatly and interpreted the initials of Rashi to mean, *"Rabban shel Yisrael,"* the teacher of Israel.

selections from RASHI'S COMMENTARIES

Thou Shalt Love the Lord. Fulfill His commands out of love, for one who acts out of love is not like him who acts out of fear.

All Thy Soul. Love the Lord even if He takes your life.

All Thy Might. With all thy property. There are people to whom wealth means more than life. Another explanation: Thou shalt love Him whatever measure it may be that He metes out to Thee, whether it be the measure of good or the measure of calamity.   *Deut. 6, 5*

He is a Man of War. But His name is the Lord (the God of Mercy); even at the time when He battles against and avenges Himself upon His enemies He retains His attributes showing pity to His creatures and feeding all the inhabitants of the world; not as is the nature of the kings of the world each one of whom when he is engaged in war turns aside from all other engagements, and has not the power to do both this and that.   *Exodus 15, 3*

Shall be Called Woman. Here we have a kind of play upon words (the words *isha* and *ish* sounding similar);
126

hence we may learn that the language used at the time of the Creation was Hebrew. *Gen. 2, 23*

Moses Feared. He (Moses) felt distressed because he saw that there were wicked men among the Israelites— common informers. He said; since this is so, perhaps they are not worthy to be delivered from bondage.

Exodus, 2, 14

And I Bear You on Eagles' Wings. As an eagle which bears its fledglings upon its wings. Scripture uses this metaphor because all other birds place their young between their feet since they are afraid of another bird that flies above them, but the eagle fears none except man—apprehending that perhaps he may cast an arrow at it—since no bird can fly above it; therefore he places it (its young) upon its wings, saying: "Better that the arrow should pierce me than my young." *Exodus 19, 4*

In the Beginning. What is the reason that the Torah commences with the account of the Creation? Because . . . should the peoples of the world say to Israel, "You are robbers, because you took by force the lands of the seven nations of Canaan," Israel may reply to them, "All the earth belongs to the Holy One, Blessed Be He. He created it and gave it to whom He pleased." *Gen. 1, 1*

God of the Spirits of all Flesh. Moses said to God: "Lord of the Universe, the dispositions of every one are manifest to Thee, and Thou knowest that these are not similar one to the other. Appoint a leader for them who will bear with each person according to his disposition." *Num. 27, 16*

The Words of the Wise Spoken in Quiet. How different is the power of Moses from that of other great kings. Great kings make decrees which are forgotten as soon as they die.

Moses' decrees, however, have been taken over by Israel
for ever.   *Ecc. 9, 17*

Whilst I am Asleep My Heart is Awake. The Lord who
is the Rock of my heart and my portion He is awake to protect me and bestow kindness on me.   *Song of Songs, 5, 2*

The Lord Trieth the Righteous. It is the way of God to
subject the righteous to affliction and trial, not, however,
the wicked. He is like the man who handles flax; so long as
he knows that the flax is good, he beats it little lest it fall
apart.   *Ps. 11, 5*

These are the generations of Aaron and Moses. Mentions
only the sons of Aaron, but they are called also the sons of
Moses because he (Moses) taught them the Torah. This
implies that whoever teaches the Torah to the son of his
fellowman Scripture regards him as if he had begotten him.
                                                San. 19b. Num. 3:1

Wise men . . . and understanding (men). What is the
difference between wise men and understanding men. A
wise man is like a rich money changer. When people bring
him dinars (coins) to examine he examines them; and
when they do not bring them to him, he sits and does nothing. An understanding man, however, is like an energetic
merchant or money changer; when they bring him coins to
examine he examines them; and when they do not bring
him any, he goes about and secures some on his own in-
itiative.   *Sifre. Deut. 1:13*

And Thou shalt Love. Fulfill his commands out of love,
for one who acts out of love is not like him who acts out of
fear. He who serves his master out of fear, if he (the master) burdens him overmuch, he (the student) leaves him
and goes away.   *Sifre. Deut. 6:5*

The Sacrifice of Isaac

After these words. Some of our teachers explain the expression: "after the words of Satan," who said to God: Of all his meals Abraham sacrifices nothing to Thee, neither a bull nor a ram. He would sacrifice his son, replied God, if I told him to do it. Others say: "after the words of Ishmael," who boasted of having undergone circumcision when he was thirteen years old, and to whom Isaac answered: If God demanded of me the sacrifice of my entire being, I would do what he demanded. *Abraham said: Behold, here I am.* Such is the humility of pious men; for this expression indicates that one is humble, ready to obey.

God said: Take now. This is a formula of prayer; God seems to say to Abraham: I pray thee, submit thyself to this test, so that thy faith shall not be doubted. *Thy son.* I have two sons, replied Abraham. *Thine only son.* But each is the only son of his mother. *Whom thou lovest.* I love them both. *Isaac.* Why did not God name Isaac immediately? In order to trouble Abraham, and also to reward him for each word, etc. *Gen. xxii. 1*

A Psalm of David

A Psalm of David. Our rabbis say: The formula "Psalm of David" indicates that David at first played the instrument, then was favored by Divine inspiration. It, therefore, signifies, Psalm to give inspiration to David. On the other hand, when it is said "To David, a Psalm," the formula indicates that David, having received Divine inspiration, sang a song in consequence of the revelation.

The Lord is my Shepherd; I shall not want. In this desert in which I wander I am full of trust, sure that I shall lack nothing.

He maketh me to lie down in green pastures. In a place to dwell where grass grows. The poet, having begun by comparing his sustenance to the pasturing of animals, in the words, "The Lord is my Shepherd," continues the image. This Psalm was recited by David in the forest of Hereth, which was so called because it was arid as clay (*heres*), but it was watered by God with all the delights of the next world (Midrash on the Psalms).

He will restore my soul. My soul, benumbed by misfortunes and by my flight, He will restore to its former estate. *He will lead me in the paths of righteousness* along the straight highway so that I may not fall into the hands of my enemies.

Yea, though I walk through the valley of the shadow of death, I will fear no evil. In the country of shadows; this applies to the wilderness of Ziph. The word *tzalmoveth* here employed always signifies "utter darkness"; this is the way in which it is explained by Dunash ben Labrat. *Thy rod and thy staff they comfort me.* The sufferings I have undergone and my reliance, my trust, in Thy goodness are my two consolations, for they bring me pardon for my faults, and I am sure that *Thou wilt prepare a table before me,* that is, royalty. *Thou hast anointed my head with oil,* I have already been consecrated king at Thy command. *My cup runneth over.* An expression signifying abundance.

Yehudah Halevi

Few details are known about the life of Yehudah Halevi, one of the greatest poets in the Hebrew language, often called "The Sweet Singer of Zion." On the basis of contemporary records which have been accepted by scholars as authentic, Halevi was born in Toledo, Spain, about 1080 or 1085. He knew Arabic and Castilian as well as the Hebrew Bible and Rabbinic literature; and was familiar with Arabic poetry, Hebrew grammar, philology, Greek philosophy and medicine. His poetry attracted the famous poet Moses ibn Ezra, who invited him to Granada. Halevi went, but eventually returned to Castile. It is difficult to trace Halevi's wanderings. His poems indicate that he spent time in Lucena and in Seville; and settled apparently in Cordova. His circle of friends must have been wide, for his written work deals at considerable length with friends. But there is little about his own family; his silence about his wife indicates that she must have died before he left Spain.

131

In maturity, his old desire to see Palestine grew stronger. Precisely when he left Cordova is unknown, but it seems to have been soon after the death of his friend Moses ibn Ezra, about 1138. From Spain he travelled to Egypt and visited Alexandria, Darmietta and Cairo. He was warmly received everywhere, and treated with great honor. His history after Cairo is a complete blank. About Yehudah Halevi's death there are many legends. According to one version, as he approached the gates of Jerusalem an Arab horseman rode him down and pierced him with his spear.

THE KUSARI

Jacob B. Agus

If, by some catastrophe, all Jewish books from the Bible to the last Yiddish daily were lost, and only the *Book of the Kusari* were left, it would be possible for the historian to reconstruct with fidelity the diverse strands of thought and sentiment which enter into the making of the traditional Jewish mentality. For Yehudah Halevi, the author of this volume, did not set out to defend the philosophy of the Jewish religion against the challenge of the metaphysicians and logicians of his day. He began and ended his quest with the concerns of the living Jewish people, so that his volume faithfully reproduces that cluster of ideas and feelings which rose to the surface of consciousness, whenever intelligent Jews reflected on the peculiar destiny of their people among the nations. Where other philosophers responded primarily to the challenge of the ideas of their day, Halevi was profoundly troubled by the unequal contest between the powerful nations and dominant faiths, and the feeble, odium-laden faith of the Jewish people. Thus, the focus of his convictions and reflections was no abstract dogma or philosophical principle, but the

133

sorry state of the Divinely chosen and blessed people, a
bitter paradox of which sensitive Jews were profoundly
aware.

One of the extant manuscripts of this volume carries on
its frontispiece the heading, "In defense and proof of the
Despised Faith," a phrase which reveals the polemical, de-
fiant spirit of the author. Why did the true faith of Judaism
command the loyalty of only a small, despised, persecuted
minority in every land, while its daughter-religions divided
the Western world among them? Did Judaism lack the
power to appeal to the objective mind? If so, then the con-
sensus of world opinion would seem to indicate that Judaism as a faith need no longer be taken seriously.

Nor could it be maintained that Judaism was uninter-
ested in the conversion of non-Jews, since it would then
stand convicted of misanthropic clannishness and atavistic
tribalism. To rationalistic thinkers, approval would appear
to be of minor importance, since truth cannot be tested
by resort to popular referendum. To an Aristotle or a
Maimonides, it was axiomatic that the capacity for true
knowledge is limited to the chosen few. But Halevi, too
much a man of the world to hold it in contempt, was concerned with the concrete situation in which the Jewish
faith, beginning with so impressive a start over its rivals,
nevertheless lagged so miserably behind them in its manifest appeal to the pagan mind. He chose as the setting for
his work, therefore, the one striking mass-conquest by Judaism since the appearance of both Christianity and Islam so
as to indicate that, in any fair contest, Judaism could well
hold its own against the competition of other faiths and the
attraction of pure philosophy.

The conversion of the King of the Khazars to Judaism is

supposed to have taken place about 740, some four hundred years prior to the composition of this work (1130-1140). In Cordova, where the author lived and worked, the tale of the Khazars was a vivid reality, since a number of Jewish families in that city claimed descent from the Khazars. It was, therefore, quite natural for Halevi to relate his philosophy to the reputed triumph of the Jewish religion in the debate held at the court of Bulan, King of the Khazars.

The author begins by telling of a persistent dream which came to the just and enlightened King Bulan, in which the pagan seeker for truth and justice was admonished that "his intentions were acceptable, but his deeds were not." This heavenly warning, in Halevi's account, is the more significant in that the one document upon which it is based, the letter of Joseph, King of the Khazars, to Hasdai ibn Shaprut, reports the heavenly voice as saying "I see your ways and like your deeds." Halevi's alteration of this admonition reflects the basic tone of his entire exposition, in that the argument is shifted from consideration of dogmas and principles to analysis of the validity of the specific practice and ritual of each living faith.

Already at that time, the metaphysical systems of Judaism, Christianity and Islam were beginning to approach a degree of uniformity, so that it was possible for intellectuals to argue that God may be approached through the rites of any and all faiths, provided heart and mind were attuned to the love of truth. "Once you have achieved this exalted faith," says the philosopher, "do not be concerned with the question of which religion or faith, or set of deeds and words, you practice, or the language in which you pray. You may even invent a religion to serve your own special needs. . . . For the fundamental rule is to seek purity of heart in whichever way it may be attained, once the basic principles of philosophy are understood in truth" *(Kusari, 1, 1).* Naturally, this lofty attitude militated effectively against the continued adherence of Jewish people to their ancestral faith. If, to the enlightened, all paths lead to God, why continue to pay so great a price for loyalty to the practices of Judaism? As a matter of fact, we learn from the later history of Spanish Jewry that, when the crucial test of persecution came, the philosophically trained Jews, with few exceptions, deserted the fold, while the naive, unsophisticated believers retained the time-tested Jewish power to live and to die for the sanctification of the Holy Name.

Halevi's reply to the challenge of philosophy is offered in the principle that only God Himself can tell how He may be properly worshipped. As the nature of God may not be understood completely by man, so the things of God, the *mitzvoth* of religion, cannot be man-made. If it be granted that the Will of God is inscrutable, then it is logical to assume that He has His own ideas as to the manner in which He should be served. Manifestly, these meta-rational ideas, grounded in the completely undetermined Divine Will, cannot be discovered by reason or speculation and can only be known by the direct act of revelation.

Thus, if one relied on sheer speculation, one would maintain that God could best be served through the methods of the ascetic, who renounces the pleasures and comforts of the world for His sake. Actually, "the observance of the Sabbath brings one closer to the Creator than renunciation and asceticism," though it is a most pleasing observance. For religious observances must strike a balance between "fear, love and joy." Indeed, "pure spiritual joy is the very acme of religious experience." And "if your joy becomes so intense as to pass into song and dance, then you have reached the height of service of and communion with the Divine Power" *(2, 50)*. In so complex a matter, rational speculation is therefore useless. Only through revelation could the pathway to God be known. Accordingly the argument descends from the ethereal heights of philosophy to the earthly contest between the contending religions, each claiming to contain the one and only true revelation.

Insofar as Halevi was concerned, the claim of Judaism was challenged seriously only by the Christian and Moslem faiths. Since these two faiths admitted that Judaism did contain true revelation in the past, maintaining only that their own subsequent revelations superseded that of Judaism, it is obvious that the burden of proof rests upon the so-called daughter-religions. The presumption of truth is held by Judaism, while the challenging faiths could prove their case only by demonstrating that God declared Judaism to be no longer valid by an act of revelation as striking and certain as that by which He made His Will manifest to Israel in the first place.

When the Torah was given to the Israelites at Sinai, God's revelation was made evident in the presence of 600,-000 adult male observers, who saw the smoke and holy fire, and heard the thunder and the Voice of God. Neither Christianity nor Islam even so much as lay claim to a revelation given with so much eclat and in the presence of so many people as the original, admittedly true, revelation at Sinai. Hence, their claims are discounted by the King of the Khazars, who undertakes thereupon to examine the faith of Judaism with great care and scrutiny.

In logical order, the author seeks to prove first the truth of Judaism as a living faith. Though he assumes the revelation at Sinai to be a universally accepted, and therefore unquestioned fact, he nevertheless realizes that in the course of time even the truest Divine treasure could be corrupted by uninspired human hands. Accordingly, he marshals evidences from the Bible and Talmud in proof of his contention that Divine inspiration departed only slowly and not yet altogether from the Jewish people. Thus he cites the rabbinic statement that the number of prophets in Israel was in excess of a million souls. When the gift of prophecy ceased to function, by virtue of the confiscation of the Holy Ark, the spirit of holiness in lesser forms continued to manifest itself in the life of saints and sages. The codification of the Mishnah, for instance, was a divinely inspired act, "for flesh and blood cannot compose such a treatise, save with the help of God" (3, 67). All *Takkanath* or rabbinic regulations, were similarly enacted with the aid of the felt Divine Presence (3, 49). Thus, Judaism, in all the stages of its development, from Moses to the last Responsa of the Gaonic academies, was divinely inspired.

But how are Jewish people so certain of the unique truth and inspiration of their tradition? At this point, the author falls back upon the mystical experiences of his own soul, representing them to be the exclusive property of Jewish people. The God of philosophy may be proved by arguments and disproved by the same means, but the personal God of Israel is directly apprehended by Jewish people. Endowed by a special Divine intuition, as it were, the Jewish people "taste" and "see" the holiness of God, so that they cannot possibly doubt His Presence or permanently refuse to succumb to His Will. "Thus, I understand the dif-

ference between the God of Abraham and the God of Aristotle, for to the former souls are drawn by sight and taste,
whereas the latter is the goal of dialectics. This direct ap-
prehension of the Divine leads those who experience it to
surrender their souls voluntarily for their love of God, and
even to die for Him" *(4, 16)*. Already, in the days of Halevi,
the martyrdom of Israel for the sanctification of the Holy
Name, was an awe-inspiring and reverence-compelling
reality, suggesting the thought that there was something
peculiarly intimate and unique in the relationship between
the Jew and God. "And in truth, He is called the God of Israel because this perception of the Divine is lacking among
non-Jews."

Naturally, the King of the Khazars would not allow the
doctrine of Israel's superiority to go unchallenged. Why
should the good God, Who loves all men, single out one
people for special distinction and endow them with an intuition for the Divine? Halevi counters with the explanation
that originally this intuition was the prerogative of all mankind, but that through the fall of Adam and the subsequent
degeneration of his descendants, the special Divine intuition came to be limited to the Jewish people. Even the
righteous proselytes, like the King of the Khazars, cannot
expect to attain the gift of intuition, since it is a hereditary
quality of the race *(1, 196)*. On the other hand, in propi-
tious circumstances the majority of Jewish people may expect to develop their inborn intuition virtually to the point
of prophecy *(1, 103)*. When this happens, "they are elevated
above their species, in the refinement of their souls and in
their longing for the highest levels of mystical communion
with the Divine in humility and purity. . . . Then, their
only longing is to return the soul to its Divine state, when it

is entirely separated from the senses, beholding the upper worlds, enjoying the perception of angelic light and listening to the Divine speech."

To ask why this prophetic gift was not conferred upon all men is to question the wisdom of Providence in creating this supremely variegated world. As well might one inquire why all creatures were not endowed with the gifts of speech and reason. All Jews are potentially prophets, and prophets constitute a supra-human species, in the scale of being, adapted for the perception of Divine "lights," in a manner which cannot be understood by the rest of mankind, even as the blind cannot understand the sense of sight.

Does it mean, then, that the Jewish people were designed by God to be the "master-race," lording it over the other nations? By no means. On the contrary, the proof of the election of Israel is the historical fact of its being immediately and ruthlessly punished for the slightest infraction of the Law. While other nations are left to the sway of natural law, the Jewish people are subject to the special Providence of God, Who rebukes whomsoever He loveth. Halevi maintains that humanity forms a living whole and he asserts that Israel fulfills a special function in the organic society of mankind, directing all men to the true paths of religion. Manifestly, "all the peoples of the world were groping in blindness before the appearance of the children of Israel." Through the revelation of God in the life of the Jewish people, "when the laws of nature were changed in their behalf," it was demonstrated that there is a "guardian and ruler of the universe. The hearts of all men were then directed toward the truth, to the point when today all the inhabitants of the world admit that the world is created, their proof being the historical experiences and career of the house of Israel" *(2, 54)*.

Thus Israel has been designed to function as the "heart" of the nations, reacting to all the ailments in the body of mankind, while at the same time stimulating its conscience. Both Christianity and Islam derive from the fructifying power of Jewish genius, "constituting the necessary spiritual preparation for the expected Messiah." As the seed is put into the ground, to rot there for a while, then to shoot forth into a tree with branches and leaves and flowers, which ultimately ripen into fruit, containing the same seed, so Israel has been cast into exile, rotting there to all appearances, but continuing to produce and nourish in mysterious fashion the branches and leaves and flowers of Christianity and Islam. When these flowers will ripen into fruit, the seed of Judaism will be found in their core. In this manner, even the travail of Israel in exile is an instrument for the redemption of the world. "All the vicissitudes which come upon us have the effect of purifying the spirit of Torah within us, purging us of all dross and refining the pure metal, so that through our purification and improvement, the Divine power might cleave unto the world" *(2, 44)*.

From this interpretation of the spiritual effects of Jewish travail in exile one might gather the impression that Jewish people should resign themselves to their exilic existence, since it is their "mission" to influence and elevate the great non-Jewish world. Halevi, however, steers clear with might and main away from this *"Protest-rabbiner"* pitfall. In his view, Jewish people affect the spiritual progress of the world in mystical fashion by their existence, rather than by overt missionary efforts. Hence, they owe it to themselves and to the world to rehabilitate their existence on a healthy and creative basis, by reforging their bonds with the Holy Land. Jewish people can attain their full prophetic stature only in their own land, for that "Divine intuition," which is their special gift can flourish only in the land of Israel (2, 8). Even as certain plants are adapted only to certain climates, so is the power of prophecy and the intimacy with Providence which prophecy implies capable of flourishing only in the chosen land, when it is inhabited by the chosen people. While men of colossal spiritual attainments, like "Abraham, Moses and the Messiah" might achieve the level of prophecy outside the borders of the Holy Land, lesser men cannot hope for such a consummation save by migrating to the land of their fathers. Indeed, Abraham and Moses regarded it as their life's ambition to settle in the Promised Land, and it will be the Messiah's function to bring all Jews back to their own land. Thus all prophecy is either acquired in the Holy Land or on account of it.

Since prophecy is the noble purpose for which Jewish people were designed, it follows that Jews deny their own soul and mock their own reason for existence, so long as they do not migrate to the chosen land, the air of which is "life for the soul." Indeed, Halevi is ready to concede that the Jews of his own day were in the category of the "dry bones" envisioned by Ezekiel. But, he argues, "We are not in the category of the dead, but in that of the tubercular patient, of whose recovery and life all the doctors have despaired, and who expects to be healed by a miracle which will controvert the laws of nature" (2, 34).

Obviously, no patient can expect the help of God, who does not himself strive and hope for recovery. Hence, it is the crucial sin of Israel to rest content with exilic existence and not to migrate to the land which is only one level removed from the Garden of Eden (heaven). "Your love of Torah cannot be sincere if you do not make this place your goal, your home in life and death. Don't you say, 'Have mercy on Zion for it is the home of our life' and believe that the *shekinah* returns to it? And if it were only for the fact that the *shekinah* dwelt in it approximately 900 years, noble souls should long for it, in order that they might be purified in it, as is likely to happen in the places of prophets and saints, especially since it is the gate of the heavens" (2, 23).

Thus Halevi begins by converting the Khazars to Judaism and ends by converting himself to personal Zionism. Step by step he was led inexorably to this conclusion through the unfolding inner logic of his faith. Judaism is the one true faith, as judged by the testimony of its own tradition, endorsed in a measure by the traditions of the two great related faiths. But the truth of tradition is itself attested to by personal experience, in which respect Judaism is pre-eminent, because every Jew is potentially a prophet, capable of seeing the "glory of God" and sensing the intimate presence of the Deity. And here is the rub. The potentiality of prophecy can only be realized in the Holy Land. The argument of the Jew *pro vita sua* remains, therefore, suspended in mid-air so long as he is in exile, deprived of the opportunity to "see" and "taste" the Divine.

Never was a book so utterly a part of the author as the *Book of the Kusari* was of Yehudah Halevi. The argument of the book led the author to undertake his famed journey to Zion, which was in truth an act of self-sacrifice, unique in the annals of mankind. In all literalness, Halevi undertook to go to the land then occupied by the Crusaders, who had murdered all the Jews in Jerusalem, in order that he

might "see" the "glory of God" and then die. The one moment of Divine revelation would more than compensate for
the death that was sure to follow. Tired of arguments that
lead whithersoever the contemporary winds list, Halevi determined to "see" for himself, convinced as he was that in
Palestine the gift of prophecy was ready and waiting for
those eager to receive it. The return of prophecy to Israel
would signalize the beginning of the redemption. "For the
Divine power comes to one in accordance with his preparation, whether much or little, and if we had readied ourselves for the God of our fathers with a perfect heart and
an aspiring soul, we should have encountered the same
wonders as our ancestors in Egypt." Of this preparation, no
element was as important as that of a personal pilgrimage
to Zion.

Thus once the Khazars were converted, the rabbi, feeling that his mission was completed, determined to go to
Palestine, for the "*shekinah* that is visible to the eyes is
lacking" elsewhere, even if the "hidden, spiritual *shekinah*"
attends those of true faith in all lands. What is death in the
face of so glorious an experience to crown the lifelong
search for the nearness of God! Furthermore, through his
journey to Zion he would attain not only personal salvation,
but also pave the way of redemption for all Israel. "For
Jerusalem will indeed be built when the children of Israel
will long for it with all their might and favor its sands and
stones" (5, 27).

Halevi's pilgrimage to Palestine, doomed from the start
as it was to end in martyrdom, was in a sense the seal and
stamp of his defense of Judaism. Through this final proof of
sincerity, the *Kitab al Khazari* ceased to be just another

book and became an undying clarion call, reverberating through the ages, calling for a return unto the God of Abraham, Who is nigh and close unto them that call upon Him in truth, and unto Zion, the dwelling place of His glory.

selections from THE KUSARI

Non-Jewish Religions

1. I was asked to state what arguments I could bring to bear against the attacks of philosophers and followers of other religions which differ from ours and against the sectaries who differ from the majority of Israel. And I remembered the arguments I had heard of a Rabbi who sojourned with the King of the Khazars, who, as we know from historical records, became a convert to Judaism about four hundred years ago: to him there appeared repeatedly a dream, in which it seemed as if an angel addressed him saying: 'Thy (intention) is indeed pleasing to the Creator, but thy way of acting is not pleasing'. Yet he was so zealous in the performance of the Khazar religion, that he devoted himself with a perfect heart to the service of the temple and the sacrifices. Notwithstanding this devotion, the angel came again at night and repeated: 'Thy intention is indeed pleasing, but thy way of acting is not pleasing'. This induced him to ponder over the different beliefs and religions, and finally he became a convert to Judaism together with many other Khazars. As I found among the arguments of the Rabbi many which ap-

pealed to me and were in harmony with my opinions, I resolved to write them down as they had been spoken. The intelligent will understand me.

It is related: when the King of Khazar dreamt that his intention was pleasing to God, but his way of acting was not pleasing, and was commanded in the same dream to seek the work that would please God, he inquired of a philosopher concerning his persuasion.

THE PHILOSOPHER replied:

There is no favour or dislike in God, because He is above desire and intention. For an intention intimates a desire in the intending person: by the fulfillment of this desire he becomes complete; as long as it remains unfulfilled, he is incomplete. In a similar way God is, in the opinion of the philosophers, above the knowledge of individuals, because they change with the times and there is no change in God's knowledge. He does not know thee, much less thy intentions and actions, nor does He listen to thy prayers or see thy movements. Even if philosophers say that He created thee, they only speak in metaphor, because he is the cause of causes in the creation of all creatures, but not because this was His intention from the beginning. He never created man, for the world is without beginning, and no man arose other than through one who came into existence before him; in every man we find united physical and intellectual qualities deriving from his parents and other relations not discounting the influence of winds, countries, foods and water, spheres, stars and constellations. Everything is reduced to the Prime Cause—not to a Will proceeding from it, but to an Emanation, from which emanated a second, a third, and a fourth cause. The causes and the things caused are, as thou seest, intimately connected

with one another; their connection is as eternal as the
Prime Cause and has no beginning. Therefore, every individual on earth has its completing causes; consequently
an individual with perfect causes becomes perfect and another with imperfect causes remains imperfect, e.g. the
negro is fit to receive nothing more than human shape and
speech in its least developed form; the philosopher, however, who is equipped with the highest capacity, derives
therefrom moral, intellectual and active advantages, so that
he wants nothing to make him perfect. But these perfections exist only in the form of latent powers which require
instruction and training to become active, bringing to light
this capacity, in all its completeness or with its deficiencies
and innumerable grades. To the perfect person there ad-
heres a light of Divine nature, called Active Intellect; his
Passive Intellect cleaves so closely to it that it considers itself to be one with the Active Intellect. His organs—I mean
the limbs of such a person—only serve the most perfect
purposes, at the most appropriate time, and in the best condition, as though they were organs of the Active Intellect,
not of the potential and Passive Intellect, which made use
of them at an earlier period, sometimes well, but more
often improperly. This degree is the ultimate and most
longed-for goal for the perfect man, whose soul, purified
of doubts, grasps the inward truth of science. The soul becomes the equal of an angel, and finds a place on the nethermost steps of seraphic beings. This is what is called, al-
lusively and approximately, God's pleasure. Endeavour to
reach it and to reach the true knowledge of things, in order that thy intellect may become active. Keep to the just
way, as regards character and action, because this will help
thee to effect truth, to gain instruction, and to become like

this Active Intellect. The consequence of this will be contentment, humility, meekness and every other praiseworthy inclination, accompanied by the veneration of the Prime Cause, not in order to receive favour from it or to divert its wrath, but solely to become like the Active Intellect. If thou hast reached such disposition of belief, be not concerned about the forms of thy humility, worship and benediction—nor fashion thy religion according to the laws of reason set up by philosophers, but strive after purity of the soul. Then thou wilt reach thy goal, viz. union with the Active Intellect. Maybe he will communicate with thee or teach thee the knowledge of what is hidden through true dreams and positive visions.

2. THE KHAZARI: Thy speech is convincing, yet it does not correspond to what I desire to find. I know already that my soul is pure and that my actions are directed to gain the favour of God. To all this I received the answer that this way of acting does not find favour, though the intention does. There must no doubt be a way of acting, pleasing in itself, and not through the medium of intention. If this be not so, why then do Christian and Moslem, who divided the inhabited world between them, fight with one another, each of them serving his God with pure intention, living either as monks or hermits, fasting and praying? It is, however, impossible to agree with both.

3. THE PHILOSOPHER: The philosopher's creed knows no manslaughter, cultivating only the intellect.

4. THE KHAZARI: And what could be more erroneous, in the opinion of the philosophers, than the belief that the world was created, and that in six days; or that the Prime Cause spoke with mortals—in view of the philosophical doc-

trine, which declares God to be above knowing details. Moreover, one might expect the gift of prophecy to be quite common among philosophers, considering their deeds, their knowledge, their researches after truth, their exertions and their close connection with all things spiritual; one might also expect that wonders, miracles, and extraordinary things would be reported of them. Yet we find that true visions are granted to persons who do not devote themselves to study or the purification of their souls. This proves that between the Divine power and the soul there are secret relations which are not identical with those thou mentionedest, O Philosopher!

After this the Khazari said to himself: I will ask the Christians and the Moslems, since one of these ways of acting is, no doubt, the God-pleasing one. But as regards the Jews, I am satisfied that they are of low station, few in number, and generally hated. He then invited a Christian scholar and questioned him about his doctrine and his practice.

THE CHRISTIAN SCHOLAR: I believe that all things are created, whilst the Creator is eternal; that He created the whole world in six days; that all mankind sprang from Adam, and after him from Noah; that God takes care of the created beings, and keeps in touch with man; that He is wrathful, takes delight, and is merciful; that He speaks, appears and reveals Himself to His prophets and favoured ones; that He dwells among those who please Him. In short: I believe in all that is written in the Torah and the other books of the Israelites, which are undisputed, because they are generally accepted as everlasting and have been revealed before a vast multitude. Subsequently the Divin-

ity became embodied in the womb of a noble Israelite virgin; she bore Him having the semblance of a human being,
which concealed nevertheless a divinity, seemingly a
prophet, but in reality a God sent forth. He is the Messiah,
whom we call the Son of God, and He is the Father and
the Son and the Holy Ghost. We believe in His unity, although the Trinity appears on our tongues. We believe in
Him and in His abode among the Israelites; this was
granted to them as a distinction, because the Divine influence never ceased to be attached to them—until their
masses rebelled against this Messiah, and they crucified
Him. Then Divine wrath burdened them everlastingly,
whilst the favour was confined to a few who followed the
Messiah, and to those nations which followed these few.
We belong to their number. Although we are not of Israelitish descent, we are well deserving of being called Israelites, because we follow the Messiah and his twelve Israelite
companions, who took the place of the tribes. Our laws and
regulations are derived from the apostle Simon (Petrus)
and from ordinations taken from the Torah, which we
study, for its truth and Divine origin are indisputable. It
is also stated in the Gospel by the Messiah: I came not to
destroy one of the laws of Moses, but I came to confirm
and corroborate them.

5. THE KHAZARI: Here is no logical conclusion; nay,
logical thought rejects most of what thou sayest. It is only
when both appearance and experience are so palpable that
they grip the whole heart, which sees no way of contest-
ing, that it will agree to the difficult, and the remote will
become near. This is how naturalists deal with strange
powers which come upon them unawares; they would not

believe if they only heard of them without seeing them; but when they see them, they discuss them, and ascribe them to the influence of stars or spirits, because they cannot disprove ocular evidence. As for me, I cannot accept these things, because they come upon me suddenly, seeing that I have not grown up in them. My duty is, therefore, to investigate further.

He then invited one of the scholars of Islam and questioned him about his doctrine and his practice.

THE MOSLEM SCHOLAR: We acknowledge the Unity and Eternity of God and that all men are derived from Adam and Noah. We absolutely reject embodiment (of God), and if any element of this appears in the Writ, we explain it as metaphoric, serving to make the doctrine acceptable to our comprehension. At the same time we maintain that our Book is the Speech of God, being itself a miracle which we are bound to accept for its own sake, since no one is able to produce anything comparable to it, or to one of its verses. Our prophet is the Seal of the prophets, who abrogated every previous law, and invited all nations to embrace Islam. The reward of the pious consists in the return of his spirit to his body in Paradise and bliss, where he never ceases to enjoy eating, drinking, women's love, and anything he may desire. The requital of the disobedience consists in being condemned to fire, and his punishment knows no end.

6. THE KHAZARI: If anyone is to be guided in matters divine, and to be convinced that God speaks to man, whilst he considers it improbable, he must be convinced by facts which are generally known and which allow of no refutation. And if your book is a miracle—a non-Arab, as I am,

cannot perceive its miraculous character, because it is written in Arabic.

7. THE MOSLEM SCHOLAR: Yet miracles are performed by the Prophet, but they are not used as evidence for the acceptance of his Law.

8. THE KHAZARI: Yes, the human mind does not incline to believe that God has intercourse with man, except by a miracle which changes the nature of things, so that man may recognize that God alone is able to do so, who created him from nought. Such a miracle must also have taken place in the presence of great multitudes, who saw it distinctly. Then it is possible for the mind to grasp this extraordinary matter, viz., that the Creator of this world and the next, of the heavens and lights, should hold intercouse with this contemptible subject, I mean man, speaking to him, and fulfilling his wishes and desires.

9. THE MOSLEM SCHOLAR: Is not our Book full of stories of Moses and the Israelites? No one denies what He did to Pharaoh, how He divided the sea, saved those who enjoyed His favour, but drowned those who aroused His wrath, that He granted them manna and the quails during forty years, that He spoke to Moses on the mount (Sinai), that He made the sun stand still for Joshua, and assisted him against the giants; nor do they deny what happened previously, viz., the Flood and the destruction of the fellow-citizens of Lot. Is this not so well known that no suspicion of deceit and imagination is possible?

10. THE KHAZARI: Indeed I see myself compelled to ask the Jews, because they are the descendants of the Israelites. For I see that they constitute in themselves the evidence for a divine law on earth.

He then invited a Rabbi and asked him about his belief.

The Basis of Jewish Faith

11. THE RABBI: I believe in the God of Abraham, Isaac
and Israel, who led the Israelites out of Egypt with signs
and miracles; who fed them in the desert and gave them the
(Holy) Land, after having made them traverse the sea
and the Jordan in a miraculous way; who sent Moses with
His Law, and subsequently thousands of prophets, who confirmed His law by promises to those who observed, and
threats to the disobedient. We believe in what is contained
in the Torah—a very large domain.

12. THE KHAZARI: I had intended from the very beginning not to ask any Jew, because I am aware of the destruction of their books and of their narrow-minded views, their
misfortunes having deprived them of all commendable
qualities. Shouldst thou, O Jew, not have said that thou be-
lievest in the Creator of the world, its Governor and Guide,
who created and keeps thee, and such attributes which
serve as evidence for every believer, and for the sake of
which he pursues justice in order to resemble the Creator
in His wisdom and justice?

13. THE RABBI: That which thou dost express is speculative and political religion, to which inquiry leads; but this
is open to many doubts. Now ask the philosophers, and
thou wilt find that they do not agree on one action or on one
principle, since they rely on theories; some of these can be
established by arguments, some of them are only plausible,
some even less capable of being proved.

14. THE KHAZARI: That which thou sayest now, O Jew,
seems to me better than the beginning, and I should like to
hear more.

15. THE RABBI: But the beginning of my speech was

the very proof, yea, the evidence, which makes every argument superfluous.

16. THE KHAZARI: How so?

17. THE RABBI: Allow me to make a few preliminary remarks; for I see thee disregarding and depreciating my words.

18. THE KHAZARI: Let me hear thy remarks.

19. THE RABBI: If thou wert told that the King of India was an excellent man, commanding admiration and deserving reputation, only because his actions were reflected in the justice which rules his country and the virtuous ways of his subjects, would this compel you to revere him?

20. THE KHAZARI: How could this compel me, whilst I am not sure if the justice of the Indian people is natural and not dependent on their king, or due to the king, or both?

21. THE RABBI: But if his messenger came to thee bringing presents which thou knowest to be only procurable in India, and in the royal palace, accompanied by a letter in which it is distinctly stated from whom it comes, and to which are added drugs to cure thy diseases, to preserve thy health, poisons for thine enemies, and other means to fight and kill them without battle, would this make thee beholden to him?

22. THE KHAZARI: Certainly. For this would remove my former doubt that the Indians have a king. I should also acknowledge that his dominion and his word had touched me.

23. THE RABBI: How wouldst thou then, if asked, describe him?

24. THE KHAZARI: In such terms as were quite clear to

me; and I would add such as were at first rather doubtful, but which were later affirmed by the former.

25. THE RABBI: In this way I answered thy question. In the same strain Moses spoke to Pharaoh, when he told him 'The God of the Hebrews sent me to thee'—viz. the God of Abraham, Isaac and Jacob. For the story of their life was well known to the nations, who also knew that the Divine power was in contact with the Patriarchs, caring for them and performing miracles for them. He did not say: 'The God of heaven and earth' nor 'my Creator and thine sent me'. In the same way God commenced His speech to the assembled people of Israel: 'I am the God whom you worship, who hath led you out of the land of Egypt'; He did not say 'I am the Creator of the world and your Creator'. In the same style I spoke to thee, O Prince of the Khazars, when thou didst ask me about my creed. I made mention to thee of what is convincing for me and for the whole of Israel, who knew these things, first through personal experience, and afterward through an uninterrupted tradition, which is equal to experience.

26. THE KHAZARI: Then your belief is confined to yourselves?

27. THE RABBI: Yes. Any Gentile who joins us sincerely shares our good fortune, but he is not equal to us. If the Torah were binding on us because God created us, the white and the black man would be equal since He created them all. But the Torah (is binding) because He led us out of Egypt and remained attached to us. For we are the pick of mankind.

28. THE KHAZARI: I see thee quite altered, O Jew, and thy words are poor after having been so rich.

29. THE RABBI: The poorest ones will become the rich-

est, if thou givest me thy attention, until I have expressed myself more fully.

30. THE KHAZARI: Say what thou wilt.

31. THE RABBI: The (realm of) the organic power comprises nurture, growth, and propagation with their powers and all conditions attached thereto. To this belong plants and animals, to the exclusion of earth, stones, metals, and elements.

32. THE KHAZARI: This is a maxim which requires ex planation, but it is true.

33. THE RABBI: Likewise, the realm of the soul's power, expressed in movement, willed action, external and internal senses and such like, is limited to all animated beings.

34. THE KHAZARI: This, too, cannot be contradicted.

35. THE RABBI: Likewise, the intellectual power distin guishes man above all living beings, it leads to the en nobling of his character, to the administration of his home and his country, to government and legislation.

36. THE KHAZARI: This is also true.

37. THE RABBI: And which would be the degree higher than this?

38. THE KHAZARI: The degree of great scholars.

39. THE RABBI: I only mean a degree which distinguishes those who occupy it essentially, as the plant is distinguished from inorganic things, a man from animals. The differences in quantity, however, are innumerable, but are purely accidental, and do not constitute a degree in the true sense.

40. THE KHAZARI: If this be so, then there is no degree above man among tangible things.

41. THE RABBI: And if we find a man who walks into the fire without hurt, or abstains from food for some time

without starving, on whose face a light shines which the
eye cannot bear, who is never ill, nor ages—and when he
reaches his life's end, dies spontaneously just as a man re-
tires to his couch to sleep on an appointed day and hour,
equipped with the knowledge of what is hidden as to past
and future; is such a degree not essentially distinguished
from the human degree?

42. THE KHAZARI: This degree would be divine and
seraphic, if it existed. It would belong to the province of
Divine power, not to that of the intellectual, spiritual (soul-
ful) or natural one.

43. THE RABBI: These are some of the characteristics
of the undoubted prophet. Through him God made manifest to the people that He is in connection with them, that
there is a Lord who guides them as He wishes, according
to their obedience or disobedience. He revealed that which
was hidden and taught how the world was created, how
the generations prior to the Flood followed each other and
how man descended from Adam. He described the Flood
and the origin of the Seventy nations from Shem, Ham and
Japhet, the sons of Noah; how the languages were split up,
and where men sought their habitations; how arts arose and
how cities were built—and the chronology from Adam up
to this day.

Maimonides

Moses Maimonides was born in Cordova, Spain, on Passover eve of the year 1135. His father was a noted Hebrew scholar who traced his ancestry to the House of David, but his prominent Jewish background gave him no security in Spain during a period of severe persecution and when the Jews in Cordova were offered a choice of accepting Islam or going into exile, Maimonides' father chose exile. For a decade the family of Maimonides wandered from land to land. It was during the time of homelessness that Maimonides, popularly known as Rambam, began to compose his first great work, the commentary on the Mishnah, which he completed when he was 33. It was in this commentary that he developed his famous 13 articles of faith which have been incorporated in Orthodox prayerbooks.

After his wanderings, Maimonides settled down near Cairo, Egypt, devoted himself to the practice of medicine, and became court physician to Sala-

159

din. A prodigious worker, Maimonides managed to retain his high medical post while serving as rabbi to a worshipful and large Jewish community. At the same time he continued his important writing and produced his Rabbinic code, the Mishneh Torah (Repetition of the Law) *and his* Guide for the Perplexed.

When he died in 1204, Maimonides was mourned by Mohammedans as well as Jews, and in Jerusalem a general fast was observed. He was buried in Tiberias. In our own time his grave still attracts many visitors.

GUIDE FOR THE PERPLEXED

Jacob S. Minkin

Great books, like human beings, have souls, and long after they have seemingly passed out of existence, they continue to live. But perhaps the most curious revival —curious because the intellectual climate in which it was written has so vastly changed with the passing centuries— is that of the *Guide for the Perplexed* (*Moreh Nebukim*), by Moses Maimonides (Rabbi Moshe ben Maimon, known as *Rambam*). While the works of many other Jewish philosophers have been forgotten, this book, written nearly eight hundred years ago, is not only remembered but is gaining steadily in vogue and influence.

In a survey among scholars to ascertain the influential Jewish books of all time, the *Guide for the Perplexed* headed the list. To Jewish scholars, Maimonides has been an intriguing figure and the *Guide for the Perplexed* their favorite book of study. This work changed men's lives; it started them on new paths of thinking. It has been one of the world's most fiercely discussed, debated and attacked books. Translated into many languages, it is studied assiduously by Jewish, Christian and Moslem scholars alike. It served as the first liberal education to many a Talmud-weary *yeshiva bahur* of past ages.

The *Guide* influenced the thinking of Baruch Spinoza. Solomon Maimon became so enamored of it that he not only wrote a commentary to it but adopted the author's name. The book acted as an intellectual ferment in the career of Moses Mendelssohn who brooded over its pages so long that it ruined his health. Yet he bore the writer no ill-will, for the hunchback-philosopher wrote: "I dote on him (Maimonides), for if he was unwittingly the cause of my physical deformity, has he not compensated my soul with sublime knowledge?"

The *Guide* has both stimulated and divided the Jews of the world. It was their greatest intellectual achievement and their source of sorest contention. It was as enthusiastically received as it was fanatically opposed. Not since the Karaite doctrine in the eighth century, were the Jews of the world so divided as they were by the publication of this book. Men of learning and piety were arrayed against each other in approval or denunciation of it. The charge of heresy was raised; the air of the time was full of anathemas and counter-anathemas. The storm did not abate until the Church was called in to settle the dispute. The charge of heresy was sweet incense in the nostrils of some Christian ecclesiastics. They knew the smell of burning Jewish flesh. Why not also burn a few Jewish parchments? The affair ended as might have been expected—with "triumph" for the anti-Maimonists. But it was a pyrrhic victory which set all Israel to mourning. For the torch that was applied to the scrolls of Maimonides' writings did not stop there. Years later the Talmud itself was put to the torch.

Fortunately for Maimonides, he did not live to see the

havoc his book created; he died before the storm. But his soul must have rejoiced when many of his most violent opponents lived to regret the consequences of the fanaticism they had set in motion.

Set against the spirit of the time in which it was written, when the crudest religious superstitions were universal, this epoch-making book, preaching a faith regulated by reason, marked a milestone in human advancement. Students of Maimonides are aware of his profound influence on modern thought. Bible critics still deal with problems that disturbed Maimonides nearly eight hundred years ago. His book was translated into Latin so early that it served as a leaven to some of the best Christian minds in Europe.

A full ten years went into the making of this volume. Regarded in the light of the author's stupendous activities it is amazing to realize what energy and devotion a fragile human being is capable of expending without breaking under the strain. While life went on with its tantalizing demands on his attention, Maimonides—physician at Saladin's court, leader and teacher of his people, host of an always crowded house—found ample leisure in which to think and muse in his own world. It was a world of prophets, sages, scholars, scientists and philosophers, a world fused in a grand synthesis of which only he was capable. And when he emerged with the parchments of the *Guide for the Perplexed*, this world beheld an edifice as if hewn of granite rock.

In the centuries that have passed, some chips of that granite have fallen. Like other human creations, the book has suffered in the process of time. Though in its conception and design, the *Guide for the Perplexed* stands unmatched in history, it is questionable whether the book can still serve as guide for our own time. As Cecil Roth said: "Every age has its own vocabulary, and the vocabulary of our thinking must be our own. . . . Maimonides' words are not ours nor is his science the science of our generation. The Scriptures still 'talk the language of men,' but the language of men has changed."

The *Guide* is not a book easily or quickly summarized. It is not a book that flashes and fascinates. To win to full appreciation, one must give himself to careful study. Maimonides himself admits that he wrote his book for one man in ten thousand, and even for this one man he took the extra precaution of obscuring certain portions in order to withhold "from the multitude (*hamon*) the truths required for the knowledge of God," excusing the great care he took on the ground that "ancient philosophers and scholars of other nations were likewise wont to treat *principia rerum* obscurely and to use figurative language in discussing such subjects."

What largely gives the book its timelessness despite the mutations of centuries, is its implied call to freedom, to the emancipation of the mind from the crude beliefs and superstitions that fettered it. Maimonides was the first to attempt a philosophy of religion, the first to proclaim the sovereignty of reason, the first to explore the Bible with an open mind, the first to rationalize beliefs and practices which for a thousand years were obeyed blindly, the first to try to span a bridge between religion and reason, between Moses and Aristotle, between the Bible conception of God and the universe and that of the Greek and Arabic thinkers. It may be maintained that Saadya Gaon and other philosophers had attempted identical things. But whereas they were weak and timorous and spoke with little conviction in their hearts, Maimonides was unafraid.

Maimonides was a rationalist at a time when reason was feared. It was safer for men to believe than to think, to follow blindly than to inquire. He followed reason unreservedly when in the opinion of his opponents its paths were devious and threatened to beguile one from the well-trodden path of faith. He knew better than his contemporaries that the Torah was truth, and that truth need not fear the test of reason. Seeking God in all things, he nowhere found Him as truly as in the realm of reason. "Never should man," Maimonides wrote in his epistle to the Jews of Marseilles, "throw his reason behind him, for his eyes are not in the back, but in the front."

It was a rash adventure, this pursuit of truth and reason when both State and Church conspired against them and visited upon their wooers the dungeon and the faggots. Maimonides was fortunate that his lot was cast in a land where men were comparatively free. For the medieval mind, theological rather than scientific, static rather than progressive, was an incurably childlike mind. It loved the fabulous and fantastic rather than the real and tangible. It was a neatly arranged universe in which medieval man lived, perhaps less sane, certainly more picturesque than the world today.

At a time when the Church forbade Christians to read their Bible and priests and knights could scarcely scratch their names, even the humblest of Jews could read his prayers and had at least a rudimentary knowledge of the Torah. There was no illiteracy in the Synagogue. It furthered education and promoted scholarship. Its primary schools compared favorably with the best of the Middle

Ages, and when it came to higher education, what priest or bishop could talk as fluently about theology as the poorest *yeshiva bahur* studying his Talmud? The Synagogue was far in advance of the Church in almost everything. Its morality was higher, its freedom greater; it had a touching regard for the dignity and sanctity of the human personality.

Nevertheless, like the Church, the Synagogue was too suspicious of reason to trust it implicitly. Not only the masses of Jews, but also their teachers and leaders believed without knowledge, obeyed without reason, and carried out the precepts of the Torah without understanding. Was it not Yehudah Halevi, poet and religious philosopher though he was, who said, "He who accepts the Torah without scrutiny and arguments is better off than he who investigates and analyzes"? There was as little free discussion of religion in the Synagogue as in the Church. Problems like God, creation, the universe, the soul, immortality, resurrection, reward and punishment, were either not pondered at all, or when they were discussed it was with the naivete of children.

The fundamental concept of the medieval man, Jew or Christian, was based on the visual and the tangible. He created his God in his own image. Not only the unphilosophical masses but their teachers and scholars, who otherwise possessed keen minds, believed in the reality of miracles, clothed God in human form and had Him perform human functions. Perhaps the classic example of the Jewish negative attitude to reason is the one afforded by Abraham ben David of Posquieres who, though a great scholar, viciously attacked his near-contemporary, Maimonides, because he characterized any one as an idolater who regarded the Divine Being as having human form.

Maimonides was a rationalist who had not deviated from the teachings of the Jewish religion. He was a rationalist not because of any foreign influence, but because Judaism as a religion and the Jews as a people are fundamentally rational. Had not the Most High declared through Moses: "Surely that great nation is a wise and understanding people?" Maimonides welcomed discussion of religion, but always within the framework of Judaism. He rejected some of the rabbinic absurdities and superstitions, but held fast to the eternal validity of the Mosaic Law as explained and interpreted by the rabbis. He spoke of the Torah as his bride, "the wife of my youth, and I succumbed to her early in my life." He honored the disciplinary significance of those regulations which cannot be fathomed by the ordinary rules of reason and logic. Indeed, he chided the vainglorious attempts of those who undertook to explain everything rationally. He wrote distinctly, "Know ye that there is a stage in knowledge superior to the philosophic, namely, the prophetic."

He held the scales of reason and religion equally balanced. It was his aim to build a harmonious system in which each should play an equal part. He was not a compromiser, a metaphysical engineer who dreamed of a bridge between Athens and Jerusalem regardless of the cost to Judaism. He was not a compromiser, because in his depth of faith he believed that the goals of reason and religion are identical. But neither was he a fundamentalist who advocated blind fulfillment of the precepts of the Torah without reason or understanding. His motto was, "Israel must obey with knowledge." His ambition was to expound the truths of Judaism as he saw them in a generation in which these truths were seriously menaced. He lived in a world of unbelief and confusion when, as a result of a shallow intellectualism on one hand and a cynical disregard of religion on the other, men not only doubted and questioned but challenged the worthwhileness of Judaism. In such a time, it was well for the teacher to adopt the tools and method of the philosopher to convince a skeptical world that Judaism was indeed a religion worth living and sacrificing for.

As philosophy of Judaism, the *Guide for the Perplexed* will be best understood against the background of the author's previous works, notably the *Mishnah Commentary* and his stupendous *Mishneh Torah,* often referred to as the "Code." The philosophical genius of Maimonides is almost as fully revealed in these works as in the *Guide,* the product of his riper years. The *Commentary,* written in Arabic and completed shortly after Maimonides had settled in Egypt, is saturated with the philosophical and theological principles of Judaism as conceived and taught by its author. To this work we owe not only the philosopher's popular presentation of the ethics of Judaism under the title, *Eight Chapters,* but also his much-contested but universally adopted *Thirteen Articles of Faith* with which to this day pious Jews conclude their morning devotions.

Likewise, the *Mishneh Torah,* written in Mishnaic Hebrew and intended for non-professional students of the Talmud, is more than merely a prodigious compendium of the vast rabbinic jurisprudence. It is a brilliant survey of the theology, metaphysics and ethics of Judaism in their relation to the faith and practices of the Jewish people. It is a landmark in Jewish history and literature, a daring attempt to rationalize religion and make the speculative ideas about God, the world, and human destiny as much an integral part of Judaism as the detailed regulations of its ceremonies and rituals. In many respects, the first part of the work, *Sefer ha-Maddah* (The Book of Cognition), belongs more properly to the domain of philosophy than to practical religious guidance, dealing as it does with such metaphysical problems as the unity of God, incorporeality, etc.

The character and spirit of the author of the *Guide for the Perplexed* is reflected perhaps more clearly in his minor writings than in the books which made his name a household word. Moses Maimonides was only thirty-seven when, out of their distress, the Jews of Yemen, victimized by bigoted Moslem rulers and fraudulent messiahs, wrote to him for counsel in the grievous times that had befallen them. His reply, which became known as *Iggeret Teman* (Letter to Yemen), was so warm and tender, with a wonderful stream of fatherly compassion flowing in its every line that he was forever remembered by them in gratitude. He urged them to remain loyal to their religion and not to weaken under persecution which, he said, was "because of the divinity that lives in our midst." At the same time he warned them not to be misled by the sham messiahs, for the real Messiah will surely come in God's own time.

His famous *Letter on Apostasy* grew out of a similarly unhappy situation. The Jews of Morocco were caught in the toils of persecution. They were compelled to pay lip-service to the Mohammedan religion and attend the Mosque on Friday. And though they remained Jews in their hearts and in their homes secretly carried out the precepts of their religion, a rabbinical zealot living far from the scene of danger condemned them as apostates and traitors to their faith. Maimonides not only refuted the fanatical ecclesiastic but, quoting authorities and historical precedents, and perhaps remembering his own family's experience under similar circumstances, he absolved the Moroccan Jews from the feeling of guilt. He said that feigned transgression of the law cannot be regarded as willful departure from it. This heroic stand illustrated his liberal spirit.

Although Moses Maimonides was the most comprehensive Jewish thinker of his time, he cannot be said to have created a philosophical system. His great service to his people was the attempt to make Jewish religious beliefs more rational by harmonizing them with the rules of logic. To serve the religious needs of his time was his highest aim. As the name of his great philosophical work indicates, the *Guide for the Perplexed* was designed to deal with the religious difficulties of the orthodox Jews who fell under the influence of the current philosophical ideas. And since the Jews in the Islamic lands were more familiar with the Arabic language than with their own tongue, he wrote his book in Arabic with Hebrew characters, in the idiom they best understood.

Though not one of the traditionally written commentaries, the *Guide for the Perplexed* is as much a commentary on the Bible as it is a work of theology and philosophy. It is a commentary on the Bible in the sense that the author employs the allegorical method in explaining such Scriptural stories and incidents as cannot be taken literally, and interpreting words that have more than one meaning, Biblical idioms and expressions that seem offensive when applied to God. For the Bible is as vigorously anthropomorphic as Maimonides is vigorously rationalistic. The Bible is on terms of easy familiarity with God and cultivates a sense of personal relationship with Him. To Maimonides God is above human ken. Scripture pictures the Deity in human form, and attributes to Him the organs, faculties, and passions possessed by mortal beings. To Maimonides the belief in God as a body is worse than idolatry.

Had Maimonides limited himself to this task alone—the interpretation of the words and expressions in the Bible that are inconsistent with the spiritual essence of God—the *Guide* would not have attracted the attention it did; nor would it have raised the storm that divided Jewry into opposing camps. For the writers of Talmud, the Midrashim, and the Greek and Aramaic translations of the Bible, including Philo, the Alexandrian philosopher who lived nearly a thousand years before the author of the *Guide,* were likewise uneasy about the visual representation of the Deity, and they invented free translations of such terms to circumvent the difficulties they encountered. They considered all such indiscreet designations of the Deity as metaphors and figures of speech intended to give man some understanding of His spiritual essence. *Dibrah Torah b'lashon bnai adam,* say the Rabbis, "The Torah speaks in the language of man."

But Maimonides did more than engage in the old and venerable struggle with the anthropomorphisms of the Bible. He advocated an enlightened Judaism, probed for the philosophic spirit of the Jewish religion, to vindicate its truth and show how little it differed from the prevailing philosophical tenor of the time. In all this, students of Maimonides discovered the influence of Aristotle. And, indeed, it would be surprising if it were lacking, for the Greek philosopher dominated the thought of the medieval world. Arab and Jewish thinkers alike fell under his influence. Although the native Jewish genius was essentially religious, the Hellenic thinker had his Jewish votaries. They invented the legend that he was a Jew born in Palestine and a disciple of Simon the Just. Even the Jewish thinkers who repudiated Aristotle's philosophy respected his genius. Maimonides was among his greatest devotees. "Aristotle," he says, "supplanted all his predecessors. A thorough understanding of him is the highest achievement to which a man can attain, with the sole exception of the Prophets."

Although Maimonides admired Aristotle and assimilated his ideas, he did not accept him unconditionally. Indeed, their disagreements were at least as many as their agreements. Maimonides had too independent a mind to follow any man, however great and universal his reputation. He not only repudiated Aristotle himself when he found his thought in conflict with the Bible, but also castigated those fanatics "who consider it wrong to differ with Aristotle or think that he was ignorant or could be mistaken in anything." Maimonides did not believe that philosophy in the strict sense began with the Greeks. He held that there were philosophical ideas in the Bible which, though not written in the language of philosophy, were of profound importance. He points to the first chapters in the Book of Genesis and the vision of Ezekiel, which he interprets as the philosophy of physics and metaphysics, to the books of Ecclesiastes, Job, and others.

Solomon Goldman may overemphasize Maimonides' independence of the Greek and Arabic influence, but there is a profound lesson in his interesting observation in *The Jew and the Universe* that, while there are in the *Guide* 1900 references to Biblical and rabbinic literature, not counting the numerous quotations from the author's own

Talmudic writings, there are no more than 70 references to
all the Greek and Arabic writings.

As a philosopher, Moses Maimonides belongs definitely
to the Jewish tradition rather than the Hellenic. God was
so firmly rooted in his mind that he needed no proof of His
existence. God, he declares, not only exists—an existence
unlike any other—but He is incorporeal. When, therefore,
we read in the Bible such qualities as wisdom, goodness,
mercy, power, and will attributed to the Holy One, they
are not to be taken literally, but as pictorial images by
which man might catch a glimpse of the essence of his
Maker. For God is not man, and none of the human attributes are authentic descriptions of Him. The only knowledge we may have of God is through his acts which are
moral, and are for man to imitate.

Maimonides clashes with Aristotle on the problem of
creation. Unlike the Greek philosopher who sponsored the
doctrine of the eternity of the world, the Jewish sage clings
to the Biblical *creatio ex nihilo,* perhaps not so much for
religious reasons as for lack of sufficient proof of the contrary. The Talmudic casuist says explicitly that if the doctrine of eternity had been convincingly demonstrated, he
would have found a way to get around the Biblical text.
Maimonides is more traditionalist than philosopher when,
like Yehudah Halevi, he furnishes no better argument for
revelation and the eternal validity of the Mosaic legislation
than the fact that all Israel at Sinai heard the Divine Voice.
The truth of revelation, he says, does not depend upon
miracles; it is a matter of history. Miracles in general are a
sore point with our philosopher, who dismisses them as
visionary and fantastic, except where they are positively
proven.

Maimonides is original in his theory of Providence, which he considers to be not universal but graded, i.e., extended to all living things but in degree of their mental and spiritual attainment. Thus, while Providence orders the preservation of animals only in their species, or *genus,* men enjoy its benefits in their individual capacity. But even in the case of man, the degree of Providence depends upon the intellectual and moral development. Maimonides meets the problem of evil and the baffling enigma of the wretchedness of the good and the prosperity of the wicked, by declaring that evil is not a positive but a negative quality, in the same measure as darkness is not a positive being, but is the abyss of the lack of light and struggle for light.

Man's ethical perfection, his character and conduct, depend upon his freedom of action, and he is therefore responsible for his own deeds and misdeeds. For if man's moral and spiritual personality were foreordained, he could not help acting as God long ago foreknew he would act, and reward and punishment, whether administered by God or man, would be wrong and unjust.

It is quite natural that the man for whom the intellectual contemplation of God was the highest goal of life, should regard the eternity of the soul not as an absolute but as a potential condition. In Maimonides' view it was pithily put, "Man must become superman to inherit eternity." It is only by man's intellectual and moral discipline that his soul is made worthy of uniting with the all-governing world-soul thus to attain immortality. It is characteristic of Maimonides, aristocrat-philosopher that he was, that he should have anticipated Nietzsche by nearly a thousand years in making the world exist solely for the few chosen spirits who acquired what he calls "true ideas," with all others to serve them.

The most novel and interesting of Maimonides' psycho-philosophical theories was that prophecy depended upon the cultivation of one's rational and imaginative faculties. Neither exclusively a free gift from on high nor attainable without divine influence, prophecy is the result of the sum total of one's intellectual, moral, and spiritual faculties, charged by an active imagination. The prophet is superior to the philosopher. He is the master, leader, and lawgiver of the world, for in him all the conditions of the most perfect life—intelligence, fantasy, and ethical conduct—are merged. Maimonides enumerates eleven degrees of prophecy with Moses on the highest level.

Maimonides signifies his acceptance of change and development in Judaism by rejecting the inherent value of sacrifices. He explains them as a concession on the part of God to the primitive level of Jewish civilization. He accounts for the unexplained precepts of the Pentateuch described as *hukim,* remnants of heathen Sabean practices, and he takes a rational view of some other precepts of the Torah. For instance, he interprets the dietary laws as having been promulgated for reasons of health; and the pilgrim festivals were designed, he maintains, to promote fellowship among the Israelites. Scholars doubt that Maimonides accepted individual immortality and bodily resurrection without inner protest.

It was a bold, awakening note that Moses Maimonides struck in the *Guide for the Perplexed,* an undertaking for which his time was little prepared. He raised Judaism to its highest level by demanding that reason and logic be applied to the study of the Bible and of religion generally.

He concludes his great work on its highest note by out-lining four steps man may take to attain perfection. They are: the acquisition of external things that contribute to his personal comfort and satisfaction, such as money, property, etc., the attainment of the animal wants of his body which, as a living being, he needs for his self-preservation, such as health, etc.; the cultivation of his faculties as a moral, so-cial being in relation to his fellowmen. The highest degree of perfection, however, for which Maimonides would have man strive, so that he may know God, is the development of his intellectual and spiritual qualities, for they alone give him immortality, and on account of them he is called man. "Having acquired this knowledge," says Maimonides, "he will then be determined always to seek lovingkindness, judgment, and righteousness, and to imitate the ways of God."

Moses Maimonides was fifty-two years old when, in 1190, he climaxed his literary career with the publication of the *Guide for the Perplexed.* He still had fourteen years more to live before he died in December, 1204. This time he de-voted to the Fostat Jewish community where he lived, to his medical practice, and the writing of his medical books, some of which were in considerable vogue when they ap-peared in Latin translation. The *Guide* was dedicated to Joseph Ibn Aknin, Maimonides' favorite pupil who had emigrated from Morocco on account of religious per-secution.

The book appeared in many translations and was studied widely by Christian and Mohammedan theologians. It was Maimonides' good fortune to have lived to see his work translated twice into Hebrew by Samuel Ibn Tibbon and Judah Alharizi. Urged to translate his book himself, Mai-

monides declined because of lack of time. When Moses
Maimonides died, all Israel went into mourning. His remains were taken for burial to Tiberias, where his tomb
became a place of pilgrimage. The universal regard in
which he was held by his contemporaries and by succeeding
generations, has been expressed in the popular saying,
"From Moses to Moses there was none like unto Moses."

After almost a thousand years, Moses Maimonides
emerges as a titanic figure of the age in which he lived, and
with his death a period in Jewish history may be said to
have closed. He was the last and greatest of the Jewish
Golden Age, and he lived and wrought in the evening glow
of its fame and glory. His reputation is great, and his influence deep and lasting. Not only Jews but mankind in general have felt the effects of his genius. His place among
the chosen spirits has not been seriously disputed. He was
not an aloof philosopher, indifferent to the needs and interests of his generation, but a kind, warm-hearted man
who wanted men to be free, and being free, happy. When
he saw religion neglected and the Torah in danger of becoming forgotten, he did the brave thing, creating a philosophy by which reason and religion might live together
in harmony.

But did he succeed? He breathed new life into the old
faith by introducing the scientific spirit into Judaism; he
served as protest against the puerilities and superstitions
that corroded religion by making Jews think more rationally about their religious tradition. He wrote the *Guide*
which quickly became a classic, and many of the finest
spirits, both Jewish and non-Jewish, walked in its light.
The extent of his success may be measured by the fact that

nearly half a century ago, Moritz Steinschneider listed over sixty commentaries on the book.

But he may also be said to have failed, although the failure was due not so much to the method of the *Guide* as to the time in which it was conceived. As far as the Jews were concerned, the challenge of the time was not one of reason but of faith. When in the Christian countries of Europe the Jews were being massacred by the thousands, and paralyzing terror seized upon their brethren in Moslem lands, what comfort or consolation could they derive from the rationalistic demonstrations of their faith? Of what help was "scientific insight" to men living on the brink of destruction? When, therefore, the *Guide* was bitterly opposed, it was not because of its liberal attitude but because they who suffered and waited found it to be a futile answer to their cry.

Yet the *Guide for the Perplexed* is one of the great challenging works in Jewish literature. If it did not contribute to the preservation of Judaism, it certainly helped to make it more reasonable and enlightened. It raised the Jewish religion to a level that commanded the respect of all thinking, unprejudiced minds. Through its Hebrew translation it became accessible to large sections of the Jewish world community. Many a Jew, strong in his faith yet inwardly conscious of the conflict between faith and reason, blessed the time in which the book was written. To them the *Moreh Nebukim,* is indeed a *Guide for the Perplexed,* a stimulating experience, a beacon.

selections from MAIMONIDES

THE EXISTENCE OF GOD, HIS UNITY AND IN-
CORPOREALITY. *Maimonides' discussion of this subject
covers a wide range of proofs and arguments of a metaphysical nature, contained principally in* Yad ha-Hazakah *or*
Mishneh Torah, *chap. I, Introduction to his Commentary on
the* Mishnah, Helek *(i.e., Sanhedrin, chap. IX), and Part II
of the* Guide.

"The foundation of foundations and the pillar of the sciences is to know that there is a First Being and that He
caused the existence of all things; and all things that exist
from heaven and earth and intervening space only exist
from the reality of His existence. If it could be supposed
that He is non-existent, nothing else could possibly exist
. . . For all things existing are dependent upon Him, but
He (Blessed be He) is not dependent upon them . . .
Therefore His reality is not like the reality of any one of
them . . . This Being is the God of the world, Lord of the
whole earth. He controls the Universe with a power to which

there is neither end nor limit, with a power unceasing."
(*Yad, Yesode ha-Torah I*)

"It is therefore certain that there must be a being which
has absolute independent existence, and is the source of the
existence of all things, whether transient or permanent."
(*Guide II, 152*)

"God is one; He is not two, but one. The oneness of any
of the single things existent in the Universe is unlike His
Unity. He is not one as a species since this includes numerous individuals; nor one as a body since this is divisible
into parts and sections, but a Unity which is unique in the
world. If there were several deities they would necessarily
be corporeal, because things that can be numbered . . .
are distinguishable one from another by accidents which
occur in bodily forms. If, then, the creator were corporeal,
He would have limitations, because it is impossible for a
body to be without a limit, and every one whose body has
a limit must likewise be limited in power." (*Yad, Yesode
ha-Torah*)

"For in the same way as all people must be informed,
and even children must be trained in the belief that God
is One, and that none besides him is to be worshiped, so
must all be taught . . . that God is incorporeal; that there
is no similarity in any way between Him and His creatures;
that His existence is not like the existence of His creatures,
His life not like that of any living being, His wisdom not
like the wisdom of the wisest of men. . . ." (*Guide I,
35*)

"If it be so that He is incorporeal, what of the Scriptural
phrases, 'Under His feet' (*Ex. XXIV, 10*), 'Written with the
finger of God' (*ibid. XXIV, 18*), 'the hand of the Lord'
(*Deut. XI, 22*), 'the eyes of the Lord' (*XI, 12*), 'the ears of

the Lord' (*Num. XI, 18*), and other expressions like these?
All these terms are used in accordance with the mental
capacity of human beings who can only comprehend corporeal beings. The Torah therefore speaks in human language, and all these are merely metaphorical expressions."
(*Yad, Yesode ha-Torah, I, 8 f.*)

THE ATTRIBUTES OF GOD. *Having disposed of the anthropomorphisms of the Bible, Maimonides takes up the question of God's attributes, and declares that the only true
attributes of God are the negative ones.* "Thus, those who
believe in the presence of essential attributes in God, viz.,
Existence, Life Power, Wisdom and Will, should know
that these attributes, when applied to God, have not the
same meaning as when applied to us, and that the difference does only consist in magnitude, or in the degree of
perfection, stability and durability . . . I mean to say that
all men must understand that our wisdom and His, or our
power and His, do not differ quantitatively or qualitatively,
or in a similar manner . . . Anything predicated to God is
totally different from our attributes." (*Guide I, 35*) "Know
that the negative attributes of God are the true attributes.
They do not include any incorrect notions or any deficiency
whatever in reference to God; while positive attributes im-
ply polytheism and are inadequate." (*Guide I, 58*)

THE ORIGIN OF THE WORLD. *Between Aristotle's Eternity
of the Universe and the Bible doctrine of Creation there
seems to be no agreement possible. Maimonides, admitting
the difficulty of the problem, treats it with extreme caution,
emerging, however, in the end as sponsor of the Scriptural
account of Creation.*

"It is well known to all clear and correct thinkers who do not wish to deceive themselves, that the question, viz., whether the Universe has been created or is eternal, cannot be answered with mathematical certainty; here human intellect must pause . . . The philosophers have for the last three thousand years been continually divided on that subject, as far as we can learn from their works and the record of their opinions." (*Guide I, 71*) "We do not reject the Eternity of the Universe because certain passages in Scripture confirm the Creation, for such passages are not more numerous than those on which God is represented as a corporeal being; nor is it impossible or difficult to find for them a suitable interpretation . . . But there is no necessity for this expedient, so long as the theory has not been proved. As there is no proof sufficient to convince us, this theory need not be taken into consideration; we take the text of the Bible literally, and say that it teaches us a truth which cannot be proved." (*Guide II, 25*)

DESIGN, MIRACLES, REVELATION, MAN. "Everything is, according to Aristotle, the result of a law of Nature, and not the reuslt of the design of a being that designs as it likes, or the determination of a being that determines as it pleases . . . We, however, hold that all things in the Universe are the result of design, and not merely of necessity; He who designs them may change them when He changes His design . . . the Universe gives evidence of design." (*Guide II, 19*) "Accepting the Creation we find that miracles are possible, that Revelation is possible, and that every difficulty in this question is removed (*ibid. II, 25*)." ". . . according to Aristotle, who assumes the eternity of the Universe, there is no occasion for the question what is the object of the existence of the Universe. But those who accept our theory that the whole Universe has been created from nothing . . . assume that the whole Universe was created for the sake of man that he might serve God. Everything that is done, they believe, is done for man's sake; even the spheres move only for his benefit, in order that his wants might be supplied." (*ibid. III, 13*)

DIVINE PROVIDENCE, FREE WILL, REWARD AND PUNISHMENT. *Aristotle asserted that humanity as a whole, and not the individual, is guided and protected by Divine Providence. The Mu'tzila, a Moslem religious sect, held that God takes notice of the falling leaf and the destruction of the ant. In contradistinction to them, Maimonides teaches:* "In the lower or sublunary portion of the Universe, Divine Providence does not extend to the individual members of species, except in the case of mankind. It is only in this species that the incidents in the existence of the individual beings, their good and evil fortunes, are the result of justice . . . Divine Providence is connected with divine intellectual influence, and the same beings which are benefited by the latter so as to become intellectual, and to comprehend things comprehensible to rational beings, are also under the control of Divine Providence . . . I have been induced to accept this theory by the circumstance that I have not met in any of the prophetical books with a description of God's Providence otherwise than in relation to human beings." (*Guide III, 17*) "There are in Scripture . . . many passages expressing the principle that men enjoy Divine protection in proportion to their perfection and piety." (*ibid. 18*)

"Man has free will . . . This is our theory, or that of our Law . . . The theory of man's perfectly free will is one of

the fundamental principles of the Law of our Teacher
Moses, and of those who follow the Law. According to this
principle, man does what is in his power to do, by his nature, his choice, and his will; and his action is not due to
any faculty created for the purpose. All species of irrational
animals likewise move by their own free will. This is the
will of God, that is to say, it is due to the eternal divine will
that all living beings should move freely, and that man
should have power to act according to his will within the
limits of his capacity." (*Guide III, 17*)

THE EVIL AND SUFFERING *in the world seem to be in direct
contradiction to Maimonides who proclaims God as the
ultimate cause of all that exists. He circumvents this, however, by stating that evil is not a positive but a negative
condition for which man, not God, is responsible.* "All evils
are negations . . . It cannot be said of God that He directly creates evil . . . this is impossible. His works are
perfectly good. He only produces existence, and all existence is good." (*Guide III, 10*) "Many frequently think that
the evils in the world are more numerous than the good
things . . . The origin of the error is to be found in the
circumstance that the ignorant man . . . judges the whole
universe by examining one single person. For an ignorant
man believes that the whole universe exists only for him
. . . If, therefore anything happens to him contrary to his
expectation, he at once concludes that the whole universe is
evil . . . The numerous evils to which individual persons
are exposed are due to the defects existing in the persons
themselves. We complain and seek relief from our faults;
we suffer from the evils which we, by our own free will, in-
flict on ourselves and ascribe them to God, Who is far from

being connected with them." (*ibid. III, 12*) "All the difficulties and troubles we meet . . . are due to the desire for
superfluous things; when we seek unnecessary things, we
have difficulty even in finding that which is indispensable.
For the more we desire to have that which is superfluous,
the more we meet with difficulties; our strength and possessions are spent in unnecessary things, and are wanting
when required for that which is necessary." (*ibid. III, 10*)

PROPHECY *in Maimonides' view is not an endowment
freely bestowed by God irrespective of the one's moral and
intellectual fitness, but a gift that must be cultivated. Wisdom, imagination, cheerfulness, courage, and perfect development of the physical, moral and rational faculties are
some of the requisites for prophecy.* "Prophecy is in truth
and reality, an emanation sent forth by the Divine Being
through the medium of the Active Intellect, in the first instance to man's rational faculty, and then to his imaginative
faculty; it is the highest degree and greatest perfection man
can attain . . . Prophecy is a faculty that cannot in any
way be found in a person, or acquired by a man, through a
culture of his mental and moral faculties . . . unless they
were combined with the highest natural excellence of the
imaginative faculty . . . a person must satisfy the following conditions before he can become a prophet . . . no
part of his body must suffer from ill-health; he must in addition have studied and acquired wisdom, so that his rational faculty passes from a state of potentiality to that of
actuality; his intellect must be developed and perfect as human intellect can be; his passions pure and equally balanced; all his desires must aim at obtaining a knowledge of
the hidden laws and causes that are in force in the Universe; his thoughts must be engaged in lofty matters; his

attention must be directed to the knowledge of God, the consideration of His works, and of that which he must believe in this respect. There must be an absence of the lower desires and appetites, of the seeking after pleasure in eating, drinking and cohabitation." (*Guide II, 36*)

"We must believe that he (Moses) was the father of all the Prophets before him, and those who came after him were all beneath him in rank. He was chosen by God from all the human kind. He comprehended more of God than any man in the past or future ever comprehended or will comprehend . . . he reached a state of exaltedness beyond the sphere of humanity, so that he attained to the angelic rank and became included in the order of angels. There was no veil which he did not pierce. No material hindrance stood in his way, and no defect whether small or great mingled itself with him." (Com. *Mishnah, Helek*)

INTELLECTUAL WORSHIP OF GOD. *Maimonides, who conceived God rationally, demanded that the worship of Him be intellectual instead of emotional.* "We must bear in mind that all such acts as reading the Torah, praying, and the performance of other precepts, serve exclusively as the means of causing us to occupy and fill our mind with the precepts of God and free it from worldly business . . . If we, however, pray with the motion of our lips and our face toward the wall, but at the same time think of our business; if we read the Torah with our tongue whilst our heart is occupied with the building of our house, and we do not think of what we are reading . . . we are then like those in reference to whom Scripture says, 'Thou art near in their mouth, but far from their reins' . . . When you are alone by yourself, when you are awake on your couch, be careful to meditate in such precious moments on nothing but the intellectual worship of God, viz., to approach Him and to minister before Him in the true manner which I have described to you—not in hollow emotion." (*Guide III, 51*) "What is the end of serving God? He does not become perfect if all His creatures serve Him and comprehend Him as far as possible . . . It might perhaps be that the service of God is not intended for God's perfection; it is intended for our perfection—it is good for us; it makes us perfect." (*Guide III, 13*)

THE TORAH: ITS PURPOSE AND USEFULNESS. *In Part III of the* Guide, *Maimonides discusses the purpose of the Divine precepts and their usefulness for the individual and human society.*

"All of us, the common people as well as the scholars, believe that there is a reason for every precept, although there are commandments the reason of which is unknown to us . . . But our Sages generally do not think that such precepts have no cause whatever and serve no purpose; for this would lead us to assume that God's actions are purposeless. On the contrary, they hold that even these ordinances have a cause, and are certainly intended for some use, although it is not known to us; owing either to the deficiency of our knowledge or the weakness of our intellect." (*Guide III, 26*)

"The general object of the Law is twofold: the well-being of the soul, and the well-being of the body. The well-being of the soul is promoted by correct opinions . . . The well-being of the body is established by a proper management of the relations in which we live one to another . . . The reason of a commandment, whether positive or negative, is clear, and its usefulness evident, if it directly tends to remove injustice, or to teach good conduct that furthers the well-being of society, or to impart a truth which ought to be believed either on its own merit or as being indispensable for facilitating the removal of injustice or the teaching of good morals." (*ibid. 28*) "For all moral principles concern the relation of man to his neighbor; the perfection of man's moral principles is, as it were given to man for the benefit of mankind. Imagine a person being alone, and having no connection whatever with any other person, all his good moral principles are at rest, they are not required, and give man no perfection whatever. These principles are only necessary when man comes in contact with others." (*ibid. 54*) "Every narrative in the Law serves a certain purpose in connection with religious teaching. It helps to establish a principle of faith, or to regulate our actions, and to prevent wrong and injustice." (*ibid. 50*)

SACRIFICES NOT ESSENTIAL. *Maimonides dared the criticism of his contemporaries when he declared that sacrifices were not expressly commanded by God, but were a concession to wean away the primitive Israelites from idolatrous worship.*

"The Law intended to give its followers purity and holiness by teaching them to suppress sensuality, to guard against it and to reduce it to a minimum" (*Guide III, 33*). ". . . the Prophets in their books are frequently found to rebuke their fellow-men for being overzealous and exerting themselves too much in bringing sacrifices; the Prophets thus distinctly declared that the object of the sacrifices is not very essential, and that God does not require them." (*ibid. 32*) They were however tolerated, because "It is contrary to man's nature that he should suddenly abandon all the different kinds of the Divine service and the different customs in which he has been brought up, and which have been so general that they were considered as a matter of course." (*ibid.*)

MAN'S QUEST FOR PERFECTION. *Maimonides concludes the Guide for the Perplexed by describing what he believes should be man's striving for perfection by examining the types of perfection proposed by the philosophers. He dismisses the first, which relates to man's material acquisitiveness (money, property, etc.). He likewise discards the second, which has to do with the care and perfection of one's body and its comforts. The moral development of one's character is the higher goal to strive after.*

"The fourth kind of perfection is the true perfection of man; the possession of the highest intellectual faculties; the possession of such notions which lead to true metaphysical opinions as regards God. With this perfection man has attained his final object; it gives him true human perfection; it remains in him alone; it gives him immortality, and on its account he is called man. The last kind of perfection is exclusively yours; no one else owns any part of it . . . The Prophets have likewise explained unto us these things and have expressed the same opinion as the philosophers. They say distinctly that perfection in property, in health, or in character, is not a perfection worthy to be sought as a cause of pride and glory to us; that the knowledge of God, i.e., true wisdom, is the only perfection which we should seek and in which we should glorify ourselves. Jeremiah, referring to these four kinds of perfection, says: 'Thus saith the Lord, Let not the wise man glory in his wisdom, neither let the mighty man glory in his might, let not the rich man glory in his riches; but let him that glorieth glory in this, that he understandeth and knoweth Me that I am the Lord Who exercises lovingkindness, judgment and righteousness in the earth; for in these things I delight, saith the Lord'."

(*Editorial commentary by Jacob S. Minkin*)

Moses de Leon

The authorship of the Zohar contin-
ues to puzzle scholars to this day. It is generally acknowledged that Moses de Leon, who compiled
and published the Zohar in Spain at the end of the
13th century, was also its author. De Leon himself
attributed authorship to Rabbi Simon bar Yohai,
who lived in Palestine in the 2nd century. But it
appears likely that de Leon attributed the mystic
volume to Simon bar Yohai in order to give the
book the sanctity of age and the authority of a
rabbi known for his mystic knowledge and miraculous deeds. Bar Yohai, who hid in a cave from the
Romans for 13 years (he is the hero of an excellent
novel by Harry Sackler, entitled Festival at Meron),
is said to have occupied himself with speculations
of a secret nature and to have penetrated the mys-
teries of heaven and earth.

But Graetz insisted, and most recently Gershom
Scholem in Major Trends in Jewish Mysticism attempted to prove in detail, that Moses de Leon was

the true author of the Zohar. *He was in possession of the original work and circulated it from 1280 on. From 1286 on he composed his "own" writings, according to Scholem. He was born at Leon, Spain, about 1250 and died in 1305. He mastered not only the Bible, the Talmud and other Rabbinic works but also Jewish mystic literature and the philosophy of Solomon ibn Gabirol, Yehudah Halevi and Maimonides. Various scholars besides Graetz and Scholem have credited him with authorship of the* Zohar.

THE ZOHAR

Jacob B. Agus

As one of the great classic works of Judaism, the *Zohar* is unique. While its authority was based upon a pious fraud, its influence upon Jewish thought was for many centuries wide and deep. Acclaimed as the most intimate revelation of the secrets of the faith, it actually reintroduced into Judaism powerful echoes of pagan, mythological thought. Reserved for the study of the elite among the pious, the *Zohar* became in time the major textbook of exotic, pseudo-messianic mass movements. Dedicated to the glorification of Jewish piety and the mystical exaltation of the Jewish people, this paradoxical volume was for many generations studied arduously by Christian savants, who were convinced that it "proved" the truth of Christianity. So ambivalent was its influence, so ambiguous its intent and so darkly shadowed the world of ideas in which it was conceived and written! Yet we cannot treat this volume as a mere historical curiosity, for it has become part of the warp and woof of more than six centuries of Jewish life.

Let us, therefore, become acquainted with the more salient features of its composition, message and influence.

To begin with, the *Zohar* is not really one book, but a compilation of books, fragments and comments, that are arranged as homilies for the Pentateuch, The Song of Songs and other Biblical passages. Attributed to Rabbi Simon bar Yohai, a rabbi who lived in Palestine in the second century, the Zoharic fragments were circulated for the first time by Rabbi Moses de Leon, a Spanish Kabbalist, in the eighties of the thirteenth century. The authenticity of the *Zohar* was doubted by leading authorities at the time of its appearance. But so powerful was the impact of the ideas and sentiments which it represented, that among the faithful, all criticism was soon silenced. The glaring anachronisms of the *Zohar,* such as its mention of the names of rabbis who lived centuries after Rabbi Simon bar Yohai, were transmuted into marvelous evidences of its divine origin by the peculiar magic of naive faith. Said the Hassidic saint, Rabbi Nahum of Chernobil, who lived in the Ukraine in the early part of the nineteenth century: "How is one exalted by the Torah? By rising, through its study, to the hidden light, whereby one can see from one end of the world to the other. . . . For the power of this light penetrates all things, so that past, present and future are one to it. This is how Rabbi Simon bar Yohai could say in the *Zohar* that which Rabbi bar Honoh was to say centuries later. Thus, too, Moses saw what Rabbi Akiba was to accomplish ages after him, for, through their Torah they attained the hidden light, in regard to which there is no distinction between the present and the future. . . ." ("M'or Ainayam," *Tzav*)

More sober pietists, like Rabbi Moshe Hagiz, recognized that the *Zohar* was a compilation of documents that were put together long after the death of its reputed author. Nevertheless, they too reaffirmed its authority as a body of divinely revealed knowledge, saying, "Whoever dares to doubt it is as one who doubts the *Shekinah.*" (*Mishnath Cha-chomin*, 332, 339) Even the great Orthodox scholar, Rabbi Jacob Yavetz, a contemporary of Moses Mendelssohn, who wrote an excellent critique of the *Zohar,* maintaining that Rabbi Simon bar Yohai did not write it, nevertheless concluded that "essentially the book of the *Zohar* is holy, as pure as the substance of the heavens." Concerning the Kabbalah based upon it, he wrote, "As to the root of the Kabbalah, the wisdom of truth, no man in Israel may doubt its truth, for it is the soul of the Torah without the least shade of doubt whatsoever." (*Mitpachas S'forim*) This general acceptance of the *Zohar* prevailed down to the opening of the modern era, with the few dissenting opinions being overridden by the immense authority of this chief text of Kabbalah, which was third only to that of the Bible and the Talmud. Even the fact that it was not regarded as an authoritative source of Halakah was due at least in part to the reputed authorship of Rabbi Simon bar Yohai, whose legalistic decisions seldom prevailed in the discussions of the Talmud. It was believed that in the sphere of the "revealed," Bar Yohai's authority was comparatively weak, while in the sphere of the "hidden," he attained the loftiest possible heights, having been vouchsafed by God "secrets" which were never previously given to mortals.

Modern critical studies make it certain that the Zoharic literature did not attain its present form until the end of the thirteenth century. Prof. Gershom Scholem of the Hebrew University in Jerusalem maintains that Rabbi Moshe

de Leon authored every part of the *Zohar,* inventing names
and characters, secret documents and commentaries upon
them by the free use of his prolific imagination. Other
scholars subscribe to the more moderate view that de Leon
edited the fragments and documents which were produced
and studied in the school of Nachmanides, writing many
parts himself, transcribing other parts and giving the
Zohar its final shape. In any event, on any modern view,
the *Zohar* is a medieval product, reflecting the shadowy
currents of thought which flowed through subterranean
channels for many centuries before coming to the surface.

What was the secret of that peculiar fascination which
the *Zohar* exercised over the minds of the Jewish people
for many centuries? Doubtless, it was the whole-souled re-
affirmation of the supreme worth of Judaism, at a time
when the Jewish faith was challenged at every step. The
Zohar was taken to be a new revelation, confirming every
belief in Judaism, strengthening every hope in the breast
of the Jew and inflating the importance of every aspect of
Jewish life into cosmic proportions. In a motherly spirit,
wiping away the tears of her beaten child, the *Zohar* con-
jured up an aura of cosmic glory to balance the deepening
tragedy of Spanish Jewry. As the unhappy lot of medieval
Jewry reached successive depths of misery in the fourteenth
and fifteenth centuries, the *Zohar* grew in popularity, dis-
placing the works of the rationalists whose philosophy
seemed pale and ineffectual in a trying age, offering but
cold comfort to bruised souls.

Following the supreme tragedy of 1492, the brutal expulsion from Spain, the *Zohar* was exalted to the highest pin-
nacle of esteem, the unhappy exiles finding in its pages the
assurance of speedy redemption and the knowledge that

their daily sacrifices for the faith were fully justified. In the "revealed" world of physical existence, the Jew was a wretched pariah, homeless, helpless and adrift, but in the "hidden" world, as it was depicted with powerful pathos and rich imagery in the *Zohar*, the Jew held in his hands the trembling scales, in which the fate of the universe was weighed; he was the high-priest of humanity, the destiny of creation and even the state of the immanent Deity varying in accord with his actions. As the very existence of the Jewish community depended upon the thread of faith, the *Zohar*, in all its irrationality and näiveté, may well have supplied that magical increment of fervor which made the difference between survival and extinction. Said a Hassidic rabbi of the middle of the eighteenth century, Rabbi Pinhas of Koretz, a contemporary of Israel Baal Shem Tov, "I thank God every day that I was not born at the time when the *Zohar* was not yet revealed, for it was the *Zohar* which held me to the Jewish faith."

Thus it was impossible to study the *Zohar* without being transported into a world in which fears were allayed, hopes fulfilled, tragedies glorified, and the golden future of the prophetic vision turned into a flesh and blood reality of the living present.

Quite apart from the complex dogmas of Kabbalah, which were woven into its texture, the *Zohar* breathes with a unique awareness of the immediate presence of the Deity. The noble pathos of intense piety virtually leaps at you from every page, demanding, cajoling, threatening, musing, dreaming—yet again and again harping upon the theme of serving Him "with love and fear." The central religious experience of the "nearness of God" is difficult to convey in the clear language of discursive thought. Symbols, myths,

hints and a generally obscure style may to the cold logic
of reason hide a spiritual experience that awakens powerful echoes in the sensitive reader. For in the logic of
emotion, the rabbinic saying holds true, "Words which
come from the heart enter the heart." No one may read the
Zohar even today without sensing the overwhelming spell
cast by the religious consciousness in action. What must
seem "foolishness" and "a stumbling block" in any rational
view, is a vigorous emotional reality, noble in its way, and
attaining depths of insight that rationality would never
fathom.

It is in its violent struggle against the spirit of rationality,
that the central impetus of Zoharic thinking may be recognized. Whatsoever the theme may be which engages the attention of the authors, the foe against whom their darts are
steadily aimed is the questioning, analytical mind, which
dwells within their own being. The *Zohar* is not an expression of naive faith, which, in its simplicity, is completely
unaware of hostile criticism or stubborn facts. The minds
of the authors, as well as those of the majority of their readers, were stirred by the rational spirit and deeply wounded
by it. For in those dark, wretched years, the Jewish faith
could ill afford the luxury of rationality. Accordingly, the
Zohar sets out to woo the anxious souls, troubled by logic
and reflection, by offering a boldly conceived metaphysical
system and a fanciful reconstruction of reality, in which the
Jewish faith is utterly vindicated. The Zoharic philosophy
is essentially an elaborate defense of naive faith, a counter-
revolution against the inroads of rational thought.

Rationality has always been the glory of Judaism. It was
a powerful rationalistic effort which lifted the Jewish faith
above the beguiling meshes of pagan thought and set forth

the basic tenets of monotheism. All through the early period of Judaism, the spokesmen of the Jewish faith employed the weapons of rationalism to batter down the gods of the heathen world. It was not without historical justification that an Alexandrine Jewish writer described Aristotle as exclaiming in astonishment "that all Jews are philosophers." For in their arguments against the pagan world, the Jews stood on the side of reason.

In later years, when Christianity and Mohammedanism disputed the right of Judaism to exist, it was still the lot of the Jew to champion the rationalistic approach to faith. Against Mohammedanism, Jewish spokesmen spoke in terms of historical criticism and in the accents of philosophy. Against Christianity, the spokesmen of Judaism were able to direct all the weapons of the rationalistic armory. Is it logical to assume the simultaneous reality of the same Being as One and as Three? Is it logical to believe that God could enter into a woman's womb and emerge as a baby? In his famous debate before the King of Aragon, Nachmanides declared "that the mind of a Jew cannot possibly tolerate such an irrational doctrine." Allied to logic is the sense of justice. Jews could and did question the injustice implied in the doctrine of "original sin," "justification by faith," and the condemnation of all unbaptized humanity, including infants, to "eternal damnation and hellfire." Thus, the impact of Judaism upon the intellectual scene in Europe was largely in line with the impetus of rationalism.

However, in the setting sunlight of the Spanish Golden Age, it became ever clearer that rationalism weakened the bonds of Jewish loyalty. To the philosophical Jew, God was a benevolent Deity, who endowed man with the power to achieve immortality by perfecting his mind and heart; to this end, the rituals of the faith are very helpful, but only insofar as they serve to discipline man's passion and to direct his thought into noble channels; other nations and faiths could well make use of other rituals and ceremonies to attain the same goal. These are indeed noble conceptions of God, Torah and man. But, consider their effect in a situation where Jewish loyalty had to be paid for in the precious coin of life and limb. Why risk so much to live as a Jew, when the rituals of Christianity could be made to serve as instruments of human advancement? If it is the intent of the act that matters, not the act itself, how is Jewish martyrdom justified? Thus, the rationalistic spirit tended to weaken the readiness of the Jew to seal his faith with his blood.

As one of the refugees from Spain put it, "I am one of the exiles from Spain, driven out of that land on account of sin and failure. All who prided themselves on wisdom, or nearly all, forfeited their honor in that bitter day, while the women and the ignorant people willingly sacrificed their wealth and even their lives for the Holy Name of their Creator." (*Joseph Ya-avetz, Oz Ha-Hayim, Ch. 2*)

The Kabbalists, in general, and the authors of the *Zohar* in particular, set out to restrain and modify the rationalistic spirit in Judaism so as to build up the kind of sacrificial loyalty that the circumstances of their time required. In their zeal, they frequently inclined the scales in the other direction, so that it is not difficult to find passages in the *Zohar* which reflect Christological and even pagan thought. On the whole, Kabbalistic thought wrestles bravely with the problems of existence, containing a profound and patiently worked out metaphysics. In this essay we shall confine ourselves to the "reasons for the Commandments" that the *Zohar* set out to supply. Is being a Jew really important? Are the *mitzvoth* (commandments) truly so significant as to justify the daily trials of *Kiddush ha-Shem*? (Sanctification of the Name)

The focal effort of Kabbalistic thinking is to demonstrate that the *mitzvoth* are "needed by Him that is above" even more than they are needed by us who are below. Through their observance, the whole of existence is maintained; without them, neither the heavenly powers nor man could possibly exist. Thus, the observant Jew is placed in the living center of creation. Upon his labors, all depends: can he possibly be denied his reward?

This theme is worked out in a thousand different variations. First, the Deity is conceived in a double aspect. In His own Being, God is Infinite and completely incomprehensible, while in His relation to the universe, He is divided into many different powers, which function for good only when they are harmonized and united. Second, one phase of the Deity is so completely identified with the Jewish people and with the Torah as to be a representation of the living spirit of Israel. Accordingly, Jewish people in their totality are divine in a very real sense, while Jewish saints wield the key to the upper as well as to the lower worlds. Third, the souls of Jews are derived from the Deity, while the souls of the nations are derived from "the other side." Fourth, the patriarchs and Moses have become identified with certain phases of the Deity. Fifth, every *mitzvah* is like a chain, with one end being expressed in an action here on earth while the other end is directly connected with the heavenly powers. When the chain is moved "below," the other end, "above," is affected correspondingly.

The net result of all these doctrines is to exalt the *mitz-*

voth into a supreme cosmic force, affecting the destiny of man, the world and even of the Deity, as it were. A basic symbol of this relationship is a burning candle—the wick which is being consumed is the people of Israel, the dark flame which surrounds the wick is the *Shekinah,* the immanent Presence of God in the world, the bright flame which rises above the dark flame is the "higher *Shekinah,*" which in turn is associated with the endless phases of the Deity which transcend reason and shade off into eternity.

The rich imagery of the *Zohar* could not possibly be conveyed through selections. It is so easy to misinterpret the fanciful speculations and "mysterious" language of this classic text of the "wisdom of the hidden." Nevertheless, we cite a few passages in illustration of the ideas mentioned in this essay:

"Come and see: the soul of man cannot be known save through the limbs of the body, which are only steps leading to it or instruments of its will. Therefore, the soul is both known and unknown. Even so, the Holy One, Blessed be He, is both known and unknown, because He is the soul to the soul, the spirit of spirit, hidden and concealed from all; but through the same gates which lead to the comprehension of the soul, the Holy One, too, is known."

Zohar I, 103b

"Happy are the righteous in this world and in the world to come for upon them all who are above and below are dependent. Thus, it was said, 'the righteous is the foundation of the world.'"   *Zohar I, 245b*

"If Torah is studied without fear and love, it does not ascend above."   *Tikkunim, 51*

"The lands of the other nations were given over to powers who were appointed over them . . . Woe to the world

that draws its sustenance from that side . . . When Israel
is in exile they derive their power indirectly, as from another domain . . . But, you, the truly righteous, holy and
exalted, sons of the Holy King, do not draw from that side,
but from the holy source that is above . . ."

Zohar I, 95b

"He who desires to understand the wisdom of holy unity
let him contemplate the flame which rises from coal or
from a candle, for the flame rises only when it is attached
to a material thing. Come and see: in the rising flame there
are two lights, one a white shining light, and the other a
dark bluish light that holds on directly to the candle. The
white light is above, and rising straight up, while beneath
it, serving as its foundation is the blue or black light, the
two lights mingling and uniting, so as to be one. . . . The
blue-black light sometimes turns to red, but the white light
above it remains white. . . .

"Come and see: there is no stimulus for the kindling of
the blue light that it might provide the basis for the white
light save through the people of Israel who cleave unto it
from below. Behold further: though it is the nature of the
blue-black light to consume all that is below it, the people
of Israel unite with it from below and continue in their en-
durance . . . And above the white light there rests a mysterious light which envelops it on all sides. Here, we arrive
at the highest secret. . . ."

(The blue light is the immanent Presence of the Deity,
which becomes destructive, because of God's austere judgment, unless it is united with the transcendent Grace of the
Almighty, which is the white light, shading off into the Infinite. Divine mercy becomes ever more pronounced, as we
rise in the comprehension of His nature. It is through Is-

rael, that the *Shekinah* is enabled to mediate between the white light of Grace and the material universe. Through the Torah and the *mitzvoth*, Israel transforms the severity and wrath of judgment into the sweetness and grace of mercy.)

"Rabbi Simon lifted up his hands and rejoiced, saying—'surely, this is the right time to reveal secrets, for the hour requires it. We have learned—at the time when the Ancient, Holy One, the most hidden of all that is hidden, sought to achieve perfection, He arranged the totality of His self-revelation in a manner corresponding to male and female. . . .'"

"Thus, you will find in the arrangements of the totality that is the self-revelation of the Deity—a mother and a father, a son and a daughter."

"These things can only be revealed to exalted saints. . . ."

Zohar III, 290a

(The expressions male and female, father and mother, son and daughter, were not intended to be taken literally—but in an abstract, metaphysical sense. Yet, this symbolism is not merely a convenient language, for, in the basic logic of Kabbalah, there is a continuous channel of influence from the physical symbol to its remote spiritual counterpart. Hence, the whole import of the Zoharic message is couched in language and logic reflecting this male-female symbolism.)

(The righteous saints in their totality build up the spirit of Israel making it possible for it to serve as a channel of Grace for Israel and all of humanity. The observance of the *mitzvoth* helps to bring about "unifications" in the heavenly spheres, enabling the flow of Grace to descend upon Israel. By the same token, the non-observance of the *mitzvoth* causes "blemishes" in the upper spheres, preventing such "unifications.")

This entire system of interpretations is based upon the testimony of an esoteric tradition.

"For he who says, in matters of Torah, that which he does not know and did not receive from his master—concerning him it is written, 'Thou shalt not make unto thyself any image or statue.'" *Zohar II, Yithro*

"Truly deserving of the stature of men are the masters of Kabbalah, for they are above all . . ."

Zohar III, 134b, Ki Taizai

"'Not in vain,' says the Holy One, Blessed Be He, 'he who busies himself with the Torah and the practice of charity and worships with the public, I account it for him, as if he had redeemed me and my son from among the heathen. Many there are who labor in the Torah and practice charity and worship; yet, the Holy One and His *Shekinah* and Israel were not redeemed. Man's purpose must be to labor in the Torah in order to unite the *Shekinah* with the Holy One, Blessed Be He.'" *Zohar III, 136a*

(The "son" is a symbolic representation of the immanent aspect of the Deity, in His active phase, as the *Shekinah* is a representation of the passive phase. The *Shekinah* is also the spirit of Israel and is in exile along with the people of Israel.)

"Nothing in the world is ever lost; every word, every sound does not fall into a vacuum, but there is a definite place for all things." *Zohar II, 100b*

"The lower world depends upon the upper world, and the upper world functions in accordance with the behavior prevailing in the lower world." *Zohar III, 40b*

"This secret I found in the book of Chanoch—all the

words of the righteous exist as ornaments before the Holy
One, Blessed Be He, who plays with them. Thereafter, they
come down and stand before Him in the shape of the saint,
who said them, and the Lord delights in that shape. Then,
they are written down in a book of remembrance, which is
kept before Him always."   *Zohar II, Va-yachel*

These passages from the vast literature of the *Zohar* il-
lustrate the twofold impetus of Zoharic thinking. As the
mystical comforter of Israel's bruised soul, the *Zohar* was
an important source of strength in the long, dark centuries
of the late medieval and the early modern period. Also, as
a record of man's desperate striving for the "nearness of
God" and for the knowledge of God's ways, the *Zohar* contains profound insights and brilliant flashes of thought. On
the other hand, the impact of the *Zohar* upon Jewish life
has in a sense been regressive and regrettable. To overcome the challenge of philosophy, the Zoharic authors
evoked from the depths of the religious consciousness the
long slumbering pagan and gnostic ways of thought, bringing back into Judaism ideas and concepts which the up-
ward surge of Jewish faith had long ago overcome. The
Zohar employs expressions and ideas which constitute the
framework of Christianity, because Christianity, too, arose
out of a similar revolt against normative Judaism and its in-
veterate rationalism. How bitterly ironical are the strange
workings of the human mind!

It was through the *Zohar* and the vast literature center-
ing around it that the pseudo-messianic movements of Sab-
batai Zevi and Jacob Frank arose in the latter part of the
seventeenth century and in the first half of the eighteenth.
The Frankist movement, in particular, set the *Zohar* over
against the Talmud, and, when they accepted Catholicism,

the Frankists insisted on studying the *Zohar,* in secret. Several generations after this conversion, the Frankists continued to study the *Zohar* assiduously. A visitor in Prague around the beginning of the nineteenth century describes these weird sectarians as follows, "The ordinary conversation of their women is not like the usual feminine patter, for the spirit of the *Zohar* and the Kabbalah rests upon them and the terms of the Kabbalah are household words to them. . . ."

Quoted in Zinberg's Geschichte, VII, p. 18

Is it to be wondered then that the writers of the "enlightenment" period condemned the *Zohar* and Kabbalah in the most vigorous fashion? The awakening of reason and reflection in the nineteenth century led to a steady decline of Kabbalah even as it brought about increasing interest in the classics of Jewish philosophy. Thus, the historian Graetz writes of the *Zohar* with unrestrained contempt, attributing the degeneration of latter-day Judaism to its baneful influence.

On the other hand, the Hassidic movement in all the beauty of its naive faith derived its inspiration very largely from the *Zohar* and the commentaries of Luria. Thus, the romantic writers of our day who love to glorify the folk-genius that is implicit in Hassidism, dwell with unbounded admiration on the *Zohar* and its attendant works. In this vein, Hillel Zeitlin, the neo-Hassid wrote, "What is the *Zohar*? A divine exalted soul which descended suddenly from the ethereal world, to be revealed to the eyes of men in millions of brilliant lights and shades and nuances of color. The Holy One took one precious stone from his crown and threw it to the ground; the stone scattered into a multitude of radiant fragments, delighting in their multi-

farious beauty, which derive from eternity, in order to il-
lumine all the dark corners; in order to satiate all who thirst
for light and in order to vitalize all that the coldness of
science had deadened. . . ."

Quoted in *Mishnath Hazoar, p. 65*

Is the opinion of the rationalists to be accepted or that of
the romanticists? The scope and depth of Judaism is fortunately spacious enough to include all that is human and
creative.

selections from THE ZOHAR

Serve the Lord with Gladness

It was incumbent on the High Priest to enter the Temple with gladness, and when he stood before His Presence in that holy place, all things round about were bound to express gladness. So it is written: "Serve the Lord with gladness; come before His Presence with singing" [*Ps. 100: 2*]. This is so for the reason that in the service of the Lord, there is no place for a dejected heart.

One may ask, If a man be deeply troubled and sunk into sorrow, and his heart is heavy, yet because of tribulation he feels the urge to go to the heavenly King to seek solace; is he then to desist from praying because of his sorrowfulness? What shall he do, since he cannot help it that his heart is heavy?

The answer is that "from the day of the destruction of the Temple, all gates to heaven have been closed, but the gates of tears have not been closed," [1] and suffering and sadness are expressed in tears. Standing over the gates of tears are certain heavenly beings, and they break down the bars and locks of iron, and allow the tears to enter, so that

---

[1] Talmud, *Berakot 32b*.

the entreaties of the grieving supplicants go through and reach the holy King, and the place of the Divine Presence grieved by the sorrow of him who prays, as it stands written: "In all their afflictions He is afflicted" [*Isa. 63: 9*]. . . .

And when the King, entering the place of the Presence, finds her grieving, then all her desires are granted to her. Hence the supplication of him who sorrows does not revert empty to him, but the Holy One, be blessed, has pity on him. Blessed is the man who sheds tears as he prays before the Holy One, be blessed.

An Allegorical Explanation of Jonah

The story of Jonah may be construed as an allegory of the course of a man's life in this world. Jonah descends into the ship: this is parallel to man's soul descending to enter into his body in this world. Why is the soul called Jonah [lit., aggrieved]? For the reason that she becomes subject to all manner of vexation when once she enters into partnership with the body. Thus, a man in this world is as in a ship crossing the vast ocean and like to be broken, as it is written, "so that the ship was like to be broken" [*Jonah 1:4*].

And then too, man in this world commits transgressions, for he supposes the Master to be disregarding the world and His Presence able to be eluded. Thereupon the Almighty stirs up a raging storm; that is, the judgment of a man, which stands always before the Holy One, be blessed, and relentlessly seeks his punishment. This it is then that strikes at the ship, and remembering man's sins, seizes him; then the man is caught in the tempest and illness fells him, just as Jonah "was gone down into the innermost parts of the ship; and he lay, and was fast asleep" [*ibid. 1:5*]. Though the man thus lies felled, still his soul makes no move to return to his Master, to return and atone for his sins. Hence "the shipmaster came to him," that is, he who is the all-around helmsman, and the Good Inclination, "and said unto him: What meanest thou that thou sleepest? arise, call upon thy God" [*ibid. 1:6*]; this is no time for sleeping: you are about to be taken up to stand trial for all your deeds in this world. Repent of your wrongdoing. Bend your mind to these matters and return to your Master.

"What is thine occupation," that is, in which you are engaged in this world, and confess now in relation to it before the Master; "and whence comest thou"; namely, from a rank droplet, and therefore refrain from arrogance before Him. "What is thy country"—consider how you came from the dust and to dust will return; "and of what people art thou" [*ibid. 1:8*]; that is, consider if you are able to place hope on being protected by virtue of your ancestors' merits.

When he is brought before the heavenly tribunal to be judged, the tempest, which was in reality the doom of judgment as it lashed out at him, calls upon the King to punish all the King's prisoners. Then the King's counsellors come before him in turn, and the tribunal is constituted. Some plead for the accused, others against him. If the man be found guilty, as with Jonah, then "the men rowed hard to bring it to the land; but they could not"; thus, they who plead for him present arguments in his favor and seek to return him to this world, but in this they fail; "for the sea grew more and more tempestuous against them" [*ibid. 1:13*]; that is, the prosecution is roused to fury against him, overwhelms the defense, and the man stands convicted of his transgressions. Thereupon three picked emissaries descend upon him. One of them draws up a balance of all the man's good deeds and all his misdeeds in this world; one takes the tally of his days; the third is he who has been constantly with the man, from the period when he was enclosed in his mother's womb.

As has been said, the judgment doom is calmed only when "they took up Jonah" [*ibid. 1:5*], when they convey the man from his home to the burial ground. Then a proclamation is sent forth concerning him, saying, if he had lived a righteous life: Honor to the image of the King! "He entereth into peace, they rest in their beds, each one that walketh in his uprightness" [*Isa. 57:2*]. But for a wicked man when he dies, it is proclaimed: Woe to this man, better for him had he never been born! Concerning this sort of man, it stands written, "and they cast him forth into the sea; and the sea ceased from its raging" [*Jonah 1:15*], which means, the doom of judgment will halt in its raging only when they have finally lowered him into the grave, which is the place of judgment. And, in truth, the fish that swallowed Jonah is the grave; and "Jonah was in the belly of the fish" [*ibid. 2:1*], which is identified with the "belly of the netherworld," as we see by the passage, "Out of the belly of the netherworld cried I" [*ibid. 2:3*].

"Three days and three nights" [*ibid. 2:1*]: which means the three days that a man is in his grave before his belly bursts apart. At the end of the three days, it casts forth its putrescence onto his face, saying: Receive back that which you put into me; all day long you ate and drank, nor ever gave a thing to the poor; like feasts and holidays were all your days, but the needy did not share your food and were left hungry. Receive back that which you put into me. . . .

And, three days more having elapsed, the man is punished in each organ, in his eyes, his hands, his feet. For thirty days, then, the soul and the body receive punishment together. Therefore does the soul tarry during this time on earth below, and does not ascend to her sphere, as a woman is isolated through the period of her impurity.

Then the soul does ascend, and the body continues to molder in the earth, and there will lie until the hour when the Holy One, be blessed, shall rouse up the dead. At that time a voice will be heard ringing through the graves, and proclaiming: "Awake and sing, ye that dwell in the dust—for Thy dew is as the dew of light, and the earth shall bring to life the shades" [*refaim; Isa. 26:19*] This will be when the Angel of Death shall vanish from the world, as it stands written: "He will swallow up death for ever; and the Lord God will wipe away tears from off all faces; and the reproach of his people will He take away from off all the earth" [*ibid. 25:8*].

It is that event which is alluded to in the words: "And the Lord spoke unto the fish, and it vomited out Jonah upon the dry land" [*Jonah 2:11*]; when the graves hear the trumpeting of that voice, they will promptly eject the dead bodies that lie in them. And the dead will assume their pristine bodily condition, as is indicated by the word *refaim* [shades] which is related to *rafah* [healing]. . . .

So we see that the story of that fish holds words of solace for the entire world. No sooner had it swallowed Jonah than it died, yet three days later it was restored to life, and vomited him forth. And in like manner, in the future, the land of Israel will be roused first to new life, and then "the earth shall bring to life the shades."

Joseph Karo

Joseph Karo, author of the Shulchan Aruch, *was born in Spain in 1488. Four years later, like many thousands of Jews, his father fled the Spanish Inquisition, taking Joseph to Portugal. When the boy was eight, they were driven out of Portugal, too, and this time migrated to Constantinople. After the death of his father, young Karo settled in Adrianople where, in 1522, he began the composition of his main work. In 1523 he was called to head the yeshiva in Nikopolis and in 1536 he settled in Safed, then the center of Talmudic scholarship and Kabbalistic mysticism. Karo devoted twenty years to his work* Beth Yosef *and twelve more years to its revision (1522-1542 and 1542-1554). The first and second parts were published in Venice in 1550-1551; the third and fourth parts in Sabbionetta in 1553-1559. His fame rests on the* Shulchan Aruch, *based largely on the* Beth Yosef. *It was published in Venice in 1565. Following the publication of his books, Karo was honored by the world Jewish community and won recognition as a great scholar. He died in Safed, Palestine, in 1575.*

THE SHULCHAN ARUCH

Oscar Z. Fasman

About 400 years ago a Jewish DP by the name of Joseph Karo compiled a book of laws that became the standard of religious practice among Jews all over the world. Its name, *Shulchan Aruch* (The Prepared Table) has become synonymous with authoritative, and the term implies the accepted norm of conduct, the recognized fount of decision. A scholar who is a master in its interpretation can be ordained as a rabbi, an accredited teacher of the Jewish way of life. It would, therefore, be as impossible to understand the Jew of today without some knowledge of the sixteenth century *Shulchan Aruch* as it would be to understand the modern American without some knowledge of his eighteenth-century Constitution. There is, however, one major distinction: the men who drew up the Constitution, honored though they are in the history of America, sought to protect certain viewpoints of their class interests, while the author of the *Shulchan Aruch* dedicated himself to the task of systematizing the accumulated wisdom of Jewish law without the slightest attempt to grind an individual or group ax. So unique was this aspect of his work

216

that tradition even speaks of an angel who guided him, for how else could one explain his sublime self-submersion?

Joseph Karo became a wanderer at the age of four. In the very year that Columbus' *Pinta* crossed the Atlantic, Karo's parents fled the persecutions of Spain, taking him to Portugal. There he developed into a brilliant scholar and mystic. Above all, he attempted to be both thorough and clear in presenting the traditional teachings in the many fields of Jewish law. He prepared for the writing of his immortal classic by producing a profoundly erudite commentary on the code that was known as the "Four Rows." Those who have been initiated into the secrets of Talmudic reasoning regard the commentary as a demonstration of the amazing power of an extraordinary mind to control vast areas of learning. Most Jews are unfamiliar with this astonishing volume. Equally unknown to them, but revered by every Talmudist, is his spirited defense of the Code of Maimonides in his commentary, *Kesef Mishnah*. What they know is the uncomplicated language of the *Shulchan Aruch* that dropped the legal discussions, passed over the debates of the sources, and clearly pronounced what is proper and improper, what is approved or rejected, what is permissible or forbidden or desirable in daily Jewish practice.

Joseph Karo spent his latter years in Palestine among the dreamers of Safed, where he took part in a strange battle of history that may have a significant echo in the Israel of today. One of his teachers, Jacob Berab, concluded that students like Karo could be given the full *semicha* (ordination), recognized in the old days of Hebrew independence. On the other hand, Levi Habib, the rabbi of Jerusalem, regarded the attempt to restore definitive authority as premature. A similar difference of opinion is beginning to appear in our day on the advisability of centralizing religious authority in the rabbinate of the Holy Land. For our present purposes, it is important merely to remember that the author of the *Shulchan Aruch* was considered worthy of the highest honor Judaism could bestow on a scholar.

The *Shulchan Aruch* consists of four sections: *Orach Chaim*—The Way of Life—dealing with the laws of prayer, benedictions, and festivals; *Yoreh Deah*—The Guide to Knowledge—dealing with the laws of dietary practice, family purity, vows, mourning, etc.; *Even Ha-ezer*—The Rock of Assistance—dealing with the laws of marriage and divorce; and *Choshen Mishpat*—The Breastplate of Judgment—dealing with civil and criminal laws.

To reach a decision on a problem in any of these fields by consulting the pages of the Talmud frequently involves a lengthy study of four or more passages in different volumes, plus a search of numerous commentaries written about each passage. The student may even then become confused by the variety of interpretations and differences of opinion. The *Shulchan Aruch* makes it possible, for most purposes, to turn to one paragraph in it to know the answer. It is like an electric calculator into which one throws a whole list of figures to be added and multiplied, touches a button, and sees the result on the sheet before one; the machine performs all the operations that would otherwise have consumed so much time.

Joseph Karo's *Shulchan Aruch,* to be sure, did not remain unchallenged. Because Karo was closer to the Spanish and African authorities, many scholars in Central Europe found it necessary to add to or modify some of his decisions. Rabbi Moses Isserles of Cracow became the

most widely recognized of these, until over the "Prepared
Table" of Karo there was always spread Isserles' commentary, "The Tablecloth," and the two are invariably printed
together. Actually, in speaking of the *Shulchan Aruch,* we
mean the work of Joseph Karo together with the commentary of Moses Isserles.

Woven around their writings one finds the dicussions
of the later *Poskin* (Codifiers). Many volumes have been
written which expand upon the work of Karo and Isserles.
So long as the genius of the Jewish mind and the dedication of the Jewish soul do not forsake the study of religious
law, there will be this continuous process of expansion and
growth. It is the greatness of Joseph Karo to have closed
one epoch of scholarship, the age of the early codifiers, and
to have opened a new epoch, the age of the later codifiers.
If a classic is defined as a contribution that marks a permanent turning point in literature, then the *Shulchan Aruch* is a
superb classic endowed with the sanctity of permanently
influencing religious practice and thought. If a classic
is defined as a lucid presentation of any extensive system
of conduct, then the *Shulchan Aruch* is perhaps unique;
for many classics—like Plato's *Republic*—describe some
great hope or dream, while the *Shulchan Aruch* sets forth
a course of life actually followed by large numbers of living
people. And if a classic is defined as an accurate portrayal
of a great social philosophy, then the *Shulchan Aruch* is a
true classic in its formulation of Jewish laws on such matters as charity, labor, family relationships, worship, communal institutions and duties.

A word of explanation may be necessary to meet the
questions that the term "philosophy" might stir up. The
Jewish religion builds attitudes out of actions. It tells a

man what to do, and assumes, with ample psychological justification, that he will thereby learn what to think. In the libraries of famous rabbis through the ages one could find, for every book about meditation and religious thought, a hundred books about what is to be done in a given set of circumstances. Instead of preaching to a husband for example, about the reverence he should show toward his wife, Judaism limits his claims, controls his demands, surrounds his wife with legal protection to guard the independence of her person—thus making reverence flow in a natural stream out of the system in the home. Orthodox Jews have the profoundest faith in this arrangement, because it is much more than humanly wise; it is divinely ordained. Thus the *Shulchan Aruch* embodies a philosophy which can only be summed up by the word Torah—the art of living according to a heavenly pattern, and the intellectual, emotional and moral response to the universe growing out of it.

The *Shulchan Aruch* nevertheless differs from the Torah in that the former has never been acknowledged to be totally infallible. If a competent scholar can establish that the Talmud on a given point leads to a conclusion that contradicts the *Shulchan Aruch,* he must give judgment in accordance with the Talmud. Such instances are so rare that only an extraordinary student will check back on a decision of the *Shulchan Aruch* to be sure it is right, although it is frequently necessary to analyze the Talmudic sources to be sure the decision covers a particular case. The conscientious student of the Halakah (Jewish law) may accept the *Shulchan Aruch* as a sufficient summary of all that preceded it, yet he must be familiar with the operation of

Talmudic logic to recognize whether the given paragraph
fits the circumstances under analysis.

In other words, the *Shulchan Aruch* has not become in
Judaism, as is sometimes asserted, what the papal office
became in Catholicism. It is not only permissible but desirable to be conversant with the wellsprings of tradition
that streamed into it, just as it is a sign of aristocracy in
the congregation today to be able to discuss with the rabbi
the original passages of halachic writing supporting his
decision. Democracy in Judaism reaches its loftiest alti-
tudes in these spheres where the meekest person upheld
by a Talmudic conclusion may call halt to the most exalted
Hebrew judge who happened to overlook it; where, furthermore, respect for the rabbi is not accorded on an
arbitrary basis but given in recognition of his ability to
interpret the sources correctly. Power of discernment into
implications of a pronouncement, whether in the Talmud
or the *Shulchan Aruch,* ranks higher than broad memory
of its phraseology; so that the *Shulchan Aruch* has become,
in addition to a normative code, a testing ground of judicial
insight, an arena of halachic jousting where the champions
of latter generations prove the agility, subtlety and depth
of their minds. Knowledge and the wisdom of knowledge
are the only passwords required for entrance, and Rabbi
Joseph Karo must be credited with having measured off a
magnificent field for trying out candidates.

Precisely this quality in the approach to any work of
halachic scholarship protected the *Shulchan Aruch* from
becoming a rigid and unimaginative factor in Jewish society. Ample room was left for the creative intellect of
later students, and the presentation in its context of total
rabbinic literature allowed for sufficient elasticity to keep

the program of the community dynamic. Joseph Karo renders a decision, but does not bring down the gavel on it. For him who wants to know immediately whether he may or may not make a given move, there is the decision; but for him who wants to analyze the decision, the poised gavel grants an opportunity to summon the opinions of preceding authorities. Whether the author himself intended that there be elaborate discussions about almost every paragraph is a moot question. His introduction indicates that he expected the *Shulchan Aruch* to be accepted as an adequate summary of earlier codes, while the introduction of his earliest critic, Rabbi Moses Isserles, takes exception to his attitude of finality. Yet one might argue that Karo only wished to put into easily accessible form the headlines, as it were, of Jewish practice. He even suggests that his volumes be divided into thirty equal parts, so that all of Jewish law may be reviewed every month by covering one part each day. In the last resort, less importance should be attached to what he hoped would occur than to what did happen. The *Shulchan Aruch* became both the authority and the starting point of new developments in legal thinking.

How strong its hold became upon the people is to be seen from the fact that they succeeded in having it reduced to an abridgement known as the *Kitzur Shulchan Aruch*. In the ordinary Jewish home this little volume came third, after the *Siddur* (Prayer Book) and the *Chumash* (Pentateuch), and all the protests of the erudite against this oversimplification could not interfere with the dissemination of what became the most popular handbook of Judaism. That it played a major role in scholarly circles is obvious; a judge in Israel is required to know the codes thoroughly, and the *Shulchan Aruch* in particular. Magnificent merit must be attributed to a literary work that can embrace both the upper and lower cultural planes of a nation. Since religion functions similarly, it must be concluded that not the mechanical but the spiritual characteristics of the *Shulchan Aruch* put their stamp upon the Jewish people. They recognized a sincere piety in the *Shulchan Aruch* and the Jewish sages long ago observed that what goes forth from the heart of the speaker goes into the heart of his audience.

The people went further. In the latitudes where they could evolve their own *minhagim* (folkways) they added to the *Shulchan Aruch*. Wherever there were no particular limitations, the accepted custom, having taken root, was considered a ramification of Rabbi Joseph Karo's code. The common man in Israel thus became a partner of the immortal author, and together they produced new forms in the service of the Almighty. If the *Shulchan Aruch* was in one way the destination of a religious search, it was in another a signpost pointing to unexplored areas of the spirit yet to be conquered.

A final observation may be made about the role of the *Shulchan Aruch* as a unifying force during the last four centuries. Historians never cease to marvel at the survival of a scattered people that retained its sense of cohesion despite the wide differences of civilization and cultural patterns among its branches in various countries. The answer lies in the uniformity of a religious code that included practice along with theology. When the modern world introduced divergent nationalisms to replace the common experiences of European society, it was imperative that the adherents of Judaism discover additional sources of unity.

The *Shulchan Aruch* thus came as a well-timed blessing. It reminded Jews in every corner of the globe of their harmony of purpose and singleness of goal. It gave them a literary banner around which to rally the program of living sacred to all of them alike. It created a spiritual focus.

The *Shulchan Aruch* is today the embodiment of Jewish practice, the beacon of the Hebrew faith. The emergence of the State of Israel offers greater opportunities than ever for its application on a broad national scale, and Jews rejoice that something native to their own genius presents an alternative to Roman jurisprudence or British common law building the new government. Both outside the boundaries of Israel and within them it serves as the high tower of positive Jewish attitudes, the constant summons to the devotion of our people to our Torah and to our way of life.

selections from THE SHULCHAN ARUCH

Laws about Benedictions

A cantor should be a person proper for the office. Who is proper? One who is free of sins, and about whom evil reports have not circulated, not even in his youth; one who is humble, and whom the congregation likes; one who has a voice that is sweet and pleasant; one who is wont to study Holy Writ.

If it is impossible to find one with all of these qualifications, then let the congregation select the best man in wisdom and generous deeds. *Rama*: If there is available an older man of pleasant voice whom the people want, but he is an ignorant man; and on the other hand, there is a lad of thirteen whose voice is not equally pleasant, but he understands the prayers, the latter should be given the precedence. He who committed a sin unintentionally—for example, he killed somebody accidentally—and completely repented, may be a cantor; but if he committed a sin maliciously, he ought not be selected as a cantor, despite repentance, since an evil report did circulate about him. . . .

A cantor who draws out his prayers so that the people will hear his voice and its sweetness, because his heart

225

rejoices in the praises he utters to the Almighty, is worthy
of divine benediction, since he prays with earnestness,
trembling and fear; but if his purpose is to make his voice
heard, and he rejoices in the sound of his voice, then his
action is deplorable. In all cases, it is not a good thing to
draw out the services to too great length, for one should
always avoid imposing upon the patience of the congregation. . . .

A cantor is not to be removed from his office, unless
something dishonorable is found in his character. *Rama*:
He is not to be removed on the basis of a mere rumor that
he conducted himself immorally or unethically; but if authentic testimony is produced, he should be removed. If
the cantor also performs duties in the slaughterhouse, he is
not to officiate in the garments he uses there; and if he is
careless in this matter, he should be removed. A cantor who
uses his voice to sing lewd songs or speak in immoral language is to be warned against continuing to do so; if he
disregards the warning, he is to be removed. If a cantor
becomes old and desires to have a son assist him in con-
ducting worship, if the son be capable in the many aspects
of the office, even though his voice is not quite so pleasant
as that of the father, the son deserves first consideration,
and the congregation ought not challenge the father in the
choice.

Whenever a congregation has established a tradition
that officeholders are limited to a fixed term, and at the
end of the term the former officeholders step down and
new men take over, whether as a cantor, trustee of charity,
or other public position, paid or unpaid, then even men
who assumed office without it being expressly stated that
the term is limited must step down at the end of the tra-

ditional period. *Rama*: There is a source that recommends that the cantor shall lead the services from a prayer book specifically designated for the use of the congregation.

Laws about Charity

It is a positive commandment to give charity in accordance with one's means, and frequently does the Torah command it. There is also a negative commandment concerning him who shuts his eyes against almsgiving, as it is said in Scripture, "Thou shalt not harden thy heart nor shut thy hand" (*Deut. 15, v. 7*). Whoever shuts his eyes against charity is to be designated as "wicked," and he is to be reckoned as an idol-worshipper. Let a man be extremely careful in this matter, for its neglect can lead to actual bloodshed; for example, where a poor man starves to death because the donor was not prompt enough in extending aid. . . .

A man will never become impoverished because of his gifts to charity, nor will any evil or damage befall him as a consequence of it, for it is said in Scripture, "And the work of righteousness shall be peace."   (*Isaiah 32, v. 17*)

The Holy One Blessed Be He is merciful to the one who is merciful to poor people. *Rama*: Let a man consider that every moment he seeks his livelihood from the Holy One Blessed Be He, and even as he desires that the Holy One Blessed Be He shall hear his cry, so let him hear the cry of the poor. Let him furthur consider that fortune is a wheel that keeps turning in the universe, and the end of man is that he or his son or his son's son will come to a similar state—men take pity on those who have shown pity for others.

Charity wards off evil decrees, and in a time of famine it rescues from death, as happened to the woman of Zarephath. (See *First Kings 17, v. 8-16*) *Rama*: And it also makes one wealthy. One is not permitted to put the Holy One Blessed Be He to the test, except in the matter of charity, as it is said in Scripture, "And try me now therewith, etc." (*Malachi 3, v. 10*); others say, only in the gift of the tithe is it permissible to put the Holy One Blessed Be He to the test, but not in other forms of charity.

Every man must give charity; even the poor man who is supported by charity must donate from that which he is given. Whoever gives less than what he should is to be compelled by the court to do his share. He is to be flogged until he gives what is estimated as his fair share, and the court may even seize some of his possessions in order to take what is the proper amount for him to donate. . . .

A noble person who gives more than his share or one who injures himself by gifts beyond his reach in order not to be embarrassed when the trustee approaches is not to be solicited in the collection for charity; and a trustee who approaches him for a donation or embarrasses him will be called to account by the Holy One Blessed Be He.

Whoever wishes to win moral merit for himself should overpower his evil inclination and be generous. Whatever is for a religious purpose shall be of the best and most beautiful. If he builds a synagogue, it shall be more attractive than his own residence; if he gives food to the hungry man, let it be of the best and sweetest on his table; if he clothes the naked, let the garment come from the best in his wardrobe; if he dedicates something to a holy cause,

let it be from the choicest of his goods; and so does the
verse say, "All the fat is the Lord's."   (*Leviticus 3, v. 16*)

Laws about Building a Family

A man should not marry a woman whose origin is
suspected to be of forbidden relationship. *Rama*: . . . A
man's family may protest against his marriage to a woman
of doubtful background, and if he disregards the protest,
let them record in some manner that they do not want their
descendants marrying with any of his. If a man was promised large sums to wed a girl, and her family later refuses
to pay, let him not make his fiancee suffer because of it, and
let him not quarrel over the dowry; for those who do so
will not prosper and will not enjoy happy family life;
money received because of taking a girl is not noble
money, and he who does these things may be described
as one who marries for money (of whom it has been pre-
dicted the offspring will not be upright). Rather let a man
receive with good spirit whatever the parents of the bride
give him, and then will they prosper in their marriage. . . .

A man ought always to strive to win in marriage the
daughter of a Torah scholar, and to give his daughter in
marriage to a Torah scholar. If he cannot find the daughter
of a Torah scholar, let him seek to marry the daughter of
renowned communal leaders; if he cannot find one of these,
let his choice be the daughter of a congregational leader;
if not one of these, then the trustee of a charitable fund; if
not one of these, let him select the daughter of an elementary Hebrew teacher, but let him not marry off his daughter
to an ignorant man. *Rama*: . . . This term means one who

is so ignorant that he is indifferent in obedience to the commandments of our faith. . . .

A young man ought not marry an old woman, nor should an old man marry a young girl, for such things usually lead to infidelity.

A man should not marry a woman if his advance intention is to divorce her later; but if he tells her beforehand that their marriage will be only for a limited period and she nevertheless consents, it is permissible for them to be married.

A man should not marry a woman in one country and marry a second woman in another country (if the first has died or been divorced) lest the children of one wife intermarry with the children of the other, thus leading to the forbidden marriage of a brother and sister. If, however, he is a man of reputation, so that his children are widely known (and such a mishap cannot occur) he may marry a second wife in another country.

Laws about Judges

It is not permissible to hold court on the Sabbath or during Festivals, but if the judges did nevertheless render a decision on those days, the decision stands.

It is not proper to hold court on the eve of the Sabbath or Festivals. If a man is summoned on such a day to appear before the court, he need not do so; even more, if the summons is delivered on such an eve for appearance after the Sabbath or Festival, and he does not appear at the appointed time, he is not to be fined. (Commentaries explain: He can argue that in the rush of preparing for the Sabbath or Festival, he forgot about the summons.) *Rama:* Some authorities believe that in our day it is permissible to hold court on the eve of the Sabbath or Festivals in order that instructors may be able to participate in the court procedure without losing time from their classes, since lectures to students are not held on the eve of the Sabbath or Festivals. Only cases dealing with financial claims, however, may be allowed this consideration, since in matters of money the court has the power to make one forfeit his possessions; in questions of ritual this permission is withheld. I am inclined moreover to the view that even in cases of finance, such permission is granted only on occasion, but it is not proper to hold court regularly on the eve of the Sabbath or Festivals. This is now an accepted custom. *Author:* A person who does not live in the city shall not be summoned to come to court during the months of Nisan and Tishre (when many days of Festival occur) but if he is summoned during either month to appear after the month is over and he fails to appear, he is to be fined. *Rama:* There are those who say that during Nisan and during the Days of Awe nobody may lodge a claim in the synagogue, not even against the villagers who have come to attend worship in the city, but a time for the hearing is to be set after the Festival; however, where it is apparent that unfair postponement or deceit is involved, court is to be held at once. In some places the tradition is that lawsuits begun before Nisan or Tishre can be heard in those months and this tradition is valid for those places. *Author:* The beginning of a case shall not take place after dark, but cases of financial claim begun during the day may be completed after dark. *Rama:* There are those who say that if the judges disregarded this regulation and held the be-

ginning of court after dark, their decision is nevertheless
binding.

The proper time for the judges to sit is from early morning until eleven o'clock in the morning. *Rama:* After that
they are under no obligation to hold court.

Court is not to be held after twelve noon, even to complete a case already begun, until the afternoon prayer has
been recited. If, however, the judges did hold court, even
to begin a new case, they should not interrupt the session,
although the late hour for afternoon services has arrived,
so long as they can still manage to recite the prayer after
concluding the case. *Rama:* But if they began to hold
court close to the late hour for afternoon services, they
should interrupt.

What is to be regarded as the beginning of a session?
When those involved in the suit commence the presentation of their arguments, or when the judges clothe themselves in their robes of office.

(*Translated by Oscar Z. Fasman*)

Heinrich Graetz

The author of A History of the Jews
*was born in Xious, Germany, in 1817 and died in
Munich in 1891. He was enrolled in the University
of Breslau in 1842, and in 1854 became a teacher
at the newly-established Jewish Theological Seminary in Breslau. From 1869 on he was also a professor at the University of Breslau. His eleven-volume
History was his great achievement. Written in
1853-1875, it was translated into numerous languages, including French, Polish, Russian, Hungarian, Yiddish, Hebrew and English. It appeared
in English in 1891-1892.*

*Graetz, who took a stand on religious controver-
sies in the Jewish community and received his Ph.D.
for a dissertation on the subject of Gnosticism and
Judaism, was also active in the field of Bible exegesis. In 1871 he edited a translation of Ecclesiastes and The Song of Songs; in 1872 he visited
Palestine; in 1882 to 1883 his critical commentary
on the Psalms was published and a year later his
commentary on the Proverbs. He also wrote commentaries on Job and Esther.*

GRAETZ'S HISTORY

Solomon Grayzel

"Can you name a Jewish historian?" Ask
this question of any informed Jew, and you will almost invariably receive the answer: Graetz. The usual Jewish home
where Jewish books are to be found is sure to possess the
six rather stout volumes of the *History of the Jews* published by the Jewish Publication Society of America. Next
to the Bible, the Society has sold more copies of it than of
any other book it has ever published. During the past fifty
years, Graetz has been reprinted more than a score of times,
so that the plates have become worn with use. No Jewish
school or synagogue library is without it. Hardly a pupil in
a Jewish religious or Hebrew school but has been referred
to Graetz for material on a subject his teacher wanted him
to look up. Echoes of Graetz may be heard in nine out of
ten sermons concerned with Jewish history; and discussions
reminiscent of Graetz stare at you from every other page
of all popular Jewish histories. Clearly, Graetz has, for two
generations, fed our minds, molded our thoughts on Jewish
subjects and largely inspired our loyalties. It becomes im-

portant, therefore, to find out who this man was and by what merit his book has become so influential.

Heinrich Graetz was born in 1817 in a small town in the German province of Posen, where old-fashioned Orthodoxy was fighting a valiant battle against the inroads of enlightenment stemming from Germany. Young Graetz received a fair Talmudic education. Despite many difficulties, he also taught himself the languages of the West and acquainted himself with its literatures and philosophic currents. He soon fell under the influence of the writings and personality of Samson Raphael Hirsch, the foremost champion of Orthodoxy in nineteenth-century Germany; and he early identified himself with the critics of Abraham Geiger, the intellectual leader of Reform. Yet Graetz was too keenly aware of the principles of progress not to be critical of any stand-still attitude. His views, as he grew older, developed rather along lines parallel to those of the great scholar Zechariah Frankel, the founder of the historical school in Judaism.

To earn his livelihood, Graetz tried to become a rabbi. He failed, because his abilities as a preacher were not equal to the demands of the office. For some years he tried his hand at directing Jewish schools established by various Jewish communities. Not till 1853 did he find the position for which he was fully equipped, namely, the teaching of Jewish history in the newly founded Jewish Theological Seminary in Breslau, under the directorship of Zechariah Frankel. There he taught and there he completed (in 1876) his monumental work, one volume of which—the one dealing with the period of the Talmud—had already appeared in 1853.

The Jews are not only a historical people, but also a

history-conscious people. Their past never dies. The first
half of their history is, in fact, alive for non-Jews as well;
it is sacred for Christians and for Moslems. Abraham as
the founder of monotheism, Isaiah inveighing against gods
of wood and stone, the Maccabees battling for religious
freedom have a place in the story of mankind's search for
God. At one point, however, the defeat of Judea by Rome,
Judaism's history practically ended for its daughter religions; for them all that went was merely introductory to
the real drama of mankind. For the Jews, however, what
followed remained equally real. During centuries of abject
misery they recalled the glories of a past which they embel-
lished and turned into a promise for a more glorious future.
The second part of their history, moreover, the part which
the non-Jewish world refused to share, was even closer to
their daily life. For by means of the study of Talmud and
Codes, philosophy and commentary, the Jew could rise
above the walls of the ghetto which surrounded him. His
physical life might be anchored in Frankfort or in Cracow,
but his intellectual life was passed in Sura and Pumpedita.
At will, he could be the companion of Rav and Samuel, of
Saadia, of Isaac Alfasi, of Rashi, of any of the other lumi-
naries who, undimmed by time, lighted up his heavens. His
feast and fast days reminded him of ancient events, his
traditions were freighted with ancient glories. His hopes for
the future burgeoned out of his past.

Good Jewish history writing is as old as some of the
oldest parts of the Bible. The writers of the Books of Samuel
and Kings were superb historians. The authors of the Books
of the Maccabees were, within the limitations of their age,
excellent reporters of past events. Josephus' histories dating
from the first century of the Common Era were therefore,

in a sense, the continuation of a tradition in Jewish life. But then came a long gap. There were chronicles during the next eighteen hundred years, lists of names and disparate events, but few works that could be dignified by the name of history. The reasons are not far to seek. The peoples among whom the Jews lived likewise failed to produce anything but chronicles. Besides, the Jews looked upon their exile as a suspension of their history, as one long series of punishments, of martyrdoms. Their sole duty, they believed, was to keep their sacred literature alive by study, and their sacred traditions by observance.

Interest in the writing of history reasserted itself in the western world late in the eighteenth and early in the nineteenth centuries. Graetz was neither the first nor the only Jewish historian. A generation before him Marcus Jost had written a *History of the Israelites* in nine volumes. Zunz, Rappaport and many other contemporaries of Graetz were devoting themselves to research in Jewish history and biography. Yet all these others are not known except to the scholar. Why did Graetz overshadow them?

There are several reasons for Graetz's superiority: his research, his point of view, his warmth and his style. Graetz knew how to find new sources of information about the past and how to evaluate these as well as the old ones. Scattered through the length and breadth of Europe were documents, edicts, memoranda and many other references to Jews. Comparatively few of them had as yet been published. They lay buried in libraries and archives and it required prodigious effort to dig them out. Once uncovered, they had to be classified, related to other contemporary events and interpreted so as to yield their significance for the people of their day. Graetz possessed an unerring instinct for such things, a

phenomenal memory and a sense for system. Above all, he
was blessed with imagination, which enabled him to see
the meaning of a law or a decree in terms of human life.

There were, besides, literary sources of history in the
more usual sense. The Bible, for example, though not history as we now generally think of it, is a source book for
history. Graetz looked upon the Bible with the critical eye
of the historian. In some respects he was a radical higher
critic, sometimes going too far in his dissection of the Bible
text and the interpretations he put on it. But his comments
are always brilliant and often convincing. The Talmud is
another literary source for Jewish history. Here, too, Graetz
brought order and system into the unorganized mass of Talmudic names and of references to historical events. He did
the same for the medieval material: the poetry, philosophy,
exegesis, law and commentary. The result was a body of
fact, and inference based on fact, which permitted the telling of the long story of the Jewish pilgrimage through the
ages without too many gaps. He succeeds in giving his
reader the conviction that his account is substantially what
must have happened and that his explanations reveal the
motives for and the results of what happened.

One cannot read Graetz's *History* without feeling that
he is describing the fate of a single people—a people moreover, that is not standing still, but traversing a definite
road and, in the face of obstacles, making unmistakable
progress. The facts he recounts are not disparate, unre-
lated. They form a whole. Not even the tragedy of the destruction of the State by Rome causes a break in the continuity of the Jewish adventure, as Christian historians
had been blandly assuming. The only difference it makes
is to turn Jewish history into the history of intellectual and

religious life—a spiritual story—to a greater extent than
before. For Graetz saw in the history of the Jews even before this event a unique story of a people motivated by
ideas, by a hunger of the spirit. Physically, the Jews thereafter suffered great hardships; but they compensated for
this by a deeper mind, by a more sensitive soul. Graetz's
pen therefore made of the history of the Jews a history of
suffering and cultural grandeur. Its great heroes were the
martyrs and the authors. Since these aspects of Jewish life
were world-wide, it was possible for Graetz to give a unified picture of the long story of the Jews.

A living thing makes decisions that lead to action; that
which is only acted upon, carried along by the current, is
essentially dead. Because of his desire to represent the Jewish people as a living entity, Graetz played down the effects
on the Jews of those historical currents which affected all
nations or which resulted from the decisions of those nations among whom the Jews lived. He insisted rather on
portraying the Jews as molders of their own destiny. In this
respect Graetz was inferior to Jost. It brought down upon
him the criticism of some of his contemporary Christian
historians, but it made him an effective forerunner of a
Jewish renaissance which insisted on self-determinism.

Of course, no Jewish history can be written as though
the Jews lived in a vacuum. It is obvious that the movements both for good and for evil which sweep across the
world affect the Jews as they do everyone else. Graetz was
interested in and made a point of showing how richly the
Jews contributed to the positive forces in the development
of civilization and to what extent they, more than others,
suffered from the destructive forces. The point is that he
was less interested in the movements than in the Jews. He

loved his people, and the warmth of this affection exudes from his every page.

The past was real to him. One gains the impression that the historical characters actually stood before him as heroes or villains. He all but talks to them, praising or scolding, showing them off or treating them with contempt.

His attitude of warm argumentation was reinforced by the needs of the times. Much of the historical research of that age was motivated by the desire to explain the Jewish people to their neighbors. Emancipation, to the extent to which the Jews of Germany ever attained it, came to the Jews during the very period that Graetz was writing his *History*. It was necessary to explain why Jews lived and acted as they did; it was imperative to refute the charges made and the insults implied. The Jews themselves needed such refutations quite as much as the Christians. Their self-respect had to be bolstered. Graetz's work was in large measure a defense of Jews and Judaism. He undertook to parade Jewish virtues and to explain how it came about that the entire Christian world was wrong about the numerous faults it attributed to the Jews. Graetz therefore spoke his mind about the persecutors of the Jews. He did not spare the warriors and the nation-builders whom the Christian Germans venerated, and he did not mince words about the Church upon whom he laid the responsibility not only for persecuting the Jews, but also for blackening Jewish character. Graetz decidedly did not make himself popular with his Christian contemporaries.

And not with the Christians alone. Graetz was not free of prejudices regarding Jews as well. Having been born near the Polish border, a Prussian in citizenship and a German by choice of culture, he possessed little sympathy for East-

European Jews and their type of Judaism. In fact, he said
as little as possible about them, thus practically neglecting
a large and vibrant segment of the Jewish people. He fully
shared the attitude toward Eastern Europe which then prevailed in Germany, where East-European Jews were considered uncouth and uncultured. Graetz further justified his
prejudices on the ground that East-European Judaism was
steeped in mysticism. For Graetz lived in a rationalistic
age. A medieval Jewish author of a philosophical or gram-
matical work was held up to admiration in his *History;* but
a mystic was given scant consideration. The outstanding
illustration of this attitude was Graetz's treatment of the
Zohar, that foremost work of Kabbalah, or Jewish mysticism, and its reputed author or compiler, Moses de Leon
of the twelfth century in Spain. There were few semi-polite
expressions of abuse which Graetz did not hurl at the book
and the author. He called the latter an impostor, a plagi-
arist, a charlatan. It stands to reason that the Kabbalists of
later generations fared no better; and it follows that Graetz
found Hassidism little to his taste.

His fellow German Jews and many other Jews of Western
Europe in his day easily forgave his derogation of East-
European Jewry. They could not pardon his treatment of
Reform in Judaism. He accused Reform of superficiality and
irresponsibility, and spoke slightingly of the Reform Move-
ment's heroes. In the subsequent English translation of his
History these judgments were somewhat moderated.

He thus earned for himself a considerable number of
critics, if not enemies. Nevertheless, his Jewish contemporaries read him avidly. For Graetz knew how to write. Although his work represented the results of wide and
thorough research, it was anything but dry. He had a happy

gift for imagery and he could make controversy interesting.
It may be a fault for a historian to display emotion, but it
makes for a wider reading public. The result was that his
History became popular even while he was writing it.

Translations of it in various languages began to appear
without much delay, considering the vastness of the task.
The fourth volume, dealing with the Talmudic period,
which had been the first to appear (1853), was the first to
be translated into English. It was done by the Reverend
James K. Gutheim, then rabbi in New Orleans. It was published in 1873 by the Jewish Publication Society, the second
of that name, which had been organized only two years
earlier and was soon to go out of existence. The transla-
tor's style was heavy; nor did the volume's external appearance make it attractive. In a sense, it may have been
fortunate that the translation of the other volumes into English was not undertaken at that time.

As soon as the third Jewish Publication Society, the one
still in existence, felt itself firmly established, it began to
lay plans for the publication of Graetz's entire *History*. The
English philanthropist, F. D. Mocatta, was just then plan-
ning to do the same thing at his private expense. Graetz
himself had, upon Mocatta's invitation, prepared a manuscript especially for this purpose. Exercising many lengthy
quotations and some detailed, scholarly but by no means
essential passages, he had succeeded in reducing the size of
the original German work by about a third. Moreover, he
brought the manuscript up to 1870, the German edition
having concluded with the events of 1848. The remaining
two-thirds were put in the hands of Miss Bella Loewy for
translation. She translated only volume one; the rest, done

by a number of others, were revised by her. She may have had the advice of Graetz himself, but certainly that of Israel Abrahams. The Society succeeded in obtaining the American rights to the work from Mocatta. Miss Loewy's manuscript was then gone over carefully by a number of the American directors of the Society, but chiefly by its secretary, Miss Henrietta Szold. It is her style, simple, lucid and dignified, that seems to pervade the whole. She, too, made up the comprehensive index which, with the addition of a biographical memoir by the rabbi of Posen, Philip Bloch, a pupil and friend of Graetz, makes up the sixth and last volume of the American edition. Graetz probably saw only the first English volume, which appeared in 1891; the publication of the rest took place during the next few years, volume six being published in 1898.

In his introduction to the English edition, Graetz expressed himself as gratified, "for in countries where English is spoken, books are not only bought, bound and placed in libraries, but are also read, taken to heart and acted upon." Thus, apparently even historians think that the grass is greener in other pastures. And yet, there can be no doubt that this book has been among the most influential published for Jews in the English language.

It remained popular in the United States, as elsewhere, despite the fact that its faults became increasingly evident. The most obvious fault was that it no longer brought the story up to date. The English edition continues to 1870; but the past seventy years have been among the most significant in the long, eventful history of the Jewish people. Moreover, the twentieth century has belied some of the hopes and conclusions of the nineteenth. Some of what Graetz's generation thought important we consider trifling;

some of what he minimized we have promoted to first rank. Besides, Graetz himself was responsible for a spurt in historical research, so that a vast amount of information has been accumulated on various subjects bearing directly or indirectly on Jewish history. Finally, the Jewish community of the United States, not to mention similar if smaller Jewish communities in the rest of the Americas, in the South Pacific and in Africa, have come into being.

The easiest thing to do and the most immediately necessary was to tell the story of Israel during the last half of the nineteenth and the first half of the twentieth centuries. The Society felt that this was an obligation which it had to assume. The late Professor Ismar Elbogen was picked for the work, and he produced the stout volume which goes by the name *A Century of Jewish Life,* published in a format corresponding to the six volumes of the *History.*

The larger problem, however, still exists. Someday soon the history of the Jewish people will have to be rewritten on the basis of the new material and in accordance with new historical methods. Never again, in all likelihood, will a single genius arise who, like Graetz, will master all that has to be known for this purpose. It will have to be done by a group of scholars, each an expert in a tiny area of the vast field.

In the meantime, Graetz's *History,* despite all its faults, continues to serve an eminently useful purpose—to inspire, inform and, to some extent, encourage research. In fact, now that there are so few men able to refer to the original and unabridged German edition, it has been thought desirable to re-translate the complete German text, with all its footnotes and long, learned excursuses. The Society has undertaken this task too. It is no slight undertaking, and it will not be completed for some years to come.

For no matter what replaces Graetz's *History* as a book of reference, it will always remain a classic. It tells a glorious story with warmth and vigor. It continues to implant loyalty to the ideals of a heroic people. It makes the past speak to the present in terms that challenge men and lead them to noble action.

The Return From Babylon

After forty-nine years of exile, in the same month (Nisan) in which their ancestors had departed from Egypt some eight or nine centuries before, the Judaeans now left the land of Babylonia. It was the spring of the year (537) when they marched forth to take possession of their dearly-beloved home, of the much longed-for Jerusalem. It was a significant moment, carrying thousands of years in its bosom. Not like trembling slaves, just freed from their chains, did they go forth, but full of gladness, their hearts beating high with lofty hopes and swelling with enthusiasm. Singers, with stringed instruments and cymbals, accompanied them on their way, and they uttered new songs of praise, beginning and ending with the words:

"Give thanks unto the Lord, for He is good, for His mercy endureth for ever."

Those Judaeans who remained in Babylonia—and they were not a few—rich merchants and landed proprietors—evinced their sympathy for their brethren by escorting them part of the way, and by presenting them with rich gifts for the new buildings in their own country. Cyrus sent an escort of a thousand mounted soldiers to defend the Judaeans from the attacks of predatory tribes upon the way, and also to ensure their being able to take possession of Judaea. The prophecy but lately spoken was now to be realised:

> "In joy shall ye depart, and in peace shall ye be led home." *Isaiah iv. 12*

In peace and in safety the travellers completed the six hundred miles from Babylonia to Judaea, protected by the Persian escort. The exodus from Babylonia, unlike the one from Egypt, has left no reminiscences; it seemed needless to record the various halting-places, as, in all probability, no noteworthy incident occurred on the way.

> "God led them by the right path, and brought them to the place of their longing." *Psalm cvii. 7, 30*

When the travellers approached the land of their passionate desire, after a march of four or five months, their joy must have been overwhelming. The prophecies that had been uttered, the hopes they had cherished, the visions they had indulged in were realised. Meanwhile their happiness was not undimmed. The Holy City, the chief object of their longing, was desolate. A great part of the country was inhabited by strangers; in the north were the Samaritans, or Cuthaeans, in the south, the Idumaeans. But these races were soon obliged to give place to the descendants of Judah, who, with the tribe of Benjamin, returned to their ancient dwelling-places. The beginning of the new Judaean commonwealth was indeed humble and small. The people could not occupy the whole of the country which had once constituted the kingdom of Judah. A population of 40,000 was not numerous enough to settle a large territory. The colony was thus compelled to group itself round the capital at Jerusalem. This concentration of forces was, in some respects, advantageous, inasmuch as the whole population, being thus brought near to the capital, could take part in all its affairs. But, though the extremely confined territory of the new colony, and the small number of members in the community were calculated to depress the lofty hopes that their prophets in Babylonia had awakened, and fill the arrivals with gloom, unexpected circumstances arose to re-inspire them with energy. From many countries to the east, west, south, and north, from Egypt, Phoenicia, and even from the Greek coasts and islands, whither they had gone of their own free will or had been sold as slaves, Judaean exiles streamed back to crowd like children around their resurrected mother, Jerusalem. These new Jewish arrivals were accompanied by large numbers of strangers, both "great and small," illustrious and obscure, who collected round them. They were received with rejoicing, for they all acknowledged the God of Israel, and were ready to follow His laws. These new proselytes not only added strength to the young community, but also inspired the settlers with greater self-reliance, who, with their own eyes, saw words of the prophets fulfilled.

At the approach of the seventh month, in which, according to law and custom, various festivals occur, the elders of the families among all classes in Jerusalem assembled, and, marching under the command of their two leaders, the governor Zerubbabel and the high-priest Joshua, they proceeded to perform the first act of reconstruction—they erected an altar of stone. This altar was to be the nucleus of the Temple, the building of which was, for the present, impossible.

While the altar was dedicated with joyous and solemn ceremonies, the leaders were making preparations for the erection of this great and important edifice, which was to be the spiritual center of the new commonwealth. The rich gifts which they had brought with them enabled them to hire laborers and artisans, and, as in the days of King Solomon, cedar trees were procured from Lebanon; stone was brought from the mountains, and after enough had been quarried and shaped, steps were taken to lay the foundations of the Sanctuary. Not only Zerubbabel and Joshua, but also the heads of families, and a large number of the people were present at this ceremony, which was performed with great solemnity. The Aaronites again appeared in their priestly garments, sounding their trumpets; the Levites of the house of Asaph chanted songs of praise, thanking the Lord whose mercy endures for ever; and the people burst forth into a loud transport of joy. Yet there mingled with the jubilant notes the voice of regret that the new Temple was smaller and less magnificent than the old.

Jerusalem, so long mourned and wept over, began to rise from her ruins. The joyful enthusiasm called forth by the re-building of the city was, however, soon to be damped; the honeymoon of the young commonwealth waned rapidly, and anxious cares began to disturb its peace. Close to the boundaries of Judaea lived the mixed tribe of Samaritans or Cuthaeans. These people had in part accepted the doctrines taught them by an Israelitish priest at Bethel, but they had also retained many of their own idolatrous practices. Quite unexpectedly, some of the Samaritan chiefs came to Jerusalem, with the request that they might be allowed to help in re-building the Temple, and also that they be received into the Judaean community. This seemed so important a matter to the Judaeans, that a council was convoked to discuss the subject. The decision was against the Samaritans. Zerubbabel informed the Samaritan chiefs that their people neither would nor could be permitted to join in the re-building of the Temple. This decision was of great import for the entire future of the new common-wealth. From that day the Samaritans began to develop a hostile spirit against the Judaeans, which seemed to show that they had been less anxious to take part in the temple-service than to injure the community and to obstruct the re-building of the Temple. On the one hand, they tried to make those Judaeans with whom they came in contact lukewarm towards the project of building the Temple, and, on the other, they persuaded Persian officials to interfere with its execution, so that the work ceased for fully fifteen years. Again the Jews found themselves suffering evils sim-ilar to those which they had experienced after their first entry into Canaan. The neighbouring tribes envied them their strip of land,—on all sides they encountered hostility. They were powerless to defend themselves, for they lacked the means for carrying on war.

Chapter XIX

Theodor Herzl

The writer of the Judenstaat *was
born in Budapest in 1860 and died only 44 years
later, in 1904, in Vienna. The son of a prosperous
merchant, Herzl received the usual Jewish education of Reform Jews in the Vienna of his time. In
1878 he entered the University of Vienna, for his
family had left Budapest for the Austrian city. In
1884 he graduated as a Doctor of Laws and was soon
admitted to the bar. Literature, however, interested
him far more than law, and he soon gave up the bar
for writing. He was a contributor to the* Tageblatt
*of Berlin and in 1887 was made feuilleton editor of
the* Allgemeine Zeitung *of Vienna. When some of
his plays were produced, he won a rather wide literary reputation and became Paris correspondent
of the* Neue Freie Presse *of Vienna in 1892. Even
at this point he was not unaware of his Jewish
heritage, for he had written a piece on French anti-
Semitism and a play, "The New Ghetto," which
revealed his connection with his people. But it was*

251

*the notorious Dreyfus Case in 1894 which pro-
voked him into a frenzy of action and thought on
Jewish problems.*

*In 1895 he interviewed Baron de Hirsch, moved
into the field of political action and began his diaries. He also produced a pamphlet called "Address
to the Rothschilds" which, revised and enlarged,
became the famous* Judenstaat *(The Jewish State),
published in 1896.*

*The rest of Herzl's brief life was spent in trying
to rouse the Jewish people to mass action for a Jewish homeland and to interest the political leaders
of his time—Kings, Emperors, Sultans, Prime Min-
isters—in the idea of a Jewish homeland. He met
Kaiser Wilhelm and the Turkish Sultan. He
broached various ideas and always tried to raise
funds either to help Jewish immigration to Palestine, or to win the support of unconvinced political
leaders. He finally discovered that his best support-
ers were the Jewish people and found backers in*

London, in Vienna, in Berlin and in Russia. Max Nordau, a famous writer of the time, became his most enthusiastic follower. In 1897 he called the first Zionist Congress, in Basle, Switzerland, and later wrote in his diary that he felt it was at this time that he had founded the Jewish state. Because he was willing to consider Uganda and Argentina as a Jewish homeland instead of Palestine, he clashed with his fellow Zionists, but he soon swore fealty to Zion and Jerusalem. Overworked, he died at 44 in Vienna and only recently his remains were removed to a grave in Jerusalem in reborn Israel.

JUDENSTAAT (THE JEWISH STATE)

Joachim Prinz

Most great Jewish books are anonymous in a profound sense. Not that the author is generally unknown, but the details of his biography have become unimportant. At times the author's name has been forgotten, and he is remembered only by the title of his work.

But the *Judenstaat* is Theodor Herzl's book. Neither its content nor its influence can be understood without an analysis of the author. It is the first Jewish book that stirred Jewry after the Western emancipation. Not that Herzl's topic or even his approach to the Jewish problem had been utterly novel. Moses Hess wrote his *Rome and Jerusalem* in 1862, and it is far superior to Herzl's *Judenstaat*. Leon Pinsker's *Auto-Emancipation,* published twenty years later, is more concise and in parts more impressive than the *Judenstaat*. Neither of the two, however, was able to create the movement that was to implement their ideas. The *Judenstaat* did. Its consequences and its impact upon masses of people can only be compared with Karl Marx's *Das Kapital* and with the Communist *Manifesto*.

254

Three factors account for the success of the little book which Herzl called, "my pamphlet:" the unusual spiritual-political circumstances of the times; the post-emancipatory disappointment of world Jewry, and the unique personality of Theodor Herzl.

Few decades in the world history can boast of so many accomplishments in almost every field of human endeavor: Bell invented the telephone; Edison the electric bulb; Henry George wrote *Progress and Poverty* and Tolstoy preached Socialism in novels; Brahms and Wagner were but two of the galaxy of great composers; Rodin and Renoir, Toulouse-Lautrec and Degas began to emerge from the great battle of the impressionists; the great French novel (Victor Hugo and Emile Zola); the dramatic play of social significance (Shaw and Wilde in England, Ibsen and Strindberg in Scandinavia, Tolstoy in Russia and Hauptmann in Germany); the organization of trade unions; the revolutionary discoveries in chemistry; the final emergence of the middle class and the bourgeois military caste; the widening conflict between a newly awakened nationalism and the beginnings of liberalism in political as well as social thinking. It is against this background of events that the *Judenstaat* must be viewed. Is it any wonder that a generation so wide awake, so profoundly alerted to the new miracles and so piously devoted to faith in progress should have listened attentively to a call for a "new order" in the affairs of the Jewish people? Herzl himself was part of the dreams and ideals of his time.

The Jewish world was sharply divided into East and West. Oriental Jewry was not even known. Elkan N. Adler's book on Oriental Jewry came as a shocking surprise. Western Jewry looked with disdain upon the unemancipated masses of the East. Of their Jewish life, their creativity and piety and their Jewish devotion, they knew nothing. Nobody would have dared to sing a Yiddish folk song in society or at a Jewish meeting anywhere in the Western Jewish world. Of Jewish literature, only the sweetish romanticism of Karl Emil Franzos and Israel Zangwill's ghetto stories seemed acceptable. Any real contact with East European Jewry was avoided.

The reason for this lay in fear and basic insecurity. Although the decrees of Jewish emancipation had been solemnly signed and although prosperity among the Western Jews of Herzl's generation was widespread, there was a general feeling of insecurity. To determine the real Jewish situation underneath the surface happiness and success, one needed a seismograph. The slightest disturbance spelled catastrophe: the tragic comedy of Alfred Dreyfus (Clemenceau, then a young lawyer, claimed that Dreyfus was the only one who did not comprehend the anti-Semitic nature of his own case) removed at once the veneer of French civilization and good French citizens crowded the streets of Paris and yelled, *"a bas les Juives;"* an alleged shabby business deal of the Jewish ammunition manufacturer, Loewe, elevated a miserable school master, Ahlwart, to leadership of the anti-Semitic movement in Berlin; and the black Friday at the stock exchange in 1893 was the beginning of a mass movement against the "international Jew." Nor could the Jews be made to believe that these attacks upon their emancipation were caused by the base instincts of the masses. After all, Richard Wagner the composer, Heinrich Treitschke the historian, Houston Stewart Chamberlain the writer, and Adolf Stoecher the Protestant minister, were among the leaders. . . .

It was necessary for Western Jewry to comfort itself with a theory that would explain the strange "medieval movement of anti-Semitism." To the Western Jews, anti-Semitism was the manifestation of lack of enlightenment and thus they proceeded to enlighten the Christian world. This was done through the *Alliance Israelite Universelle* in Paris, the *Central Verein* in Berlin, the *Union* in Vienna, which were the leading Jewish organizations of these countries and fully represented the beliefs of the majority of the Jewish people. The magazines and books published at that time reassured the world of Jewish patriotism; recorded proudly every Jew who had died "on the field of honor" or had made an important scientific contribution; denied emphatically any tie with world Jewry; and sought to emphasize the ethical foundations of Judaism rather than the colorful customs which distinguished Judaism from Christianity. Anti-Semitism was a real force in the life of the majority of the Jews in Western countries. It was difficult to prevent Jews from intermarrying; more than one hundred twenty-five thousand had changed their religion since the emancipation was proclaimed.

Theodor Herzl, it must be remembered, was not far removed from this world. There was a time when to him, too, conversion was the only possible solution. "Two years ago," he wrote in the spring of 1895, "I meant to solve the Jewish problem with the help of the Catholic Church, at least in Austria. I meant to go to the Pope and ask him to help us in the fight against anti-Semitism. 'If you do as I say, I shall make myself the leader of a huge movement aiming at a voluntary and honest conversion to Christianity.'" His plan was to lead a solemn procession of Viennese Jews "on a Sunday morning at twelve o'clock noon to Stephan's

Cathedral with church bells ringing. It should be done un-ashamedly and proudly." Ironically enough, it took Bene-dikt, his publisher, a confirmed anti-Zionist and assimila-tionist, to convince him how undignified and impractical the plan was. "For one hundred generations your family preserved its ties with the Jewish people. Yet now, you take it upon yourself to terminate it. You can't do it. You must not do it. Furthermore, the Pope won't see you anyway." It is not clear which of the two arguments convinced him; at any rate, Herzl gave up the idea.

A few days later in a conversation with a friend, Lud-wig Speidel, music critic of the *Neue Freie Presse*, he be-gan a new train of thoughts, the first beginnings of the *Judenstaat*. He recorded it thus:

> *I begin to understand anti-Semitism. It is the con-sequence of our emancipation. . . . But anti-Semi-tism which lives in the masses as something strong and subconscious will not hurt the Jews. On the contrary, it will serve us well. . . . Hardships are good means of education. It will lead to Darwin's mimicry. The Jews will be integrated. They are sea lions which world accident threw into water. Thus they pretend to be fishes. They adopt the appear-ance and characteristics of fishes. Yet if they ever were to land again on dry land and were permitted to stay there for a few generations, their fins would change into feet. Only new pressure can remove the traces of pressure.*

Speidel was impressed with what he called "a world his-toric concept" of the Jewish problem. A few experiences

which followed this conversation are recorded in Herzl's
diary: some anti-Semitic incidents; a service at the famous
synagogue on *rue de la Victoire* in Paris; and a discussion
with Fredrich Beer who did Herzl's bust. During the ex-
cited discussion with Beer, Herzl conceived the idea of a
play which was to deal with the Jewish problem. It took
him "three glorious weeks" to write "The New Ghetto."
As a play it was mediocre, and offered no real solution.
The duel between the anti-Semitic nobleman and the Jew
ends with the death of the Jew. The death of his hero in
the play was in reality a suicide. Indeed the idea of suicide
plagued Herzl throughout his lifetime. In terms of a real
solution of the Jewish problem as a problem of the people,
personal and individual solutions meant little.

It was at that time that his plan for a pamphlet began
to be formulated. He meant to call it, "A Survey on the
Jewish People" (*Zustaende der Juden*). It represented a
reporter's approach to the problem. "I intended to visit
those places into which world-accident had scattered them:
Russia, Galicia, Hungary, Bohemia, later the Orient and the
new Zionist colonies and then again, West Europe." The
aim of this survey was to prove to the world that the Jews
were innocent victims and that "they were being slandered
without being known." This is still the ideology of the as-
similationist. It is still apologetic. The plan, however, was
dropped in favor of a novel.

A novel was closer to Herzl's heart. Alphonse Daudet,
the French novelist and an anti-Semite, reminded him of
the far-reaching influence of *Uncle Tom's Cabin* upon the
emancipation of the American Negro. The plot for the
novel was almost ready. Again suicide played a central
role. This time it is not the hero but a symbolic Jew, Sam-

uel Kohn, who commits suicide "because he was not able
to discover his Promised Land." The plot is meager and
Herzl's love for the melodrama would have made this an
almost unbearable novel. Happily, he decided upon what
he called "a practical idea." This meant a serious political
pamphlet.

Although Herzl could not account for the sudden change
to this new form, it seems abundantly clear that his letters
to Baron Hirsch and the conversation that followed, were
responsible for this. The first letter is vague. The second
(May 4, 1895), however, has all the characteristics of style
and approach of the *Judenstaat.* "So far" he writes to
Hirsch, "you were merely a philanthropist. I shall show
you how to grow." This is the almost impertinent style of
most of Herzl's letters. There is an abruptness and direct-
ness of speech which is at once insulting and appealing.
The conversation which followed was decisive. Herzl, who
during the entire period watched himself as though he were
looking at a historic drama and did things deliberately in
the light of it, played his role well. Although he did not
admit it immediately, he played the role of Moses before
Pharaoh. The real Pharaohs were yet to come. In his conversation with Hirsch he speaks almost in Biblical terms:
"I shall go to the German Kaiser. He will understand me
for he was trained to understand big things. I shall tell him,
'Let us go. We are strangers. One does not permit us to assimilate and we can't do it. Let us go.'" This role fits him
well. He begins to like it. And perhaps with a trembling
heart he pretends to be bold. His language is. "Do you have
a full hour for me?" he says to Hirsch. "If you don't, let's
not even start." Herzl's summary of the conversation is: "I
was not disappointed. On the contrary, I was stimulated."

The *Judenstaat* was the result of this stimulation. "At home something pulled me to the desk. I wrote walking, standing, in the street, at the table and at night when I could not sleep." At times he was not quite sure of his sanity. "Were it not so logical, I should call it 'compulsion neurosis.'" In older days such a state of mind was called "inspiration." In this state of exultation he wrote some seventy pages of the most fantastic plans which he wanted to incorporate into the *Judenstaat*. In the final version, however, many of these "thought splinters" were left out. They are part of what he called "Address to the Family Circle of the Rothschilds." The idea became an obsession with him that the fortune of the Rothschild family should finance his plans. As he began to think in terms of a catastrophe which sooner or later would overwhelm the Jewish people, he considered this plan the only means of saving the huge fortune of the family.

The manuscript was to be read to two friends, Rabbi Moritz Guedemann, the Chief Rabbi of Vienna, and Heinrich Mayer-Cohen, a philanthropist from Berlin. Herzl thought of a gigantic setting—the Alps in Glion, Switzerland. Only snow-covered mountains could form the proper background for an idea that tried to reach the stars and was as gigantic in his mind as the eternal snow on the mountain-tops. The plans, however, were changed and he had to choose the drab surroundings of a Jewish restaurant in Munich. The two men were impressed, even enthusiastic. Guedemann called him a Moses. It was then that he realized that his plan which he wanted subsidized by the Rothschilds, transcended the concern of one family and that it could only be carried out by the people for whom it was intended—a factor mightier than any bank or any

family fortune. The Jewish people were included in the
plans. And so, the frills and trimmings disappeared and
the *Judenstaat* was conceived and written. It is not a uni-
form book, either in style or in content. Some of the
"thought splinters" disturb the flow of the book. Yet it contains two important parts: the theory of the Jewish question
and a sketch of the apparatus which was to lead to its solution. When the English translation appeared in London in
1896, its title was, *The Jewish State—An Attempt at a
Modern Solution of the Jewish Question.*

The slightly more than seventy pages that constitute the
Judenstaat made fantastic reading. They contained the
theory of the new movement and a plan of action. Although the plan was widely discussed and formed the basis
for practical work in Palestine, it was the theory that converted Jewry to the new movement. For a theory was badly
needed, particularly in Europe where no movement could
grow without accepting a clearly defined ideology. Herzl's
Judenstaat became literally the Bible and the catechism of
European Zionism. The decades following the publication
of the *Judenstaat* were devoted to ideological discussion
rather than merely practical work. The interpretation of
this Bible of Zionism in hundreds of books and thousands
of articles, not to speak of the endless discussions at Zionist
meetings all over the world, formed the backbone of the
movement at a time when colonization and immigration
were virtually at a standstill. European Jewry in the West,
by virtue of tendencies of assimilation, in the East as a result of Haskalah, the movement of enlightenment, was passing through a crisis of Jewish religion. Zionism was the
secular substitute for it and the new ideology created by
the *Judenstaat* almost replaced the religious dogma.

The starting point of the ideology presented in the *Juden-staat* was the "understanding" and new interpretation of anti-Semitism. Herzl was not satisfied with the definition of anti-Semitism in the literature of his contemporaries. Anti-Semitism could not be due to a lack of enlightenment. Anti-Semitism was much more deep-seated and therefore beyond the reach of rational enlightenment. "The old preju-dices against us still lie deep in the hearts of the people. One only needs to listen to the people where they speak frankly and simply: both proverb and fairy tale are anti-Semitic." This anti-Semitism so profoundly imbedded in the character of the Christian world must therefore be con-sidered a reaction to the *existence* of the Jewish people rather than to any *action* on their part. This anti-Semitism causes oppression and pogroms. Since the Jewish people are not better than other people, it does not improve their character. "Oppression naturally creates hostility against oppressors and our hostility aggravates the pressure. It is impossible to escape from this vicious circle." Nor can anti-Semitism be cured by assimilation. "We have honestly tried everywhere to merge ourselves into the social life of our environment and to preserve only the religion of our fa-thers. They will not permit us to do so."

What then is the *cause* of anti-Semitism? It is contained in one sentence which we consider the basic statement in the *Judenstaat*. It became the slogan of the new movement. With this simple, short sentence which sounds trite today, Herzl began the revolution in Jewish thinking. The sen-tence reads: "We are a people—one people." Here was the theory of anti-Semitism and the explanation for the abnor-mal existence of the Jewish people. Scattered all over the globe, the Jews remained a people within the nations

among whom they lived. The proof was the existence of the
Jewish question: "The Jewish question exists. Nobody can
doubt it." The Jews remained not only *a* people among the
various nations, but also *one* people across all the borders,
transcending language, habit and national custom which
they may have accepted in the countries of their adoption.
Since the Jews constituted one people, the interpretation of
anti-Semitic phenomena by contemporary writers was wrong.
There must be an approach that would apply to the affair
of Alfred Dreyfus in France as well as to the pogroms in Russia, to the anti-Semitic movements in Germany, to the anti-
Jewish trials in Hungary and to the violent anti-Semitism in
Vienna. These were not to be regarded as isolated national
occurrences but as manifestations of a single phenomenon.
This phenomenon was called "the Jewish question," and it
was the entire problem which the *Judenstaat* proposed to
solve.

A very important point of the *Judenstaat* is usually over-
looked in the many interpretations of the book. It is what
Herzl calls "the propelling force." This is, to our mind, the
very crux of the movement which Herzl founded and without which the *Judenstaat* would have been forgotten and
the Zionist movement would not have existed. It shows not
only Herzl's daring but his understanding of the elements
of a political movement. Against the background of Jewish
prosperity in the Western countries, where Jews were suc-
cessful in contemporary banking, manufacturing, sciences,
literature and music, he dared to predict that anti-Semitism,
instead of disappearing, would increase to such an extent
as to make the life of the Jews in the West as well as in the
East, utterly unbearable. He introduced into the discussion,
a new term: *Judennot*—Jewish misery. It corresponds in his

theory to the place which the idea of the "increasing misery of the working masses" has in the socialist theory of Karl Marx. Political movements are doomed to failure if they lack the daring to predict for their whole foreseeable future, the economic and political development of the group at which they are aimed. But daring alone is not enough. Daily reality must furnish sufficient proof that the political theory is more than a sermon. The labor movement based upon the theory of the "increasing misery of the working masses" grew because the theory proved to be true. Herzl's *Judenstaat* would have remained a pamphlet and a Utopian idea without the prediction of increasing Jewish misery and without the fulfillment of this prophecy. "In Russia the Tzar will kill us, in Germany the Kaiser will issue decrees and there will be expropriation from above." These were daring words at a time when everybody was speaking of progress.

For the complexities of the Jewish question, Herzl had a relatively simple solution. "The whole plan is in its essence simple, as it must be if everybody is to understand it. Let sovereignty be granted us over a portion of the globe large enough to satisfy the rightful requirements of a nation. The rest we shall manage for ourselves. The creation of a new state is neither ridiculous nor impossible . . . the governments of all countries, plagued by anti-Semitism, will be keenly interested in assisting us to obtain the sovereignty we want."

The idea of the state is clear, yet Herzl was in doubt as to the country where the Jewish State was to be established. "Shall we choose Palestine or Argentina? . . . Argentina is one of the most fertile countries in this world, extending over a vast area. It has a sparse population and a mild climate. . . . Palestine is our ever-memorable historic home." Thus the idea of the *Judenstaat* does not necessarily mean Palestine. It aims at a state. It means sovereignty. And it means, above all, an international guarantee in the form of a charter to be obtained from one of the existing governments. But the choice of the land is left to a commission which will decide between Argentina and Palestine, or even other countries in the world. Herzl was as undecided about the country as he was about many other matters, particularly in regard to the Hebrew language. Assimilated Jew that he was, he could not conceive of Hebrew as the language of the people and was quite surprised when Dr. M. Berkowicz asked for permission to translate the *Judenstaat* into Hebrew. He was certain that one of the European languages would be acceptable to most Jews. There are other parts of the "practical plan" which make strange reading today, yet its framework remains an ingenious part of the *Judenstaat*.

Herzl envisaged the creation of two organizations: "The Society of Jews" and "The Jewish Company." It is interesting that in the German original, the two terms are used in English. Headquarters of both organizations were to be in London. Herzl was convinced that whatever country would be selected, England would play a major part in the creation of the state. "The Society of Jews will do the preparatory work in the fields of science and politics," and The Jewish Company will be responsible for the practical implementation. The Society of Jews will represent the Jewish people in the Diaspora. It will be its national address. It will take the place of the state as long as the state does not exist.

What Herzl envisaged by his Society of Jews was fulfilled by the World Zionist Organization and later by the Jewish Agency for Palestine. And his Jewish Company found its counterpart in those organizations which did the practical work in the upbuilding of the land. A good many of the details in Herzl's plan for the Jewish State became obsolete: his concept of an "aristocratic republic," his general tendency toward some mild form of dictatorship; some of his proposals for practical implementation. But the strange details did not obscure the sublime message of the *Judenstaat,* nor detract from its influence. Had Herzl limited his book to his theory of the Jewish question and to the bare outline of his plan, the *Judenstaat* would still have been the most stirring and influential of modern Jewish books. It captured the imagination of the Jewish people. It invested Jewish life with new meaning. The *Judenstaat* became the credo of the modern Jew.

selection from JUDENSTAAT

Chapter I.—Introduction

It is astonishing how little insight into the science of economics many of the men who move in the midst of active life possess. Hence it is that even Jews faithfully repeat the cry of the anti-Semites: "We depend for sustenance on the nations who are our hosts, and if we had no hosts to support us we should die of starvation." This is a point that shows how unjust accusations may weaken our self-knowledge. But what are the true grounds for this statement concerning the nations that act as "hosts"? Where it is not based on limited physiocratic views it is founded on the childish error that commodities pass from hand to hand in continuous rotation. We need not wake from long slumber, like Rip van Winkle, to realize that the world is considerably altered by the production of new commodities. The technical progress made during this wonderful era enables even a man of most limited intelligence to note with his short-sighted eyes the appearance of new commodities all around him. The spirit of enterprise has created them.

Labor without enterprise is the stationary labor of ancient days; and typical of it is the work of the husbandman, who stands now just where his progenitors stood a thousand years ago. All our material welfare has been brought about by men of enterprise. I feel almost ashamed of writing down so trite a remark. Even if we were a nation of entrepreneurs—such as absurdly exaggerated accounts make us out to be—we should not require another nation to live on. We do not depend on the circulation of old commodities, because we produce new ones.

The world possesses slaves of extraordinary capacity for work, whose appearance has been fatal to the production of handmade goods: these slaves are the machines. It is true that workmen are required to set machinery in motion; but for this we have men in plenty, in super-abundance. Only those who are ignorant of the condition of Jews in many countries of Eastern Europe would venture to assert that Jews are either unfit or unwilling to perform manual labor.

But I do not wish to take up the cudgels for the Jews in this pamphlet. It would be useless. Everything rational and everything sentimental that can possibly be said in their defense has been said already. If one's hearers are incapable of comprehending them, one is a preacher in a desert. And if one's hearers are broad- and high-minded enough to have grasped them already, then the sermon is superfluous. I believe in the ascent of man to higher and yet higher grades of civilization; but I consider this ascent to be desperately slow. Were we to wait till average humanity had become as charitably inclined as was Lessing when he wrote "Nathan the Wise," we should wait beyond our day, beyond the days of our children, of our grandchildren, and of our great-grandchildren. But the world's spirit comes to our aid in another way.

This century has given the world a wonderful renaissance by means of its technical achievements; but at the same time its miraculous improvements have not been employed in the service of humanity. Distance has ceased to be an obstacle, yet we complain of insufficient space. Our great steamships carry us swiftly and surely over hitherto unvisited seas. Our railways carry us safely into a mountain-world hitherto tremblingly scaled on foot. Events occurring in countries undiscovered when Europe confined the Jews in Ghettos are known to us in the course of an hour. Hence the misery of the Jews is an anachronism—not because there was a period of enlightenment one hundred years ago, for that enlightenment reached in reality only the choicest spirits.

I believe that electric light was not invented for the purpose of illuminating the drawing-rooms of a few snobs, but rather for the purpose of throwing light on some of the dark problems of humanity. One of these problems, and not the least of them, is the Jewish question. In solving it we are working not only for ourselves, but also for many other over-burdened and oppressed beings.

The Jewish question still exists. It would be foolish to deny it. It is a remnant of the Middle Ages, which civilized nations do not even yet seem able to shake off, try as they will. They certainly showed a generous desire to do so when they emancipated us. The Jewish question exists wherever Jews live in perceptible numbers. Where it does not exist, it is carried by Jews in the course of their migrations. We naturally move to those places where we are not persecuted, and there our presence produces persecution.

This is the case in every country, and will remain so, even in those highly civilized—for instance, France—until the Jewish question finds a solution on a political basis. The unfortunate Jews are now carrying the seeds of Anti-Semitism into England; they have already introduced it into America.

I believe that I understand Anti-Semitism, which is really a highly complex movement. I consider it from a Jewish standpoint, yet without fear or hatred. I believe that I can see what elements there are in it of vulgar sport, of common trade jealousy, of inherited prejudice, of religious intolerance, and also of pretended self-defense. I think the Jewish question is no more a social than a religious one, notwithstanding that it sometimes takes these and other forms. It is a national question, which can only be solved by making it a political world-question to be discussed and settled by the civilized nations of the world in council.

We are a people—one people.

We have honestly endeavored everywhere to merge ourselves in the social life of surrounding communities and to preserve the faith of our fathers. We are not permitted to do so. In vain are we loyal patriots, our loyalty in some places running to extremes; in vain do we make the same sacrifices of life and property as our fellow-citizens; in vain do we strive to increase the fame of our native land in science and art, or her wealth by trade and commerce. In countries where we have lived for centuries we are still cried down as strangers, and often by those whose ancestors were not yet domiciled in the land where Jews had already had experience of suffering. The majority may decide which are the strangers; for this, as indeed every point which arises in the relations between nations, is a question of might. I do not here surrender any portion of our prescriptive right, when I make this statement merely in my own name as an individual. In the world as it now is and for an indefinite period will probably remain, might precedes right. It is useless, therefore, for us to be loyal patriots, as were the Huguenots who were forced to emigrate. If we could only be left in peace.

But I think we shall not be left in peace.

Oppression and persecution cannot exterminate us. No nation on earth has survived such struggles and sufferings as we have gone through. Jew-baiting has merely stripped off our weaklings; the strong among us were invariably true to their race when persecution broke out against them. This attitude was most clearly apparent in the period immediately following the emancipation of the Jews. Those Jews who were advanced intellectually and materially entirely lost the feeling of belonging to their race. Wherever our political well-being has lasted for any length of time, we have assimilated with our surroundings. I think this is not discreditable. Hence, the statesman who would wish to see a Jewish strain in his nation would have to provide for the duration of our political well-being; and even a Bismarck could not do that.

For old prejudices against us still lie deep in the hearts of the people. He who would have proofs of this need only listen to the people where they speak with frankness and simplicity: proverb and fairy-tale are both Anti-Semitic. A nation is everywhere a great child, which can certainly be educated; but its education would, even in most favorable circumstances, occupy such a vast amount of time that we could, as already mentioned, remove our own difficulties by other means long before the process was accomplished.

Assimilation, by which I understood not only external conformity in dress, habits, customs, and language, but also identity of feeling and manner—assimilation of Jews could be effected only by intermarriage. But the need for mixed marriages would have to be felt by the majority; their mere recognition by law would certainly not suffice.

The Hungarian Liberals, who have just given legal sanction to mixed marriages, have made a remarkable mistake which one of the earliest cases clearly illustrates; a baptized Jew married a Jewess. At the same time the struggle to obtain the present form of marriage accentuated distinctions between Jews and Christians, thus hindering rather than aiding the fusion of races.

Those who really wished to see the Jews disappear through intermixture with other nations, can only hope to see it come about in one way. The Jews must previously acquire economic power sufficiently great to overcome the old social prejudice against them. The aristocracy may serve as an example of this, for in its ranks occur the proportionately largest numbers of mixed marriages. The Jewish families which regild the old nobility with their money become gradually absorbed. But what form would this phenomenon assume in the middle classes, where (the Jews being a bourgeois people) the Jewish question is mainly concentrated? A previous acquisition of power could be synonymous with that economic supremacy which Jews are already erroneously declared to possess. And if the power they now possess creates rage and indignation among the Anti-Semites, what outbreaks would such an increase of power create? Hence the first step towards absorption will never be taken, because this step would involve the subjection of the majority to a hitherto scorned minority, possessing neither military nor administrative power of its own. I think, therefore, that the absorption of Jews by means of their prosperity is unlikely to occur. In countries which now are Anti-Semitic my view will be approved. In others, where Jews now feel comfortable, it will probably be violently disputed by them. My happier coreligionists will not believe me till Jew-baiting teaches them the truth; for the longer Anti-Semitism lies in abeyance the more fiercely will it break out. The infiltration of immigrating Jews, attracted to a land by apparent security, and the ascent in the social scale of native Jews, combine powerfully to bring about a revolution. Nothing is plainer than this rational conclusion.

Because I have drawn this conclusion with complete indifference to everything but the quest of truth, I shall probably be contradicted and opposed by Jews who are in easy circumstances. Insofar as private interests alone are held by their anxious or timid possessors to be in danger, they can safely be ignored, for the concerns of the poor and oppressed are of greater importance than theirs. But I wish from the outset to prevent any misconception from arising, particularly the mistaken notion that my project, if realized, would in the least degree injure property now held by Jews. I shall therefore explain everything connected with rights of property very fully. Whereas, if my plan never becomes anything more than a piece of literature, things will merely remain as they are. It might more reasonably be objected that I am giving a handle to Anti-Semitism when I say we are a people—one people; that I am hindering the assimilation of Jews where it is about to be consummated, and endangering it where it is an accomplished fact, insofar as it is possible for a solitary writer to hinder or endanger anything.

This objection will be especially brought forward in France. It will probably also be made in other countries, but I shall answer only the French Jews beforehand, because these afford the most striking example of my point.

However much I may worship personality—powerful individual personality in statesmen, inventors, artists, philosophers, or leaders, as well as the collective personality of a historic group of human beings, which we call a nation—however much I may worship personality, I do not regret its disappearance. Whoever can, will, and must perish, let him perish. But the distinctive nationality of Jews neither can, will, nor must be destroyed. It cannot be destroyed, because external enemies consolidate it. It will not be destroyed; this is shown during two thousand years of appalling suffering. It must not be destroyed, and that, as a descendant of numberless Jews who refused to despair, I am trying once more to prove in this pamphlet. Whole branches of Judaism may wither and fall, but the trunk will remain.

Hence, if all or any of the French Jews protest against this scheme on account of their own "assimilation," my answer is simple: The whole thing does not concern them at all. They are Jewish Frenchmen, well and good! This is a private affair for the Jews alone.

The movement towards the organization of the State I am proposing would, of course, harm Jewish Frenchmen no more than it would harm the "assimilated" of other countries. It would, on the contrary, be distinctly to their advantage. For they would no longer be disturbed in their "chromatic function," as Darwin puts it, but would be able

to assimilate in peace, because the present Anti-Semitism
would have been stopped for ever. They would certainly be
credited with being assimilated to the very depths of their
souls, if they stayed where they were after the new Jewish
State, with its superior institutions, had become a reality.

The "assimilated" would profit even more than Christian
citizens by the departure of faithful Jews; for they would
be rid of the disquieting, incalculable, and unavoidable
rivalry of a Jewish proletariat, driven by poverty and political pressure from place to place, from land to land. This
floating proletariat would become stationary. Many Christian citizens—whom we call Anti-Semites—can now offer
determined resistance to the immigration of foreign Jews.
Jewish citizens cannot do this, although it affects them far
more directly; for on them they feel first of all the keen
competition of individuals carrying on similar branches of
industry, who, in addition, either introduce Anti-Semitism
where it does not exist, or intensify it where it does. The
"assimilated" give expression to this secret grievance in
"philanthropic" undertakings. They organize emigration so-
cieties for wandering Jews. There is a reverse to the picture
which would be comic, if it did not deal with human beings. For some of these charitable institutions are created
not for, but against, persecuted Jews; they are created to
dispatch these poor creatures just as fast and far as possible. And thus, many an apparent friend of the Jews turns
out, on careful inspection, to be nothing more than an Anti-
Semite of Jewish origin, disguised as a philanthropist.

But the attempts at colonization made even by really
benevolent men, interesting attempts though they were,
have so far been unsuccessful. I do not think that this or
that man took up the matter merely as an amusement, that

they engaged in the emigration of poor Jews as one indulges in the racing of horses. The matter was too grave and tragic for such treatment. These attempts were interesting, in that they represented on a small scale the practical forerunners of the idea of a Jewish State. They were even useful, for out of their mistakes may be gathered experience for carrying the idea out successfully on a larger scale. They have, of course, done harm also. The transportation of Anti-Semitism to new districts, which is the inevitable consequence of such artificial infiltration, seems to me to be the least of these evils. Far worse is the circumstance that unsatisfactory results tend to cast doubts on intelligent men. What is unpractical or impossible to accomplish on a small scale, need not necessarily be so on a larger one. A small enterprise may result in loss under the same conditions which would make a large one pay. A rivulet cannot even be navigated by boats, the river into which it flows carries stately iron vessels.

No human being is wealthy or powerful enough to transplant a nation from one habitation to another. An idea alone can achieve that: and this idea of a State may have the requisite power to do so. The Jews have dreamt this kingly dream all through the long nights of their history. "Next year in Jerusalem" is our old phrase. It is now a question of showing that the dream can be converted into a living reality.

For this, many old, outgrown, confused and limited notions must first be entirely erased from the minds of men. Dull brains might, for instance, imagine that this exodus would be from civilized regions into the desert. That is not the case. It will be carried out in the midst of civilization. We shall not revert to a lower stage, we shall rise to a

higher (ne. We shall not dwell in mud huts; we shall build
new more beautiful and more modern houses, and possess
them in safety. We shall not lose our acquired possessions;
we shall realize them. We shall surrender our well earned
rights only for better ones. We shall not sacrifice our beloved customs; we shall find them again. We shall not
leave our old home before the new one is prepared for us.
Those only will depart who are sure thereby to improve
their position; those who are now desperate will go first,
after them the poor; next the prosperous, and, last of all,
the wealthy. Those who go in advance will raise themselves
to a higher grade, equal to that whose representatives will
shortly follow. Thus the exodus will be at the same time an
ascent of the class.

The departure of the Jews will involve no economic dis-
turbances, no crises, no persecutions; in fact, the countries
they abandon will revive to a new period of prosperity.
There will be an inner migration of Christian citizens into
the positions evacuated by Jews. The outgoing current will
be gradual, without any disturbance, and its initial movement will put an end to Anti-Semitism. The Jews will leave
as honored friends, and if some of them return, they will
receive the same favorable welcome and treatment at the
hands of civilized nations as is accorded to all foreign visitors. Their exodus will have no resemblance to a flight, for
it will be a well-regulated movement under control of public opinion. The movement will not only be inaugurated
with absolute conformity to law, but it cannot even be carried out without the friendly cooperation of interested Governments, who would derive considerable benefits from it.

Security for the integrity of the idea and the vigor of its
execution will be found in the creation of a body corporate,

or corporation. This corporation will be called "The Society of Jews." In addition to it there will be a Jewish company, an economically productive body.

An individual who attempted even to undertake this huge task alone, would be either an impostor or a madman. The personal character of the members of the corporation will guarantee its integrity, and the adequate capital of the Company will prove its stability.

These prefatory remarks are merely intended as a hasty reply to the mass of objections which the very words "Jewish State" are certain to arouse. Henceforth we shall proceed more slowly to meet further objections and to explain in detail what has been as yet only indicated; and we shall try in the interests of this pamphlet to avoid making it a dull exposition. Short aphoristic chapters will therefore best answer the purpose.

If I wish to substitute a new building for an old one, I must demolish before I construct. I shall therefore keep to this natural sequence. In the first and general part I shall explain my ideas, remove all prejudices, determine essential political and economic conditions, and develop the plan.

In the special part, which is divided into three principal sections, I shall describe its execution. These three sections are: The Jewish Company, Local Groups, and the Society of Jews. The Society is to be created first, the Company last; but in this exposition the reverse order is preferable, because it is the financial soundness of the enterprise which will chiefly be called into question, and doubts on this score must be removed first.

In the conclusion, I shall try to meet every further objection that could possibly be made. My Jewish readers will, I hope, follow me patiently to the end. Some will naturally make their objections in an order of succession other than that chosen for their refutation. But whoever finds his doubts dispelled should give allegiance to the cause.

Although I speak of reason, I am fully aware that reason alone will not suffice. Old prisoners do not willingly leave their cells. We shall see whether the youth whom we need are at our command—the youth, who irresistibly draw on the old, carry them forward on strong arms, and transform rational motives into enthusiasm.

Ahad Ha-am

Asher Ginzberg, who used the pen-name of Ahad Ha-am (One of the People), was born in Russia in 1856. His father was a wealthy merchant, a Hassid of great learning. Young Asher was therefore brought up in a bookish atmosphere and, at 16, was an accomplished Talmudist—and a husband. Filial piety kept him in his parental home for a dozen years after his marriage, but in 1884 he left for Odessa and it was only at the age of 30 that he began to lead his own life. Having absorbed a good deal of secular knowledge, European culture was his ideal until the savage pogroms in Russia in 1881. He realized that the Haskalah (the period of Enlightenment) was no real solution for the Jewish problem and began to think about Zion. Odessa was then a center of the Hibbat Zion movement and Ginzberg soon became an active member of the group, and a member of its central committee. Under the name of Ahad Ha-am he wrote an article called Lo Zeh Haderech *(This*

281

is Not the Way) for the Hebrew periodical Hame-
litz, *which played a decisive role in his life. It won
him foes and friends, made a writer out of him and
an active leader in Zionism. For the rest of his life
he was, as he himself realized, a man of strife and
contention.*

For six years he edited Hashiloah, *one of the
great Hebrew magazines, and was a director of the
publishing company* Ahiasaf. *He wrote exclusively
in Hebrew and is considered to have been one of
the greatest editors in the history of Hebrew letters.
On several occasions, he visited Palestine and wrote
his impressions of the country in influential essays
which later appeared in his books. He attended the
first Zionist Congress and was one of the few Zionists who resisted the glamor of political Zionism.
He was the prime advocate of cultural Zionism and
frequently fought and opposed Theodor Herzl.
After the six momentous years with* Hashiloah, *he
returned to business in 1903. Eventually he moved*

to London and this departure from his familiar environment served to curtail his activities in Zionist and Hebrew cultural movements. The climate affected his health, thus ending his hope of emerging from semi-retirement. Virtually an invalid, in 1921 he left London for Tel Aviv. He died in January, 1927 and was buried in a Tel Aviv cemetery.

AHAD HA-AM'S ESSAYS

Harry Essrig

> *Since first thy light broke on us, we behold*
> *Master! in thee the Paladin of truth,*
> *And champion of the spirit; clear of vision,*
> *Modest and pure in every thought and deed;*
> *Secure in thine own truth, not caring aught*
> *How others judge; treading thy chosen path*
> *With firm step and unflinching gaze, as one*
> *Who carries in his soul the sacred flame*
> *And guards the last sole spark of heavenly fire.*
>
> (From a poem by C. N. Bialik;
> translated by Leon Simon)

> *He was, I might say, what Gandhi*
> *has been to many Indians, what Maz-*
> *zini was to young Italy a century ago.*
> (Chaim Weizmann)

There is no thinking Jew of this century who has not been exposed in some way to the impact of the philosophical insights and Zionist concepts of Ahad

Ha-am. If Herzl be considered the father of the modern nationalist movement of the Jewish people, then Ahad Ha-am may well be regarded as its mentor and oracle, its most prominent and original thinker, whose ideas have played a strategic role in the shaping of Jewish reality. His sensitivity to the plight of Judaism in its modern setting, his impassioned concern for the survival of the standard-bearers of this unique tradition, and his incisive explorations into the complex of issues that spelled life or immediate extinction for the Jewish entity—all these stamp him with the mark of greatness.

Although for the general public his chief distinction is as a merciless critic of the early Messianic pretensions of political Zionism, he was far more. He formulated a view of Jewish nationalism, which was grounded in the philosophical and scientific atmosphere of his time. He sought to plumb the depths of the historic enigma of Jewish survival in order better to plot a blueprint for the future rehabilitation of the communal structure; and broke new trails in exploring the dynamics of Jewish creative expression.

Before judgment can adequately be made on the structure of his world outlook, one must first clarify the many-sided personality of Asher Ginzberg, who assumed the modest and unpretentious pseudonym "Ahad Ha-am" (One of the People) on what he then expected to be his only appearance in print. What a curious and delicate mixture of contradictions this prophet of the Hebraic renaissance represented! He was a leader of men and an expounder of daring views, an iconoclast and a loving, even reverent believer in the power of ideas, a cautious, seemingly pessimistic surveyor of his world and a builder of a comprehensive rationale for the Jewish future. In perennial pursuit of order in his thinking, he worked toward synthesis of ancient ideas and current needs, toward a combination of the nationalist and universalist motifs in Jewish history that would guarantee survival without at the same time erecting cultural and spiritual ghettos between Jews and the rest of the world. Equilibrium and the attempt to weave diverse strands into unity: these were the characteristics of his thought and life.

He reflected the anguish of the modern Russian Jews, in whose minds two hostile cultures clashed; yet more successfully perhaps than any of his contemporaries he resolved this spiritual conflict. In his public and literary life he bridged the gap between the piety of his Hassidic ancestors and the world-shaking discoveries of Darwin and Herbert Spencer, between the intellectual isolation of his birthplace in the darkness of Czarist Russia and the fermenting cultural centers of London and Odessa. Powerful forces played upon his mind and soul; the result was vital and original. Like a fresh gust of wind he entered into the dust-laden atmosphere of Jewish thought.

Writing only when prompted by a pertinent issue or the need to convey a specific message, Ahad Ha-am was essentially a publicist. His philosophical speculations were therefore always the result of his reaction to the pressing practical problems of Jewish existence and to controversies which found their clearest expression in the Hebrew periodicals of his time. He looked upon the writer's craft with awe, refusing to earn a livelihood from it, and was compelled to dissipate most of his energy and time in commercial endeavors. Yet during the six years that he served as editor of the *Hashiloah*, he became a dominant force in Hebrew literature and nursed an entire generation in the

canons of taste and literary esthetics. Though he often referred to his dream of preparing a comprehensive, book-
length study of Jewish morals, he produced only four
slender volumes of collected essays, which had originally
appeared in various periodicals. The first volume was published in 1894, the second in 1903, the third in 1904, and
the fourth in 1913. These were fittingly called, *Al Parashat
Derahim* (At the Parting of the Ways).

His essays may be classified into those dealing with
philosophical and social ideas and those whose focus is
the Jewish national movement. In the former, he deduced
from general principles some particular lesson or moral for
improving the status of Jewish life; in the latter, he continuously agitated for a revival of the Jewish heart, for a
deeper attachment to our national life and a more ardent
desire for our national welfare. Thus all his life was of one
piece; he lived and wrote for a single purpose: to revive
the languishing Hebraic spirit through the repossession of
the ancestral home as the cultural workshop of the Jewish
nation.

It was the inner tragedy of Jewish life that struck terror
in his heart. The Jewish scene, as he surveyed it, was characterized by fragmentation, the lack of a national ideal, and
appalling impotence in the face of threats to survival as a
functioning and creative entity. The Jewish people were
split into isolated, disparate settlements throughout the
world, each differing in its thoughts, sentiments, habits
and aspirations from the others, and giving rise to a mul-
tiplicity of types of Judaism. Subject to local pressures,
these disconnected members of the Jewish body politic
could only produce individual forms lacking in homogene-
ity and common characteristics. They thus ran the risk of

absorption by the dominant majority, especially since religion could no longer fulfill its historic role as a core of
unification in the Diaspora. Under the lure of emancipation, the national instinct had likewise been attenuated.
The Jewish plight was indeed precarious. As a people, the
Jews stood in danger of losing the focus of their striving
and sense of cultural coherence; they had no alternative
but to face realistically the problem of survival as a national entity in modern times. Somehow, they had to be
welded once again into "one internally connected organism."

In answer to this alarming situation, Ahad Ha-am sought
to erect a structure of thought which might serve as a guide
to the perplexed members of his generation. In no one
place, however, did he present a systematic and logical
organization of all his concepts. His basic views are sprin-
kled throughout his four volumes of essays. Yet it is possible to trace the major threads of his reasoning through
the labyrinth of his prolific mind and catch the essence of
his vision.

It is not surprising that he tried above all to formulate
a precise definition of the meaning of nationhood. In his
opinion, a nation or people is not merely the sum of its individual members. It is an organic unity of itself, an his-
torical-psychological grouping, the possessor of an ego or
spirit that manages to retain its uniqueness through all the
metamorphoses of time. It represents a "mixture of past
and present, memories and impressions, hopes and aspirations" linked together and held in common by all the members of the group. It is a "living organism whose life is the
outward expression of a certain fundamental character" and
is actuated by a specific outlook on human problems. A

nation is likewise a spiritual-cultural body, possessing an
inner life of its own, leaving a distinctive mark on the manner of living, the mode of thinking, the language, literature, art and similar cultural manifestations which it creates in order to satisfy the needs of existence. But above all
—and this is one of Ahad Ha-am's central themes—a nation is moved by a strong biological drive, a dynamic corporate will to live which often functions most effectively
in the soul's underground.

This primitive impulse for self-preservation is always
able to discover the necessary means for its continued fulfillment. In the halcyon days of the Jewish people, when
they resided in their native land, this instinctual drive
came to natural fruition. With the destruction of the First
Temple, however, their religious heritage assumed the
function and responsibility of safeguarding the national
existence against the inroads of hostile environment, and
preserved the integrity of the group. The numerous precepts and commandments of the law served as a "protec-
tive bulwark" which shielded their national identity. In
this way the Jewish will to live withstood the pressures of
the unnatural circumstances of the "galuth." But with the
emancipation after the long night of medieval disfranchise-
ment, its devastating effects on the spiritual and ethnic
purity of the Jewish people and the weakening religious
loyalties, new realities emerged. The existence of the Jewish people now hung in the balance. The problem in modern times was to reawaken the national consciousness of
the Jewish people and strengthen their will to live.

Thus it was the Jewish collective with its subconscious
impulses to attain unfettered self-development that formed
the heart of Ahad Ha-am's *Weltanschauung*. For in his

opinion Judaism placed the accent on the welfare of the entire group, the embodiment of its noblest aspirations. It conceived of a "society in which each individual does that which is right from the point of view of the whole, without regard to his personal interest or convenience." Ahad Ha-am therefore envisaged the national ego as a complete organism, which preserves an inner sense of unity not only between its scattered contemporary parts but between all the epochs of its history. Nor are the creative personalities of the nation independent of the influence exerted by the people upon them, for they stand in an intimate relationship to the well-springs of the national spirit.

Within his philosophical framework, religion is stripped of its supernatural aura and fills a more modest role than is commonly supposed in the usual interpretations of Jewish history. Ahad Ha-am, influenced by the English and French positivists, became the first Hebrew thinker to part company with the theological rationale for Jewish survival. He phrased the significance of Judaism in its social-national version and considered religion, though the most significant of Jewish cultural products, as primarily a means for subsistence. He was not an abstract philosopher but an empiricist and psychologist, intrigued with the genetic approach to human problems and adept at tracing the roots and development of Jewish institutions and concepts. Cultural phenomena were viewed in their social context, for they derived essentially from the desire for survival and happiness. He therefore analyzed Judaism not from the dogmatic point of view in terms of its doctrinal formulation, but mainly in the light of its historical and functional significance. He evaluated it not on the basis of any special claims to validity and truth but as the national-biological

expression of a people, a body of ideals and patterns of behavior which arose out of the pressing needs of existence,
in response to specific conditions and the varying moods of
the cultural milieu.

And yet, though his theory of nationalism is couched in
so-called secularist terms, he recognized the fact that Judaism as such has exercised its own influence on the survival of the people and that it represented more than the
agglomerate of national characteristics such as language,
literature, customs, etc. It is here that we encounter the
second dominant motif in his thinking: his concept of a
"national spirit" or genius, the particular bent of a people,
the social force that expresses the very inwardness of an
historic-cultural entity. It is here that he strives to place
his finger on the essence, the truly distinctive characteristic, of the Jewish people.

The uniqueness of the Jewish people, he maintained, did
not reside in their religious attainments but in their superior
moral nature. The essence of the Jewish spirit was revealed
in the striving of this ancient people to realize in life the
ideal of ethical perfection, and in their fervent belief that
such a state of moral excellence can be achieved. They have
always stood as a protest against the sway of ruthless power
and have ever exalted spiritual values. They have suffered
from time immemorial as priests in the tabernacle of the
God of Justice but were never deterred from the fulfillment of their self-imposed obligations.

This consciousness of moral selection is rooted in the central idea of absolute righteousness, as exemplified by the
prophets: the highest type produced by the Jewish nation,
reflecting what was uppermost in the Hebraic soul. In their
teachings they defined the standard of conduct for the

people—the struggle for the ultimate triumph of right over
might—and in their life they gave testimony to the fundamental qualities of prophecy, namely the love of truth and
the refusal to compromise with expediency. They articulated the traditional hope for the establishment of absolute
justice in all of creation and fashioned a national ideal as
well as a mission.

For this ideal of ethical perfection could not survive
merely as an abstraction. It became the responsibility of the
Jews to embody this ideal and make it manifest in their
own national life as a means toward securing its acceptance
eventually by all of humanity. As a "peculiar people," Israel must indeed be among the nations of the world an
elemental force making for righteousness but it could not
fulfill its destiny in dispersion, as the exponents of Reform
Judaism intimated. Only in its historic home could its existence as "a corporate society of human beings, living out
their own life in accordance with a law that expressed their
own spiritual essence" be assured. Here it would be possible for the Jewish people to develop freely, to combine
prophetic morality with the best of European thought and
give concrete evidence of their moral essence, thus serving
in the best sense of the term as a light unto the nations of
the world. In this way the nationalist movement was transfigured by Ahad Ha-am into an instrument for the rejuvenation of Jewish morality and the fulfillment of Jewish
destiny.

The broad outlines of his views on cultural Zionism therefore emerge as a direct outgrowth of his philosophical pos-
tulates. His strictures against Herzl and his followers may
be seen to issue from his thinking on the entire panorama
of Jewish life, past and present. It is true that the sociologist

and thinker was bound to clash with the impatient weaver of dreams but it was no mere conflict of temperament or capricious splitting of hairs. An inevitable logic leads from Ahad Ha-am's grasp of Jewish history and views on the dynamics of nationalism to his insistence upon the type of haven that ought to be established in the ancient cradle of the Jewish genius.

The long-drawn-out tragedy of Jewish life confronts us with a formidable impasse. Life in the Ghetto or even under the seemingly favorable conditions of emancipation cannot provide for the unity of the Jewish people, "its renaissance and development, in accordance with its spirit, based on general human principles." What is needed is to combine the unadulterated Jewishness of the Ghetto with the breadth and freedom of modern life, and that is possible only on one's own soil. Thus the spiritual center, though it be the seat of a small settlement of Jews, can alone guarantee the survival of Jewish culture as well as make possible the national regeneration of Diaspora Jewry.

Ahad Ha-am therefore conceived of Zionism not as the answer to the economic plight of Jews or to the desperate situation of separate Jews united by a common enemy, but rather to the threat of extinction which hovered over Judaism. It was not that he disregarded the challenge of anti-Semitism or the needs of those "who cannot or will not assimilate to their surroundings"; he was basically concerned with the dwindling will to live of an historic entity. The immediate and pressing problem was not the ingathering of the exiles, since the vast majority of Jews would in any case be compelled to reside outside of Palestine and their material welfare would remain largely dependent on local conditions. It is because the circumstances of Diaspora life

cannot prevent the incorporation into Jewish civilization of
elements from the general cultural environment without
endangering its integrity that a center must be established.
Here it would be possible for the Jewish group to "fulfill
that physical natural 'mission' which belongs to every organism . . . create for itself conditions suitable to its character, in which it could develop its latent powers and
aptitudes, its own particular form of life, in a normal manner and in obedience to the demands of its nature." Here a
base of operations would be maintained for the national
spirit and for an original Jewish culture which could then
exert an integrating influence on the periphery of the Jewish settlements the world over and serve as a model for
them. In no way did Ahad Ha-am minimize the host of activities commonly subsumed under the title of political
Zionism; he merely stressed their inadequacy without a cultural foundation upon which such endeavors might rest.
"We must," he cautioned, "take hold of both ends of the
stick."

Ahad Ha-am constantly agitated for the revival of the
Jewish national spirit, for a spiritual and psychological
change, as antecedent or at least accompanying the attainment of a political home in Palestine. This inner rehabilitation of the Jewish people could not wait until after the
external solution of its problems, for Zionism's major concern was not to ameliorate the physical and economic conditions of the Jews but to heal their moral and spiritual
wounds. Now and at once must their national idealism be
increased and strengthened, for without its resurgence no
concrete achievement on a large scale and on a firm basis
was possible. This spiritual change is most urgently needed
as a prerequisite for any great material advance. "Every be-

lief or idea leading to practical deeds necessarily presupposes that the attainment of a certain end is a need felt in our hearts," he wrote. Zionism as an ideal could only be achieved by a boundless desire. This desire did not yet exist; it had to be cultivated and transformed into a powerful agency for the building of the homeland. Therefore, "the concentration of Jews in Zion must be preceded by the concentration of the hearts of the Jews in the love of Zion." The return to the land had to *follow* a radical change in the Jewish heart. Hebraism had to be grasped and assimilated as a "culture" before it could be embodied in practice. Only then could the center in Palestine be a focal point from which a regenerated vision of Judaism would radiate to the periphery of the Diaspora.

The style is the man, and in the case of Ahad Ha-am this observation is most apt. Based on the language of the Mishnah and early Agada, his writing reflected the mechanics of his mind in its terseness, its flashes of humor or irony, and even hints of warm feeling. It was a lean prose that he preferred, avoiding the flowery expression which was the legacy of the Haskalah movement. He would say: "Perfect the thought and the thought will perfect the style"; and what he wrote was characterized by the purity, logic and expert craftsmanship which establishes him at once as a model for Hebrew prose writers.

More clearly than any of his contemporaries, Ahad Ha-am defined the problems of Jewish survival and painted a tantalizing vision of what the future might be. Freethinker and saint, citizen of the world and yet Jewish in the profoundest sense, this great personality pointed to new directions on the long Jewish journey through history. His teachings have not ceased to influence Jewish thinking. There is no

Jewish ideology of any consequence that has not in some way borrowed from him. Bialik's tribute to Ahad Ha-am is as true today as when it was first written:

And if ever it happens that even in our generation
Our Holy Spirit still sparkles, revealing itself in a Jew,
Then it has never shone any brighter in any son of the Galut
Than it glistens in thy great soul.

selections from AHAD HA-AM'S ESSAYS

The Prophetic Idea

The Prophet is essentially a one-sided man. A certain moral idea fills his whole being, masters his every feeling and sensation, engrosses his whole attention. He can only see the world through the mirror of his idea; he desires nothing, strives for nothing, except to make every phase of the life around him an embodiment of that idea in its perfect form. His whole life is spent in fighting for this ideal with all his strength; for its sake he lays waste his powers, unsparing of himself, regardless of the conditions of life and the demands of the general harmony. His gaze is fixed always on what ought to be in accordance with his own convictions; never on what can be consistent with the general condition of things outside himself. The Prophet is thus a primal force. His action affects the character of the general harmony, while he himself does not become a part of that harmony, but remains always a man apart, a narrow-minded extremist, zealous for his own idea, and intolerant of every other. And since he cannot have all that he would, he is in a perpetual state of anger and grief; he remains all his life "a man of strife and a man of con-

tention to the whole earth." Not only this; the other members of society, those many-sided dwarfs, creatures of the
general harmony, cry out after him, "The Prophet is a fool,
the spiritual man is mad"; and they look with lofty contempt on his narrowness and extremeness. They do not see
that they themselves and their own many-sided lives are
but as the soil which depends for its fertility on these narrow-minded giants.

It is otherwise with the Priest. He appears on the scene
at a time when Prophecy has already succeeded in hewing
out a path for its Idea; when that Idea has already had a
certain effect on the trend of society, and has brought about
a new harmony or balance between the different forces at
work. The Priest also fosters the Idea, and desires to perpetuate it; but he is not of the race of giants. He has not the
strength to fight continually against necessity and actuality;
his tendency is rather to bow to the one and come to terms
with the other. Instead of clinging to the narrowness of the
Prophet, and demanding of reality what it cannot give, he
broadens his outlook, and takes a wider view of the relation between his Idea and the facts of life. Not what ought
to be, but what can be, is what he seeks. His watchword is
not the Idea, the whole Idea, and nothing but the Idea; he
accepts the complex "harmony" which has resulted from
the conflict of that Idea with other forces. His battle is no
longer a battle against actuality, but a battle in the name
of actuality against its enemies. The Idea of the Priest is
not, therefore, a primal force; it is an accidental complex
of various forces, among which there is no essential connection. Their temporary union is due simply to the fact that
they have happened to come into conflict in actual life, and
have been compelled to compromise and join hands. The

living, absolute Idea, which strove to make itself all-power-
ful, and changed the external form of life while remaining
itself unchanged—this elemental Idea has died and passed
away together with its Prophets. Nothing remains but its
effects—the superficial impress that it has been able to leave
on the complex form of life. It is this form of life, already
outworn, that the Priests strive to perpetuate, for the sake
of the Prophetic impress that it bears.

Other nations have at various times had their Prophets,
men whose life was the life of an embodied Idea; who had
their effect, smaller or greater, on their people's history, and
left the results of their work in charge of Priests till the end
of time. But it is preeminently among the ancient Hebrews
that Prophecy is found, not as an accidental or temporary
phenomenon, but continuously through many generations.
Prophecy is, as it were, the hallmark of the Hebrew national spirit.

The fundamental idea of the Hebrew Prophets was the
universal dominion of absolute justice. In Heaven it rules
through the eternally Righteous, "who holds in His right hand
the attribute of judgment," and righteously judges all His
creatures; and on earth through man, on whom, created in
God's image, lies the duty of cherishing the attribute of his
Maker, and helping Him, to the best of his meager power,
to guide His world in the path of Righteousness. This Idea,
with all its religious and moral corollaries, was the breath
of life to the Hebrew Prophets. It was their all in all, beyond which there was nothing of any importance. Righteousness for them is beauty, it is goodness, wisdom, truth:
without it all these are naught. When the Prophet saw injustice, either on the part of men or on the part of Providence, he did not inquire closely into its causes, nor bend

the knee to necessity, and judge the evil-doers leniently;
nor again did he give himself up to despair, or doubt the
strength of Righteousness, or the possibility of its victory.
He simply complained, pouring out his soul in words of
fire; then went his way again, fighting for his idea, and full
of hope that in time—perhaps even "at the end of time"—
Righteousness would be lord over all the earth. "Thou art
Righteous, O Lord,"—this the Prophet cannot doubt, although his eyes tell him that "the way of the wicked pros-
pereth": he feels it as a moral necessity to set Righteousness on the throne, and this feeling is strong enough to
conquer the evidence of his eyes. "But I will speak judgments with thee": this is the fearless challenge of Righteousness on earth to Righteousness in Heaven. These
"judgments" relieve his pain; and he returns to his life's
work, and lives on by the faith that is in him.

These Prophets of Righteousness transcended in spirit
political and national boundaries, and preached the gospel
of justice and charity for the whole human race. Yet they
remained true to their people Israel; they, too, saw in it
the chosen people; and from their words it might appear
that Israel is their whole world. But their devotion to the
universal ideal had its effect on their national feeling. Their
nationalism became a kind of corollary to their fundamental Idea. Firmly as they believed in the victory of absolute
Righteousness, yet the fact that they turn their gaze time
after time to "the end of days" proves that they knew—as by
a whisper from the "spirit of holiness" within them—how
great and how arduous was the work that mankind must
do before that consummation could be reached. They knew,
also, that such work as this could not be done by scattered
individuals, approaching it sporadically, each man for him-

self, at different times and in different places; but that it
needed a whole community, which should be continuously,
throughout all generations, the standard-bearer of the force
of Righteousness against all the other forces that rule the
world: which should assume of its own freewill the yoke
of eternal obedience to the absolute dominion of a single
Idea, and for the sake of that Idea should wage incessant
war against the way of the world. This task, grand and
lofty, indeed, but not attractive or highly-esteemed, the
Prophets, whose habit was to see their innermost desire as
though it were already realized in the external world, saw
placed on the shoulders of their own small nation, because
they loved it so well. Their national ideal was not "a kingdom of Friests," but "would that all the people of the Lord
were Prophets." They wished the whole people to be a
primal force, a force making for Righteousness, in the
general life of humanity, just as they were themselves in its
own particular national life.

from "Priest and Prophet"

Slavery In Freedom

Today, while I am still alive, I try mayhap to give my
weary eyes a rest from the scene of ignorance, of degrada-
tion, of unutterable poverty that confronts me here in Russia, and find comfort by looking yonder across the border,
where there are Jewish professors, Jewish members of
Academies, Jewish officers in the army, Jewish civil servants: and when I see there, behind the glory and the grandeur of it all, a twofold spiritual slavery—moral slavery and
intellectual slavery—and ask myself: Do I envy these fellow-
Jews of mine their emancipation?—I answer, in all truth

and sincerity: No! a thousand times No! The privileges
are not worth the price! I may not be emancipated; but at
least I have not sold my soul for emancipation. I at least
can proclaim from the housetops that my kith and kin are
dear to me wherever they are, without being constrained to
find forced and unsatisfactory excuses. I at least can remember Jerusalem at other times than those of "divine service":
I can mourn for its loss, in public or in private, without being asked what Zion is to me, or I to Zion. I at least have
no need to exalt my people to Heaven, to trumpet its superiority above all other nations, in order to find a justification for its existence. I at least know "why I remain a
Jew"—or, rather, I can find no meaning in such a question,
any more than if I were asked why I remain my father's
son. I at least can speak my mind concerning the beliefs and
the opinions which I have inherited from my ancestors,
without fearing to snap the bond that unites me to my
people. I can even adopt that "scientific heresy which bears
the name of Darwin," without any danger to my Judaism.
In a word, I am my own, and my opinions and feelings
are my own. I have no reason for concealing or denying
them, for deceiving others or myself. And this spiritual freedom—scoff who will!—I would not exchange or barter for
all the emancipation in the world.

from "Slavery in Freedom"

The Sabbath

Men of this kind, themselves without any vestige of true
Jewish feeling, cannot by any means be brought to understand how there can be among us intelligent men, familiar

with all the theories of the learned world about the origin of the Sabbath and the other religious observances, who know also what our author himself affects not to know, that even "the bed-rock on which the Jewish outlook is based" did not spring into being full-grown, but was gradually evolved, like the conception of the Sabbath, out of the crude beliefs and emotions of primitive man, and who can still find the Sabbath a delight, can respect and hold sacred the day which has been sanctified by the blood of our people, and has preserved it for thousands of years from spiritual degeneration, although they may not be scrupulously careful as regards all the details of the multifarious kinds of forbidden work. They cannot understand how such men, though they may not be very particular about what they eat away from home, can still observe Kashrut in their houses, because they do not wish their tables to be regarded as unclean by the Jewish public: not that they fear the public, as our author erroneously supposes in one of his essays, but that they value the national tie that unites them with it: and how even those who act otherwise would yet regard it as the height of impertinence for a Jew to boast publicly that he is no longer at one with the great mass of his people as regards his domestic life and his food.

from "A New Savior"

Jewish Bent Towards the Abstract

If the heathen of the old story, who wished to learn the whole of the Torah while he stood on one foot, had come to me, my reply would have been: " 'Thou shalt not make unto

thee any graven image or any likeness'—that is the whole
Torah, and the rest is commentary." What essentially distinguishes Judaism from other religions is its absolute determination to make the religious and moral consciousness
independent of any definite human form, and to attach it
without any mediating term to an abstract incorporeal
ideal. We cannot conceive Christianity without Jesus, or
even Islam without Mohammed. Christianity has deified
Jesus, but that is not the important thing. Even if Jesus had
remained the "son of man," had remained simply a prophet,
as Mohammed is to the Moslems, it would still be true—
and this is the significant fact—that Christianity links up
the religious and moral consciousness with the figure of a
particular man, and belief in whom is an essential part of a
religion inconceivable without him. Judaism, and Judaism
alone, depends on no such human figure. For Judaism God
is the only ideal of absolute perfection, and He only must
be kept always before the eye of man's inner consciousness,
in order that man may "cleave to his attributes." No man,
not even the most perfect, is free from shortcomings and
sins; no man can serve as an ideal for the religious sentiment, which strives after union with the source of perfection. Moses died in his sin, like any other man. He was
simply God's messenger, charged with the giving of His
Law; his image is not an essential part of the very fabric
of the religion. Thus the Jewish teachers of a later period
found nothing to shock them in the words of one who said
in all simplicity: "Ezra was worthy to be the bearer of the
Law to Israel, had not Moses come before him" (*Sanhedrin,
21a*). Could it enter a Christian mind, let us say, to conceive the idea that Paul was worthy to be the bearer of the
"message," had not Jesus come before him? And it need

scarcely be said that the individual figures of the other Prophets are not an essential part of the fabric of Judaism. Of the greatest of them, Hosea, Amos, Isaiah and others— we do not even know who or what they were; their person- alities have vanished like a shadow, and only their words have been preserved and handed down from generation to generation, because they were not their words, but "the word of the Lord that came unto them."

This applies equally to the Messiah, whose future coming is awaited. His importance lies not in himself, but in his being the messenger of God for the bringing of redemp- tion to Israel and the world. Jewish teachers pay much more attention to "the days of the Messiah," than to the Messiah himself. One of them even disbelieved altogether in a per- sonal Messiah, and looked forward to a redemption effected by God Himself without an intermediary; and he was not therefore regarded as a heretic.

This characteristic of Judaism has perhaps been the prin- cipal obstacle to its wider acceptance. It is difficult for most men to find satisfaction in an abstract ideal which offers nothing to the senses; a human figure much more readily in- spires devotion. Before the triumph of Christianity, the Greeks and the Romans used to accuse the Jews of having no God, because an incorporeal divinity had no meaning for them; and when the time came for the God of Israel to become also the God of the nations, they still could not ac- cept His way without associating with Him a divine ideal in human form, thus satisfying their craving for a less re- mote object of adoration.

from "Jewish and Christian Ethics"

Difference Between Jewish and Christian Outlook

This preference of the Jewish mind for the impersonal is equally evident in the Jewish conception of the aim of religion and morality. There is no need to dilate on the familiar truth that Judaism conceives its aim not as the salvation of the individual, but as the well-being and perfection of a group, of the Jewish people, and ultimately of the whole human race. That is to say, the aim is always defined in terms of a collectivity which has no defined and concrete form. In its most fruitful period, that of the Prophets and the divine revelation, Judaism had as yet no clear ideal of personal immortality or of reward and punishment after death. The religious and moral inspiration of the Prophets and their disciples was derived not from any belief of that kind, but from the conviction of their belonging to "the chosen people," which had, according to their belief, a divine call to make its national life the embodiment of the highest form of religion and morality. Even in later times, when the Babylonian exile had put an end to the free national life of the Jews, and as a result the desire for individual salvation had come to play a part in the Jewish religious consciousness, the highest aim of Judaism still remained a collective aim. For proof of the truth of this statement there is no need to look further than the prayers in the daily and festival prayerbooks, of which only a minority turn on the personal needs of the individual worshiper, while the majority deal with the concerns of the nation and of the whole human race.

Which of these two aims is the higher? This question has been endlessly debated; but the truth is that in this matter we cannot establish any scale of values. A man may attain to the highest level in his religious and moral life whether he is inspired by the one aim or by the other. But the individual salvation certainly makes a stronger appeal to most men, and is more likely to kindle their imagination and to inspire them to strive after moral and religious perfection. If Judaism, unlike the other religions, prefers the collective aim, this is yet another instance of the characteristically Jewish tendency to abstractness and to the repudiation of the concrete form. So long as this tendency persists—so long, that is, as the Jewish people does not lose its essential character—no true Jew can be attracted by the doctrine of the Gospels, which rests wholly and solely on the pursuit of individual salvation.

from "Jewish and Christian Ethics"

A Spiritual Centre

When we use the word "centre" metaphorically in relation to human society, it necessarily connotes a similar idea: what we mean is that a particular spot or thing exerts influence on a certain social circumference, which is bound up with and dependent on it, and that in relation to this circumference it is a centre. But since society is a complex of many different departments, there are very few centres which are universal in their function—that is, which influence equally all sides of the life of the circumference. The relation between the centre and the circumference is usually limited to one or more departments of life, outside which the two are not interdependent. Thus a given circumference may have many centres, each of which is a centre only for one specific purpose. When, therefore, the word "centre" is used to express a social conception, it is accompanied almost always—except where the context makes it unnecessary—by an epithet which indicates its character. We speak of a literary centre, an artistic centre, a commercial centre, and so on, meaning thereby that in this or that department of life the centre in question has a circumference which is under its influence and is dependent upon it, but that in other departments the one does not exert nor the other receive influence, and the relation of centre and circumference does not exist.

Bearing in mind this limitation, which is familar enough, and applying it to the phrase quoted above—"in Palestine we can and should establish for ourselves a spiritual centre of our nationality"—we shall find that the phrase is capable of only one interpretation.

"A centre of our nationality" implies that there is a national circumference which, like every circumference, is much larger than the centre. That is to say, the speaker sees the majority of his people, in the future as in the past scattered all over the world, but no longer broken up into a number of disconnected parts, because one part—the one in Palestine—will be a centre for them all and make them all into a single, completed circumference. When all the scattered limbs of the national body feel the beating of the national heart, restored to life in its native home, they too will once again draw near to one another and welcome the inrush of living blood that flows from the heart.

"Spiritual" means that this relation of centre and circumference between Palestine and the lands of the diaspora will of necessity be limited to the spiritual side of life. The influence of the centre will strengthen the Jewish national consciousness in the diaspora; it will restore our independence of mind and self-respect; it will give to our Judaism a national content which will be genuine and natural, unlike the substitutes with which we now try to fill the void. But all this cannot apply outside the spiritual side of life, in all those economic and political relations which depend first and foremost upon the conditions of the immediate environment, being created by that environment and reflecting its character. Whilst it is true that in all these relations the effects of the changed outlook (such as the reinforcement of our sense of national unity and power of resistance) will show themselves to some extent, yet essentially and fundamentally these departments of life in the diaspora will not be linked with the life of the centre. For it is absolutely inconceivable that Palestine could radiate economic and political influence throughout the length and breadth of the diaspora, which is co-extensive with the globe, in such a way and to such an extent as would entitle us to say, without inexact use of language, that Palestine was the centre of our national life in these departments also.

from "A Spiritual Centre"

Survival in the Diaspora

An attitude may be either subjectively or objectively negative. If we express disapproval or dislike of something or other, our negative attitude is subjective: it relates not to the thing itself, but only to our own reactions to it. But if we say that something or other cannot possibly exist, our negative attitude is objective: it results from an examination of the objective facts, without any reference to our own predilections.

In the subjective sense all Jews adopt a negative attitude towards the diaspora. With few exceptions, they all recognize that the position of a lamb among wolves is unsatisfactory, and they would gladly put an end to this state of things if it were possible. Those who profess to regard our dispersion as a heaven-sent blessing are simply weak-kneed optimists; lacking the courage to look the evil thing in the face, they find it necesary to smile on it and call it good so long as they cannot abolish it. But if the Messiah—the true Messiah—were to appear today or tomorrow, to lead us out of our exile, even these optimists would join the throng of his followers without a moment's hesitation.

This being so, the "negative attitude towards the diaspora" which has become a debating counter must be negative in the objective sense. To adopt a negative attitude towards the diaspora means, for our present purpose, to believe that the Jews cannot survive as a scattered people now that our spiritual isolation is ended, because we have no longer any defense against the ocean of foreign culture, which threatens to obliterate our national characteristics and traditions, and thus gradually to put an end to our existence as a people.

There are, it is true, some Jews who are of that opinion; but they are not all of one way of thinking. They belong in fact to two different parties, which draw diametrically opposite conclusions from their common assumption. The one party argues that, as we are doomed to extinction, it is better to hasten the end by our own action than to sit and wait for it to come of its own accord after a long and painful death-agony. If a Jew can get rid of his Judaism here and now by assimilation, good luck to him; if he cannot, let him try to make it possible for his children. But the

other party argues that, since we are threatened with extinction, we ought to put an end to our dispersion before
it puts an end to us. We must secure our future by gathering the scattered members of our race together in our historic land (or, some would add, in some other country of
their own), where alone we shall be able to continue to
live as a people. Any Jew who is both able and willing to
get rid of his Judaism by assimilation may remain where he
is; those who are unable or unwilling to assimilate will betake themselves to the Jewish State.

But so far both these parties remain merely parties, and
neither has succeeded in persuading the Jewish people as
a whole to accept the fundamental postulate with either
of its consequential policies. Both alike have come into
conflict with something very deep-rooted and stubborn—the
instinctive and unconquerable desire of the Jewish people
to survive. This desire for survival, or will to live, obviously
makes it impossible for the Jewish people as a whole to
contemplate the disappearance of the diaspora if that involves its own disappearance; but the case is no better if
the argument is that the diaspora must disappear in order
that the people may survive. Survival cannot be made dependent on any condition, because the condition might not
be fulfilled. The Jews as a people feel that they have the
will and the strength to survive whatever may happen,
without any ifs or ands. They cannot accept a theory which
makes their survival conditional on their ceasing to be dispersed, because that theory implies that failure to end the
dispersion would mean extinction, and extinction is an alternative that cannot be contemplated in any circumstances
whatever.

Except, then, for these two extreme parties, the Jews

remain true to their ancient belief; their attitude towards the diaspora is subjectively negative, but objectively positive. Dispersion is a thoroughly evil and unpleasant thing, but we can and must live in dispersion, for all its evils and all its unpleasantness. Exodus from the dispersion will always be, as it always has been, an inspiring hope for the distant future; but the date of that consummation is the secret of a higher power, and our survival as a people is not dependent upon it.

This, however, does not settle the question of our survival in dispersion: on the contrary, it is precisely this positive attitude towards the diaspora that gives the question its urgency. A man at death's door does not worry much about his affairs during his last days on earth; a man on the point of going abroad is not particular about the tidiness of the lodging he occupies just before his departure. But if the Jews believe that they can and must continue to live in dispersion, the question at once arises—how is it to be done? It is neither necessary nor possible for them to go on living all the time in exactly the same old way. The will to live not only persuades them to believe that it is possible to survive in dispersion; it also impels them, in the changing circumstances of successive epochs, to find always the most appropriate means of preserving and developing their national identity. Moreover, this watchful instinct is always anticipating events, always providing in advance against the future. When Titus besieged Jerusalem, we are told, the defenders always had a new rampart ready in the rear before the one in front of it was overthrown. So it is with our national survival. And now that all but the wilfully blind can see the old rampart tottering to its fall, we are

bound to ask ourselves: where is the new rampart that is
to secure our existence as a people in dispersion?

from "Diaspora Nationalism"

Our National Capital

During the period of the Second Temple, there came a
time when the Jews in Palestine realised that the territorial
basis of their national existence was slipping away from
under their feet; and fearful of losing their all with the loss
of their country, they made shift to turn what may be called
their national capital into liquid and portable assets. Since
that time the scattered fragments and the successive generations of the Jewish people have been held together and
unified by the triple bond of religion, literature and (as
the foundation of both) language. These were all originally rooted in the land of Palestine, and they could be
made portable only at the expense of shedding such of their
roots as could not be separated from their native soil. Religion had to give up the Temple and all the rites and ceremonies that could be observed only in Palestine; literature
had to forego the inspiration of contact with nature in its
native land; and Hebrew had to cease to be a language of
every-day speech. As though guided by some premonitory
instinct, the nation made the necessary preparations for its
exile well in advance. Even before the final Roman con-
quest, the centre of the religious life was gradually shifted
from the Temple to the Synagogue; in literature, works
like the Song of Songs and the Book of Ruth gave place to
legal compilations and collections of folk-lore; and Hebrew
became less and less a living language, more and more a

purely literary idiom. Thus the remnants of the national
capital were put into a form in which they could accompany
the people on its wanderings and serve to maintain its national existence through the long, dark years of exile. It was
for the most part a bare and meager existence; but the capital at any rate was kept intact. Consequently there was
never any reason, in the old days, to doubt whether the
Jews were a distinct nation, or to demonstrate their title to
be regarded as such. The national capital, however scanty,
was there for all to see in the actualities of Jewish life.

from "Diaspora Nationalism"

Chaim Nachman Bialik

Chaim Nachman Bialik was born in Radi, in the province of Volynia, Russia, in 1873. His family moved to a suburb in Zhitomir where his father was a tavernkeeper. When Chaim was seven, his father died and his mother was left with the responsibility of caring for her children unaided. In order to lighten his mother's burden, Bialik was sent to his grandfather's house where he was reared in a religious and Talmudic atmosphere; at the age of 16, he attended the yeshiva at Volozhin. After two years he went to Odessa where, in 1892, he published his first poem, "To the Bird," which was widely praised. In 1893 he was married and lived for four years as a merchant in the town of Korostishov and then three years as a Hebrew tutor in Sosnovitz. Meanwhile, he was writing his powerful poems and winning a wide audience. In 1900 his friends brought him back to Odessa where he soon became one of the major literary personalities, together with Ahad Ha-am and other impor-

*tant Jewish creative artists. With two other Hebrew
writers he established a publishing house and
edited the poetry and fiction sections of Hashiloah.*

*When the Bolsheviks won Russia, Bialik left
for Berlin, but soon thereafter went to Palestine.
On Bialik Street, in Tel Aviv, he lived until his
final illness in 1934. When he passed away all Israel
mourned him. A museum and a great publishing
house have been erected in his memory.*

BIALIK: POET AND PROPHET

Menachem Ribalow

The name of Chaim Nachman Bialik became
a legend in his lifetime. His span of life was only sixty years
(1873-1934), but he exercised a tremendous influence upon
his generation. Most of the modern Hebrew poets and
writers were guided by the light he shed, studied his poetic style, absorbed his linguistic inventions and accepted
him as their mentor.

After his death his influence became even more marked.
Countless books and articles were written about him. Anthologies were published in his memory. Jewish students
in Israel and elsewhere are taught his poetic and prose
works. Many schools are named after him. His house in
Tel Aviv is now a museum.

It can be said that a Bialik cult has arisen in modern
Hebrew literature similar to the cults of Shakespeare and
Goethe in world literature. Bialik has been accepted as a
supreme poetic personality in the Jewish cultural milieu.
His volumes of poems are among the greatest books of our
generation.

Bialik was among those creative personalities, unique

in the annals of literary history, who, when they appear, set their seal upon the life and spiritual creativeness of their generation. They impart new energy and new values to old concepts and accepted norms. They open new vistas in the life of their people. According to a Hebrew saying, they renew the works of creation. Bialik was such a force. Through his poetic creations he brought about the Hebrew literary renascence of his period and the rejuvenation of the Hebrew language. With his cry of revolt and protest Bialik quickened the pulse of his people.

In addition to his poetic genius, Bialik was endowed with the divine spark of prophecy. He was a man of inspiration. More than that he was a child of the *Shekinah*— the Divine Spirit. In his own words, "At times it seems to me that I am the only begotten son of the Holy One, Blessed Be His Name, the favorite child of His Divine Spirit." Inspiration is the heritage of any poet who sings of himself and to himself. But the Divine Spirit—the *Shekinah*—is the soul of a people, and it is revealed only to chosen ones and to prophets of God.

The poet ordinarily sings about his own life, nature, man's tribulations, or the mystery of existence. But the prophetic poet not only sings, he preaches and chastises, he lashes out against the people and its God. The artist-poet, singing his individual song, reflects upon the world and upon man who inhabits it, and he sings his song with poetic imagery. But the prophet-poet, even when he is alone, never concentrates upon himself alone. His is a three-fold visual front: himself, his people and his God. This conflict takes place in his inner soul: between himself and his people; between both and their God.

Bialik was born in a small town in the southern part of

Russia. He spent his childhood as a poverty-stricken orphan, studied in yeshivas, and was in turn a Hebrew teacher, a lumber and coal merchant, and later a publisher. But this logical personality knew how to lift himself above his environment, and to penetrate to the great beyond once trodden by the divine prophets. He took the linguistic symbolism and prophetic allegories from Amos, Isaiah, Jeremiah and Ezekiel, sparked them with new fire and hurled them into our lives, kindling our souls. He was the only one of our contemporaries who had the moral strength to open his Yiddish poem, "The Last Word" (which he called prophetic), with the daring line: "I was sent to you by God," and to complete his first stanza with these words: "And God remembered you and brought me to you." The end of the poem is reminiscent of Jeremiah:

> *And God said unto me:*
> *"And now go down to the potter's house*
> *And buy a pot,*
> *And hurl it down and say in a loud voice*
> *So that everyone may hear:*
> *Thus will you be shattered!*
> *Then speak no more.*
> *Don't cry, don't scream.*
> *Bow your head in silence.*
> *The day will dawn—it comes, it comes!"*

In his prophetic poems, Bialik heaps coals of fire upon the heads of the people as well as upon his own. The collective "I" of the people is identified with the individual "I" of the poet. He seeks and finds all the shortcomings of his people within himself. For the people's faults are his faults; and their sins, his sins.

And this individual-communal emotion makes the prophet-poet a symbol of his people, a man who bears its burden, the magnitude of its destiny. And his soul's agonized cry is the cry of a man who is "roasted alive upon his own coals."

Bialik who grew up in Czarist Russia, which taught the world a lesson in unprincipled barbarism, said of himself: "My father is bitter exile, my mother—black poverty." This was the Jew who saw his people sink to the depths, living "a life without hope and without light, the life of a chained and hungry dog. . . ." He was the greatest revolutionary in the Diaspora who called for total war against the insufferable conditions of life in exile.

He chastised his people for living such a life, he thundered against them with all the fire of his indignation; shook them with all the strength of his anger. His heart was filled with pride and dignity, which intensified his disgust with the ways of his people. He could not endure their submissiveness, their slavishness, the bending of necks beneath the yoke of their taskmasters, and their acceptance of agony with resignation. He sought to put an end to their shame, to stir again the ancient dignity of those who were being led like sheep to massacre, and who did not rise in revolt.

"The City of Slaughter," written after the Kishenev pogroms in 1904, shook the Jewish world to its foundations. Bialik was sent to the city of slaughter by the Jews of Odessa who wanted a first-hand report of what had happened there. Instead of a routine report to the committee, he let loose a thunderbolt of prophetic denunciation.

After the holocaust of Hitler, the incident of Kishenev appears pale in comparison. But in the eyes of the prophet-poet, that small-scale pogrom was a hint of what was to

come. Indeed, the "City of Slaughter" was the beginning
of those tragic circumstances in the life of the Jewish people in the European Diaspora which reached their climax
in the Hitler atrocities.

Bialik walked among the ruins of Kishenev and beheld
the maniacal fury of anti-Semitism and the bitter shame of
Israel's exile. The heart of the delegate from Odessa burst
with suppressed shame and agony. He controlled his tears,
for he knew that "the time to bellow is when the ox is
bound for the slaughter," not after.

But his heart not only writhes in pain at the sight of the
ruins and the atrocities that were visited upon his people;
it constricts at the sight of their terrible degeneration. From
the cemetery where the martyrs were buried, he comes to
the synagogue on a fast day proclaimed as a day of mourning. There he is horrified at the weeping and the wailing
of the survivors. He writes: "Thus groans a people who is
lost. . . . They beat upon their hearts and confess their
sins saying: 'We have sinned, we have dealt treacher-
ously.'" The self-accusations of a people who are butchered
alive shake him to the roots of his being. And he, as one of
the people, as its spokesman, feels his own unworthiness
and shame.

The poet, feeling the inadequacy of poetry when the dignity of man has been trampled, when the sanctity of life
has been desecrated, lifts himself above poetry and is
clothed with the spirit of prophecy. He demands retribu-
tion for all the generations put to shame from time immemorial. He grasps the pillars—not only of our national
structure—but of the universe, as if prepared to pull them
down. He flagellates himself and his people, and now he
flings defiance against the All Highest.

It is in this mood that he writes his poems "Upon the Slaughter" and "I Knew in a Dark Night." In these poems he grasps at the Throne of God in order to shake it and demand the justice due him. More than the prophets and more than Job, he challenges the Creator and his creations:

> *If Right there be—why, let it shine forth now!*
> *For if when I have perished from the earth*
> *The Right shine forth*
> *Then let its Throne be shattered and laid low!*
> *Then let the heavens, wrong-racked, be no more!*
> *While you, O murderers, on your murder thrive,*
> *Live on your blood, regurgitate that gore!*
> *Who cries Revenge! Revenge!—accursed be he!*
> *Fit vengeance for the spilt blood of a child*
> *The devil has not yet compiled . . .*
> *No, let that blood pierce world's profundity,*
> *Through the great deep pursue its mordications,*
> *There eat its way in darkness, there undo*
> *Undo the rotted earth's foundations!*

With this outburst Bialik's national poetic genius reached tremendous power. His revolt against himself, against his people and against his God, brought him nearer to the folk. The more he goaded them, the more he captured their hearts.

It seemed as if the tortured body and the sick soul of his people longed for the healing hand of the one who whipped them into action. They needed to be chastised, purified, awakened from their lethargy and aroused to revolt. His gift to national self-consciousness was of tremendous importance. Because of the world-shaking challenge in the "City of Slaughter," a Jewish army of self-defense was or-

ganized among the Russian youth. Later when other Russian cities were attacked, the "sons of the Maccabees" did
not flee for shelter in cellars or in attics. They organized
into armed squads and sallied forth to meet the enemy and
return blow for blow. These partisans later developed into
the Haganah, the Army of Israel. The partisan bands of the
ghettos of Poland and Lithuania in the days of Hitler were
the sons of the original members of the self-defense squads
inspired by Bialik's poem. The burning message of the
prophet-poet was transformed into a life-giving force of a
people yearning for redemption.

The idea of revolution in the Diaspora found epic expression in Bialik's great poem, "The Dead of the Wilderness." He based this poem on a Talmudic injunction: "Come
and I will show you the dead of the wilderness." On that
sentence he constructed a far-reaching poetic edifice.

Through the eyes of his imagination he beheld the desert
generation of those who made their exodus from Egypt;
those who died in the desert and who were not privileged
to enter the land of Israel. These dead are sleeping giants
who still wear their armor. In their lifetime they were
mighty warriors, determined to go from slavery into freedom. They were the original explorers, undaunted pioneers.
But with all their strength and determination, they could
only go out of Egypt and wander in the desert. They were
not destined to enter the Promised Land. They fell into an
everlasting sleep in the midst of the desert.

As described by Bialik, this desert—with its fearful
stretches of wasteland, its misleading lights, its brooding
silence and violent storms, its untold secrets—is the un-
charted desert of the Diaspora in which Israel wanders, lost
and in a daze for generations. But even though the Diaspora

is a curse, in the eyes of the poet it has a magnificence and
grandeur of its own. It is characteristic of Bialik that he
looked at things—even unpleasant ones—not in their insig-
nificance, but in their cosmic aspects, and in their historical
sweep.

The sleeping dead of the wilderness are not poor slaves
who compromised with their destiny. They are:

> *Crouched like dragons primeval,*
> *Things from the dawn of creation.*

They did not attain their goal because the wilderness
closed them in. But they died or fell asleep like proud
heroes, in the peace and glory of bygone aeons. And behold, after thousands of years, the great hour of redemption came, the hour of awakening for the giants:

> *And in that instant—*
> *Wakes the terrible power that slumbered in chains,*
> *Suddenly the old generation of heroes stirs and*
> *   arises,*
> *Mighty in battle: their eyes are like lightning, and*
> *   flame-like their faces*
> *Then flies the hand to the sword.*
> *Sixty myriads of voices—a thunder of heroes—*
> *   awaken,*
> *Crash through the tempest and tear asunder the*
> *   rage of the desert.*
> *Round them is wildness and blindness. And they*
> *   cry:*
> *"We are the mighty!*
> *The last generation of slaves and the first genera-*
> *   tion of freemen!"*

The last sentence has become a classic quotation in Hebrew literature and in the life of the Jewish people. It
seemed as if the thought had waited for generations for
Bialik to come and give it expression. It hovered in the air
of the Diaspora for hundreds of years waiting to be born.
And when the hour arrived, it became the battle cry for
our reborn generation.

The dramatization of the exile and the redemption is the
basis of Bialik's renowned creation, "The Scroll of Fire,"
the poem that aroused great controversy and differences of
opinion due to its multiple motifs and ideas.

It deals with the destruction of the First Temple, and the
story of the abduction of its holy altar flame. According to
legend the flame was spirited away to a secret hiding place
on a desolate island. One of the exiled sons of Judah went
out in search of the flame. The symbolism of the island and
the flame is quite clear. Just like the desert in "The Dead
of the Wilderness" the island in "The Scroll of Fire" is the
Diaspora. The flame is the spirit of the people—the soul of
its culture. And he who goes in search of it is the man of
vision who thirsts for redemption, eager to find the holy
flame which would kindle the heart of the people anew.

Bialik did not stop with this legend. He added many
more about the destruction. One of them is the meaning-
ful allegory of the two hundred youths and the two hundred maidens whom the enemy exiled from Jerusalem and
brought to the desolate island. These young exiles were the
remnants of the destruction—the youth which bore the seed
of the future within themselves. Bialik invested them with
all the depth of his yearning for redemption and with all
his soul's desire for love.

In contrast to the epic spirit of the "Dead of the Wilder-

ness" a deep lyric spirit pervades "The Scroll of Fire." In
the first poem everything is solid, stony; in the second, the
words flow from the soul full of poignant melancholy. Instead of a unified expression, there is dualism. There are
two camps: one for lads and one for maidens. There are
two extraordinary youths: one delicate, with bright eyes,
who looks up to the heavens as if seeking the star of his
life; and the other, a man of awesome aspect with stormy
eyes who looks down to earth as if seeking some precious
thing he has lost. They symbolize the tragic conflicts in
life which, pulling in different directions, make it impossible to reach a set goal. There is an autobiographic flavor in
all parts of the poem: the pain of unrequited love; the
earthly and divine aspects of love; the divine and satanic
sides of life; the loneliness of man—especially of the Jew
in exile; the thirst for beauty and perfection; the yearning
to get beyond the bounds of reality into the sphere of
dreams—these elements combine to form a beautiful tapes-
try of poetic symbolism.

The two youths who walk along the island are two aspects of man: one has faith in his heart; the other, despair.
One sings a song of hope and redemption; the other, a song
of revenge and immolation.

Even the four hundred exiles are divided by the enemy
into two camps that cannot come together. Their souls
yearn to join each other, but they find it impossible. Dis-
unity is the decree of exile, which devours the body and the
soul with the fangs of assimilation. All the promising youths
are sacrificed to the Moloch of strange civilizations.

One of the unforgettable scenes in "The Scroll of Fire"
is the procession of both camps—one facing the other. The

maidens walk with eyes closed. They do not see the deep waters at their feet; neither do they hear the warning cries of the young men. Blindly they walk until they fall into the waters. After them the young men descend with a desire to save them, only to drown together with the maidens in the waters of oblivion.

Only the delicate youth with the bright eyes remains on the island—the one who sacrificed his personal happiness on the altar of the holy flame and was sent on a long mission to be a prophet and a man of vision unto his people and to find the flame that was hidden for a future day. The figure of the youth is all gentleness and deep yearning, resembling Bialik and his poetry. It is but a reflection of himself.

Bialik also reveals himself in the poems he wrote about the yeshiva and the Beth Medrash—in "The Talmud Student," "On the Threshold of the House of Prayer," "Before a Bookcase."

"The Talmud Student" (*Hamathmid*) is the great poem about Israel's love of Torah which preserved the Jewish people throughout all the periods of the Diaspora. The figure of the student in the poem symbolizes Bialik himself and all the other Jewish Talmud students. There are both protest and compassion in the poem. He bemoans the fate of the Jewish child who devotes his days and his nights to the study of Torah and who denies himself every joy of life. There are admiration and wonder at the little hero who checks every natural instinct and isolates himself in the great ideal of studying Torah for its own sake.

The Beth Hamedrash appears as the strong fortress of the spirit of the Jewish people: It was

> *. . . The mystic fount whence*
> *Thy brethren going to their slaughter* drew
> *In evil days the strength and fortitude*
> *To meet grim death with joy, and bare the* neck
> *To every sharpened blade and lifted axe,*
> *Or, pyres ascending, leap into the flame*
> *And saintlike die with* Echad *on their lips.*

Thus Bialik bestowed a wreath of glory and heroism even upon the Diaspora, because of the great light which arose from the students of the Torah. The song from the souls of the youths and maidens who died in the sea was echoed in the chants of the yeshiva youths who sacrificed their lives on the altar of Torah. On that altar there burned the spark of the fire spirited away at the destruction of the Temple, which rolled down through the generations.

And Bialik himself, the epitome of all Talmud students, walks along the vast stretches of Israel's history, looking for the fire and collecting the fragments of light scattered in books and manuscripts.

He dreamed a great dream of collecting all the spiritual treasures of his people—from the time they were exiled; to give them a new lease of life in the form of a new canon which would nourish the spirit of his people.

Together with J. H. Ravnitzky he issued the *Book of Legends* in which the choicest legends of the Talmud were collected. After more than a generation Bialik's *Book of Legends* is still a best seller. The book draws the hearts of its readers closer to the beauty and wisdom of our ancient literary heritage.

He then began to translate and interpret the Mishnah. He also undertook to do research in medieval Hebrew poetry with marked success. He sought to reveal the literary treasures preserved in the creations of the masters of Hebrew verse in the Golden Era. Again with J. H. Ravnitzky as his collaborator, he issued and edited the poems of Solomon ibn Gabirol and Moses ibn Ezra. In the wake of these books, there arose in our own era a strong interest in medieval Hebrew poetry.

Toward the end of his life, Bialik occupied himself with writing Biblical legends which he issued in a special book entitled *Once Upon a Time*. He also wrote short stories and literary essays and translated into Hebrew such works as Cervantes' *Don Quixote* and Friedrich Schiller's *Wilhelm Tell*.

He went on to edit and publish books and anthologies; to give lectures, and to travel around the world on national missions. He visited the United States with Shmaryahu Levin in 1926. While performing these tasks, engaged in gathering Hebrew literary masterpieces, doing public work, his first and foremost interest still remained his poetic works. His poetry gained in depth and beauty with each year. His nature poems, which cannot be discussed at length here, were fresh and wholesome. The brightness and melodic quality of the music in his lines was something new in Hebrew literature. When he sings the song of "The Pool," "The Light," "The Morning Spirits," "The Songs of Summer" and the "Songs of Winter," he sees the world in all its pristine loveliness.

From these poems Bialik passed on to his poems of confession and prayer: "A Twig Fell," "May my Lot be Cast Among You," "One by One—Sight Unseen," "He Stole a Glance and Died," "Flitting by," etc. In these poems he is revealed in a new light. The Prophet becomes a Psalmist.

His song is the silent prayer of a man who has exhorted a generation and a people, who has demanded justice of God and dignity from his people—and found neither.

He begins again to write autobiographical poems, as he did in the beginning of his career. But they are different. They are profounder and permeated with sadness and wisdom, lighting up with a mysterious glow the way of man on earth. The cycle reaches its close. The poet returns to his source, to the innocence of childhood, to the meek and pure in heart, to those who "are restrained in words but overflow with beauty." One by one, in quiet sadness, imperceptibly like the stars fading before the morning star, his innermost desires die out. Loneliness encompasses him. This is the last mile of a man who has remained alone, of a man who has sung of the last generation of enslavement and the initial generation of freedom, but who himself was not destined to experience this freedom.

Thus one sees the shadow of death over him and his poems which sing of death:

> *And all shall die around me*
> *Eternal silence shall engulf me.*

He strives toward unknown, hidden worlds where time and space merge in the mystery of eternity. Upon the threshold of the final gate, the poet collapses with a prayer upon his lips, and his prayer, like his prophecy and his poetry, become integral parts of our spiritual life. The light of his personality glows over us still.

selections from POEMS OF BIALIK

If Thou Wouldst Know

If thou wouldst know the mystic fount whence
Thy brethren going to their slaughter drew
In evil days the strength and fortitude
To meet grim death with joy, and bare the neck
To every sharpened blade and lifted axe,
Or, pyres ascending, leap into the flame
And saintlike die with *Echad* on their lips;

If thou wouldst know the mystic fount whence
Thy stricken brethren, crushed and overcome
By hellish pains and fangs of scorpions,
Drew patience, firmness, trust, and heaven's comfort,
And iron might to bear relentless toil,
With shoulders stooped to bear a loathsome life,
And endlessly to suffer and endure;

If thou wouldst know the bosom whither streamed
Thy nation's tears, its heart and soul and gall,
Whither like water flowed its gushing moans,
The moans that moved the nethermost abyss,
And plaints whose terror bristled even Satan,

Rock-splitting plaints, though vain to crush the foe's
Steeled heart, more adamant than rock and Satan;

If thou wouldst know the fortress whither bore
Thy sires to havens safe their Torah Scrolls,
The sacred treasures of their yearning souls . . .
If thou wouldst know the shelter where preserved,
Immaculate, thy nation's spirit was,
Whose hoary age, thou sate with shameful life,
Did not disgrace its gracious lovely youth;

If thou wouldst know the mother merciful,
The aged loyal mother love-abounding,
Who saved her lost son's tears with tenderness,
And steadied lovingly his falt'ring steps,
And when fatigued and shamed he would return
'Neath her roof's umbrage, she would wipe his **tears**
And lull him to sweet sleep upon her knees;

If thou wouldst know, O humble brother mine,—
Go to the house of prayer grown old, decayed,
In the long nights of Tebeth desolate,
Or in the scorching, blazing Tammuz days,
In noonday heat, at morn or eventide . . .
If God has left there still a remnant small,
Thine eyes shall even to this day behold
Through sombre shadows cast by darkened **walls,**
In isolated nooks or by the stove,
Stray, lonely Jews, like shades from eras past,

Dark, mournful Jews with faces lean and wan;
Yea, Jews who bear the weighty Galuth yoke,
Forgetting toil in Talmud pages worn,
And poverty in tales of bygone days;

Who rout their cares with blessed psalmody
(Alas, how lowly, trivial the sight
To alien eyes!). Thy heart will tell thee then
That thy feet tread the marge of our life's fount,
That thine eyes view the treasures of our soul.

If with God's spirit thou art still imbued,
If still His solace whispers in thy heart,
And if a spark of hope for better days
Illumines yet thy darkness great and deep,
Mark well and hearken, humble brother mine:
This house is but a little spark, a remnant
Saved by a miracle, from that great fire,
Kept by thy fathers always on their altars.
Who knows, perchance the torrents of their tears
Ferried us safely, hither bringing us?
Perchance with their prayers they asked us of the Lord,
And in their deaths bequeathed to us a life,
A life that will endure forevermore!

(Translated by Harry H. Fein)

Upon the Slaughter

Heavenly spheres, beg mercy for me!
If truly God dwells in your orbit and round,
And in your space is His pathway that I have not found,—
Then you pray for me!
For my own heart is dead; no prayer on my tongue;
And strength has failed, and hope has passed:
O until when? For how much more, How long?

Ho, headsman, bared the neck—come, cleave it through!
Nape me this cur's nape! Yours is the axe unbaffled!
The whole wide world—my scaffold!
And rest you easy: we are weak and few.
My blood is outlaw. Strike, then; the skull dissever!
Let blood of babe and graybeard stain your garb—
Stain to endure forever!

If Right there be,—why, let it shine forth now!
For if when I have perished from the earth
The Right shine forth,
Then let its Throne be shattered, and laid low!
Then let the heavens, wrong-racked, be no more!
—While you, O murderers, on your murder thrive,
Live on your blood, regurgitate this gore!

Who cries Revenge! Revenge!—accursed be he!
Fit vengeance for the spilt blood of a child
The devil has not yet compiled.
No, let that blood pierce world's profundity,
Through the great deep pursue its mordications,
There eat its way in darkness, there undo,
Undo the rotted earth's foundations!

(Translated by Abraham M. Klein)

Go Flee, O Prophet!

> Go flee! No! Such a man as I shall not retreat.
> My flock taught me to step with gentle pace;
> Nor has my tongue learned fear or base deceit,
> My word shall fall as falls a heavy mace.

And if my strength is spent, 'tis not my wrong.
The sin is yours. Bear the iniquity!
My hammer found no anvil firm and strong,
My axe struck but the soft rot of a tree.

It matters not! I'll make peace with my fate
And to my girdle bind my tools, the same
As unpaid laborer when day grows late;
And then I'll leave as softly as I came,

Return to my own vales and habitat,
Make with the forest sycamores my stay,
But you, decaying moldiness and rot,
Tomorrow's storm shall fling you far away.

(Translated by Ben Aronin)

'Twixt Tigris and Euphrates

On a hill there blooms a palm
'Twix Tigris and Euphrates old,
And among the leafy branches
Sits the phoenix, bird of gold.

Bird of gold, go forth and find me
Him whose bride I am to be:
Search and circle till thou find him,
Bind him, bring him, bird, to me.

If thou hast no thread of scarlet,
Give him greeting without end:
Tell him, golden bird, my spirit
Pines with longing for my friend.

Tell him: Now the garden blossoms,
Closed except to his command;
Mid the leaves the golden apple
Waits and trembles for his hand.

Tell him, nightly on my pillow
Wakes the longing without name,
And the whiteness of my body
Burns my couch as with a flame.

If he comes not, hear my secret:
All prepared my coffer stands;
Linen, silk, and twenty singlets
Wrought and knitted by these hands.

And the softest of all feathers
By my mother plucked and stored:
Through the nights she filled the cushions
For her daughter's bridal hoard.

And the bridal veil of silver
Waits to deck me when I marry;
Bride and dowry, both are ready—
Wherefore does the bridegroom tarry?

Seethe and whisper, magic potion:
Thus the phoenix makes reply:
In the night to thy beloved
With my secret will I fly.

In his dreams I give thy greeting,
In his dreams reveal thy face;
Lo! Upon a broomstick mounted
Unto thee he flies apace.

And he comes and speaks: Behold me,
Oh my joy, my hope, my pride:
Not with golden gifts or dowry,
But with love become my bride.

Gold and silk I have aplenty,
Fire of youth and ringlets fine:
Both I give thee: swiftly, lightly,
Come to me, beloved mine.

When the night was dark above me
And the stars with clouds were stilled,
On his quest the phoenix vanished—
And his words are unfulfilled.

And at morn, at noon, at even,
Still I watch the clouds of fire:
Clouds above me, answer, wherefore
Comes he not, my heart's desire?

(Translated by Maurice Samuel)

Out of the Depth

I know that in the darkness of some night
Like a spent star my soul shall flicker out,
And not a star shall know its resting place.
But yet my wrath shall smolder like a crater
Whose flames have fallen; yea, my wrath shall live
While yet the thunder rumbles in the sky,
While ocean heavenward flings his troubled waves.
O God, would that my people's ageless woe
Were stored deep in the bosom of the world

To water the wide plains of sky and earth,
To nourish stars and plants, to live their life,
To pulse in all their throbbing, sense their growth,
With them to dwindle, rise and sprout afresh!
Out soaring generations, let that woe
Witness to wrong eternal. Voiceless, dumb,
Oh, let that cry ring through the deep of hell
And pierce the heavens, everlastingly
Withholding the redemption of the world.
And when, at end of days, the sun of guile
And counterfeited righteousness shall rise
Upon your slain, when crimsoned with your blood
The banner of deceit shall flaunt the heavens
Unfurled above your slayers, when their flag
Emblazoned with the spurious seal of God
Shall pierce the sun's bright eye,
When haughty dance and noisy revelry
Of lying feasts shall waken from their graves
Your hallowed bones: the firmament shall shudder
And grow dark at your agony, the sun
Shall redden to an orb of your pure blood
To brand the mark of Cain upon the front
Of all the universe, to testify
The broken arm of God. Yea, star to star
Shall flash its trembling message and cry "Behold
A world's deceit, a nation's agony!"
Until the Lord of Vengeance, stung to wrath,
Shall rise and roar and with His sword unsheathed
Go forth to strike.

(Translated by Reginald V. Feldman)

Throbs the Night with Mystic Silence

Throbs the night with mystic silence,
Hushed the weary world and still;
And the ever-flowing brooklet
Murmurs 'neath the resting mill.

Darker grows the night and darker,
Shadows upon shadows creep;
One bright star and yet another
Falls into the darkness deep.

All the world is wrapped in silence,
But my heart seeks no repose;
And within my heart a fountain
Softly bubbles there and flows.

Speaks my heart: "Son, the fulfillment
Of thy dream at length draws nigh;
Lo, a star falls! Do not tremble—
Thine yet sparkles in the sky.

"Thine is firmly fixed and shining
Yonder in its azure nest;
Lift thine eyes and see it twinkling,
Kindling hope within thy breast."

All the world is wrapped in silence,
As I sit here pensively;
One world have I—yea, no other
Than the world which lives in me.

(Translated by Bertha Beinkinstadt)

Selected Bibliography *of works in English dealing with the texts, authors and evaluations of the great Jewish books*

THE BIBLE

The Holy Scriptures, according to the Masoretic text, in an English translation completed in 1917 under Jewish auspices. The Jewish Publication Society, Philadelphia.

The King James Version

The Isaac Leeser Translation of the Bible. Hebrew Publishing Company, New York.

The American Standard Version

The Complete Bible: An American Translation, by Smith and Goodspeed. University of Chicago Press, Chicago.

The Modern Reader's Bible, by Richard G. Moulton. Macmillan, New York.

Pathways Through the Bible, by Mortimer J. Cohen. Jewish Publication Society, Philadelphia.

The Hebrew Scriptures in the Making, by Max L. Margolis. Jewish Publication Society, Philadelphia.

The Book of Books, by Solomon Goldman. Harper, New York; Jewish Publication Society, Philadelphia.

THE SIDDUR

The Authorized Daily Prayer Book. With commentary, introductions and notes by the late Chief Rabbi Joseph H. Hertz. Bloch Publishing Co., New York.

Daily Prayer Book. Translated and annotated with an introduction by Dr. Philip Birnbaum. Hebrew Publishing Co., New York.

The Standard Prayer Book. Authorized English translation by the Reverend S. Singer. Bloch Publishing Co., New York.

THE KUSARI

Kitab Al Khazari, by Judah Halevi. Translated from the Arabic by Hartwig Hirschfeld. Pardes Publishing House, New York.

Kuzari, by Jehuda Halevi. Abridged and Edited with an introduction and commentary by Isaak Heinemann. East and West Library, London.

The Kuzari, by Rabbi Judah Halevi. Adapted by Henry Biberfeld. Jewish Pocket Books, New York.

The Wisdom of Israel. Edited by Lewis Browne. Random House, New York.

THE TALMUD

The Babylonian Talmud. Translated by I. Epstein. Soncino Press, London.

The Mishnah. Translated by Herbert Danby. Clarendon Press, Oxford.

The Midrash. Soncino Press, London.

Everyman's Talmud, by Abraham Cohen. Dutton, New York.

The Talmudic Anthology, by Louis I. Newman and Samuel Spitz. Behrman, New York.

Introduction to Talmud and Midrash, by H. L. Strack. Jewish Publication Society, Philadelphia.

GUIDE FOR THE PERPLEXED

Guide of the Perplexed, by Maimonides. Translated by M. Friedlander.

Mishne Torah, by Maimonides. Edited by Moses Hyamson.

The Code of Maimonides. Book Thirteen. The Book of Civil Laws. Translated by Jacob J. Rabinowitz. Yale University Press, New Haven.

The Code of Maimonides. Book Fourteen. The Book of Judges. Translated by A. M. Hershman. Yale University Press, New Haven.

Essays on Maimonides. Edited by Salo W. Baron. Columbia University Press, New York.

Maimonides, by David Yellin and Israel Abrahams. Jewish Publication Society, Philadelphia.

The Legacy of Maimonides, by Ben Zion Bokser. Philosophical Library, New York.

RASHI'S COMMENTARIES

The Pentateuch and Rashi's Commentary, by Abraham Ben Isaiah and Benjamin Scharfman, et. al. S. S. and R. Publishing Co., New York.

Rashi, by Maurice Liber. Translated from the French by Adele Szold. Jewish Publication Society, Philadelphia.

Rashi Anniversary Volume. American Academy for Jewish Research. New York.

The Master of Troyes, by Samuel Blumenfield. Bloch Publishing Co., New York.

Pentateuch and Rashi's Commentary, by M. Rosenbaum and A. M. Silberman, London, 1932.

SHULCHAN ARUCH

Code of Jewish Law. A compilation of Jewish laws and customs by Rabbi Solomon Ganzfried. Translated by Hyman E. Goldin. Star Hebrew Book Co., New York.

The Ethics of the Shulhan 'Aruk, by Itzehak Spector. Uraitha Publishing Co., Tacoma, Wash.

Anthology of Medieval Hebrew Literature. Edited by Abraham E. Millgram. Associated Talmud Torahs of Philadelphia, Philadelphia.

The Wisdom of Israel. Edited by Lewis Browne. Random House, New York.

THE ZOHAR

The Zohar. Translated by Harry Sperling and M. Simon. Five Volumes. Soncino Press, London.

Selections From the Zohar, by Gershom Scholem. Schocken, New York.

The Talmudic Anthology. Edited by Louis I. Newman and Samuel Spitz. Behrman, New York.

The Wisdom of Israel. Edited by Lewis Browne. Random House, New York.

Major Trends in Jewish Mysticism, by Gershom Scholem. Schocken, New York.

A HISTORY OF THE JEWS

A History of the Jews, by Heinrich Graetz. Jewish Publication Society, Philadelphia.

"A Memoir of Heinrich Graetz," by Philip Bloch, in Volume Six of the Jewish Publication Society edition.

"Graetz the Jewish Historian," by Israel Abrahams, in *The Jewish Quarterly Review,* 1892.

"Heinrich Graetz Centenary," by Gotthard Deutsch, in *Year Book of the Central Conference of American Rabbis,* Volume 27.

"Graetz's History in America," by Solomon Grayzel, in *Historia Judaica,* Volume Three, 1941.

JUDENSTAAT

The Jewish State, (*Judenstaat*) by Theodor Herzl. American Zionist Emergency Council, New York.

Excerpts From Herzl's Diaries. Scopus, New York.

Old-New Land, by Theodor Herzl. Translated by Lotta Levenson, with a preface by Stephen S. Wise. Bloch Publishing Co., New York.

Theodor Herzl, a memorial. *The New Palestine.* Edited by Meyer W. Weisgal. New York.

Theodor Herzl, by Jacob De Haas. Brentano, New York.

Theodor Herzl, by Alex Bein. Translated from the German by Maurice Samuel. Jewish Publication Society, New York.

AHAD HA-AM'S ESSAYS

Selected Essays, by Ahad Ha-am. Translated by Leon Simon. Jewish Publication Society, Philadelphia.
Essays, Letters, Memoirs of Ahad Ha-am. Translated by Leon Simon. East and West Library, London.
Ten Essays on Zionism and Judaism, by Ahad Ha-am. Translated by Leon Simon. Routledge, London.

THE POETRY OF BIALIK

Complete Poetic Works of Hayyim Nahman Bialik. Edited by Israel Efros. Histadruth Ivrith, New York.
Bialik Issue. The New Palestine, 1926. New York.

About the Authors *of this book*

JACOB B. AGUS, rabbi of Beth El Congregation, Baltimore, Md., received his Bachelor's Degree from Yeshiva College in 1933 and was ordained as rabbi by the Isaac Elchanan Theological Seminary in 1935. In 1938 he earned his M.A. and a year later his Ph.D. at Harvard University. A prolific author, he has written *Modern Philosophies of Judaism* and *Banner of Jerusalem,* a life of Rabbi Kuk, as well as important essays in leading periodicals.

SAMUEL M. BLUMENFIELD, dean of the College of Jewish Studies in Chicago, is a prominent Jewish educator who has written a book on Rashi entitled *The Master of Troyes.* He has also edited works on Yehudah Halevi and on Zionism and has contributed articles to many scholarly journals. Dr. Blumenfield was educated at the College of the City of New York, at Columbia and at the Jewish Institute of Religion. He has held many educational posts in the American Jewish community and has been active in Jewish communal life.

HARRY ESSRIG is spiritual leader of Temple Emanuel, Grand

Rapids, Michigan. He is a graduate of Jewish Teachers Institute and Teachers College, Columbia University. He served as a chaplain in the U.S. Army—30 months overseas —and rose to the rank of Major as Assistant Staff Chaplain of the Ninth Air Force. He also served as a director of Hillel Foundations at the University of Chicago, at Harvard, at Radcliffe and at M.I.T. Rabbi Essrig has contributed articles to many leading Jewish periodicals and is the author of *Problems of Jewish Life* and *The American Jew Takes Inventory.* He contributed a chapter on Jewish-Americans to the volume *One America,* edited by Francis J. Brown and Joseph Roucek.

OSCAR Z. FASMAN is president of the Hebrew Theological College in Chicago, the only American-born president of an Orthodox Rabbinical yeshiva. Born and educated in Chicago, he received his college degree from the University of Chicago. From 1930-1940 he was rabbi of Congregation Bnei Emunah in Tulsa, Oklahoma. From 1940-1946 he was rabbi of United Synagogues of Ottawa, Canada and from 1942-1945 served as chaplain with the Canadian Army and was commissioned by King George as an Honorary Captain. Rabbi Fasman has written many articles and monographs for various learned journals and is the author of *Sabbath— Cornerstone of Jewish Life.*

SIMON FEDERBUSH, before coming to the United States a decade ago, held many important posts in Europe. He was Chief Rabbi of Finland, a member of the Polish Parliament, president of the Mizrachi Organization of Galicia and head of various institutions of learning in Poland. He holds a Ph.D. degree and was educated at the Universities of

Vienna, Cracow and Lemberg. He is one of the founders of the World Jewish Congress, a member of its administrative committee since its creation and presently a member of its Executive Committee. Active in Zionist work, he has held many important posts in the movement and is now honorary president of Hapoel Hamizrachi of America. He has written many books, including *Iyunim, Chikray Talmud,* and other volumes in Hebrew. His book *The Truth About the Protocols of the Elders of Zion* appeared in both Finnish and Swedish. His latest volume on the basic law of the state of Israel has been published in Israel.

SOLOMON GOLDMAN, one of the most distinguished members of the American rabbinate, has been rabbi of Anshe Emet Synagogue in Chicago since 1929. He is a former president of the Zionist Organization of America and a scholar of note. Dr. Goldman's works include *A Rabbi Takes Stock, Crisis and Decision, The Jew and the Universe,* and *The Golden Chair.* In recent years he has been working on a monumental study of the Bible under the general title of *The Book of Human Destiny.* Two volumes have thus far been published: *The Book of Books* and *In the Beginning.*

SOLOMON GRAYZEL is the editor of the Jewish Publication Society of America and the author of the popular *A History of the Jews.* He was educated at the College of the City of New York, Columbia University, the Jewish Theological Seminary and Dropsie College. He also taught history at Gratz College. Dr. Grayzel has been a prolific writer for numerous journals and is the author of *The Church and the Jews in the XIIIth Century.* He has also been president of the Jewish Book Council of America and of the Board of

Education of the Philadelphia branch of the United Synagogue.

LUDWIG LEWISOHN, now a professor at Brandeis University, is perhaps the most prominent English-Jewish writer in the United States. Author of scores of books, his most influential volumes have been those on Jewish themes. His writings include *The Island Within, Upstream, Mid-Channel, These People,* and, most recently, *The American Jew.*

JACOB S. MINKIN is a graduate of Columbia University and the Jewish Theological Seminary of America. He was engaged for a number of years in the active rabbinate—in Hamilton, Ont., Rochester, N.Y. and New York City, but left the active pulpit for a writing career. Dr. Minkin is the author of *The Romance of Hasidism; Herod: A Biography; Abarbanel and the Expulsion of the Jews,* besides a great many articles on religious, historical and philosophical subjects contributed to learned and popular publications, as well as to the *Encyclopedia Americana* and the *Universal Jewish Encyclopedia.*

JOACHIM PRINZ is rabbi of Temple B'nai Abraham of Newark, N.J. Ordained at the Jewish Theological Seminary at Breslau, Germany, in 1925, he was rabbi in the Berlin Jewish community for 12 years before coming to the United States. Prominent in Jewish communal life, Dr. Prinz is a vice-president of the American Jewish Congress. His works include *Adventures of the Bible, We Jews, Stories of the Bible, Friday Night, Illustrated Jewish History,* and *Life in the Ghetto.*

MENACHEM RIBALOW, for more than 30 years editor of *Hadoar,* the only Hebrew weekly in the world outside of Israel, is perhaps the most prominent Hebrew writer in the United States. Born and educated in Russia, his literary career has been devoted largely to *Hadoar* and to his editing of various yearbooks and the writing of volumes of literary criticism. He is an expert on Bialik, whom he knew well. His works include *Sefer Hamasot* (Book of Essays), *Sofrim V'Ishim* (Writers and Personalities), *Ketavim V'Megillot* (Writings and Scrolls), *Dichter Un Shafer in Nei Hebraische*—in Yiddish—(Writers and Creators in Neo-Hebrew), and a recent volume, *Im Hakad El Hamabua* (With the Pitcher to the Fountain) which won the LaMed Prize for 1951.

SAMUEL ROSENBLATT is rabbi of Beth Tfiloh congregation of Baltimore, Md., and the author of numerous scholarly works which include *The Interpretation of the Bible in the Mishnah, Our Heritage,* and *People of the Book.* He was Hazard Fellow at the American Schools of Oriental Research at Jerusalem, Gustav Gottheil Lecturer at Columbia University and has been lecturer on Jewish literature at Johns Hopkins University since 1930. Active in the Zionist movement, Dr. Rosenblatt was a delegate to the 19th World Zionist Congress and has been a prominent leader in the American Jewish Congress, the Mizrachi, the American Academy for Jewish Research, the B'nai B'rith, and the Rabbinical Assembly of America. He was ordained at the Jewish Theological Seminary of America in 1925 and received his Ph.D. from Columbia University.

DATE DUE

OC 21 '82			
GAYLORD			PRINTED IN U.S.A.